Yankee Blitzkrieg

Maj. Gen. James H. Wilson

Yankee Blitzkrieg

Wilson's Raid
Through Alabama and Georgia

JAMES PICKETT JONES

Brown Thrasher Books
THE UNIVERSITY OF GEORGIA PRESS
Athens and London

© 1976 by the University of Georgia Press
Athens, Georgia 30602

Reprinted in 1987 by the University of Georgia Press
as a Brown Thrasher Book.

The paper in this book meets the guidelines for
permanence and durability of the Committee on
Production Guidelines for Book Longevity of the
Council on Library Resources.

Printed in the United States of America.

98 97 96 95 94   P   7 6 5 4 3

The Library of Congress has cataloged the first
printing of this title as follows:

Jones, James Pickett.
Yankee blitzkrieg: Wilson's raid through Alabama and Georgia / James Pickett
Jones—Athens: University of Georgia Press, c1976.
xiv, 256 p.: ill.; 24 cm.
Bibliography: p. [232]–242.
Includes index.
ISBN 0-8203-0370-4

1. Wilson's Cavalry Raid, 1865.   2. Wilson, James Harrison, 1837–1925.   I. Title.
E477.96.J66   973.7'38   74-15206
                                                          MARC
Library of Congress   76[7611]

ISBN 0-8203-0970-2 (pbk.: alk. paper)

To the memory of my father

"Cavalry Crossing a Ford"

A line in long array, where they wind betwixt green islands;
They take a serpentine course—their arms flash in the sun—hark
    to the musical clank;
Behold the silvery river—in it the splashing horses, loitering, stop
    to drink;
Behold the brown-faced men—each group, each person, a picture—
    the negligent rest on the saddles;
Some emerge on the opposite bank—others are just entering the
    ford—while,
Scarlet, and blue, and snowy white,
The guidon flags flutter gaily in the wind.

from *Drum Taps*
by Walt Whitman

Contents

Illustrations and Maps

Preface

Blitzkrieg has become a part of the English language and no one bothers to make the translation to "Lightning War." The dictionary says that a "blitzkrieg" is "sudden, swift, large-scale offensive warfare intended to win a quick victory." Union Maj. Gen. James Harrison Wilson had probably never heard the word when he directed his buglers to sound "Boots and Saddles" to set the Civil War's largest cavalry force in motion. Yet he was determined to move his 13,480 horsemen suddenly and swiftly to a quick victory.

The Confederacy was reeling when Wilson's raiders left their camps along the Tennessee River in March 1865 and rode south. But there was talk of prolonged rebel resistance in the deep South using the agricultural and industrial facilities of a sweep of territory that ran from Macon to Meridian. That area had hardly been touched by the war, and in Columbus, Georgia, and Selma, Alabama, the South had two of its most productive industrial communities.

Twenty-seven-year-old General Wilson was certain his large, well-officered, well-trained, and well-armed cavalry corps could deny the Confederates a redoubt in the heart of Alabama and Georgia. Wilson, like many cavalry leaders, north and south, believed the mounted arm had been grievously misused through four years of war. But in March 1865, armed with support from Grant, Sherman, and Thomas, Wilson could at last test the theory that massed heavily armed cavalry could strike swiftly in great strength and press to quick victory.

Although there would be some mounted charges to support dismounted men, the basic use of the horse was quick mobility. The hard fighting would be left to dismounted men fighting from an advantage given them by their far-ranging mounts.

Wilson's strategy was to get there "first with the most men," and it would be tested against the man who had invented the very phrase, Nathan Bedford Forrest. "That Devil Forrest," Confederate "Wizard of the Saddle," led a hopelessly outnumbered force struggling on for a dying cause. Forrest failed to halt Wilson, and he admitted to his young adversary after the fall of Selma: "Well, General, you have beaten me badly, and for the first time I am compelled to make such an acknowledgement."[1]

Selma was taken and its war-sustaining facilities destroyed. Montgomery, a city of symbolic importance, and the industrial hub of Columbus, heard the jingle of Wilson's horsemen as they rode through the streets. Two months after its inception, the raid ended with the fall of Macon. The last act in the corps's Civil War service was the capture of Jefferson Davis, Alexander H. Stephens, and numerous other Confederate leaders.

Wilson believed that his campaign, coupled with his seizure of Davis, ended all hope of Confederate resistance east of the Mississippi. Numerous contemporaries and many historians share this view. There would be no guerrilla warfare; Jeff Davis's "last ditch" was not defensible.

This book, first published in 1976, is the only study of Wilson's raid. Edward G. Longacre's 1972 biography of Wilson, *From Union Stars to Top Hat*, thoroughly explores the career of the able young Union general, but it devotes only a part of one chapter to the raid. Wilson's own description of the raid, in his autobiography *Under the Old Flag*, is a complete account, but it is highly biased. *Yankee Blitzkrieg* is an attempt to give a campaign, significant in the war's last days and significant in the history of mounted warfare, a clearer place in the history of the Civil War.

Since the initial publication of *Yankee Blitzkrieg* the raid has received attention from historians. Rex Miller has written of Wilson's lost brigade in *Croxton's Raid*. The most important work published since 1976 bearing on Wilson's Raid had been Stephen Z. Starr's monumental three-volume study, *The Union Cavalry in the Civil War* (Baton Rouge: Louisiana State University Press, 1979–1985). Starr began his three volumes with Wilson's Raid, his clear choice as the Union's most effective use of cavalry in the entire conflict. The raid "was given pride of place in the history of the Union cavalry," wrote Starr, "because this campaign, its planning, organization, tactics, and operations . . . are a model of their kind and show the officers and men of the Union cavalry in the Civil War at the height of their powers and effectiveness" (III:565). Starr's treatment of the raid is contained in pages 14 through 46 of volume I. Characterizing Wilson's campaign, the author wrote: "it was nothing less than a cavalry invasion: a raid raised to a higher power" (I:20). Starr agrees with *Yankee Blitzkrieg* that the raid would be far better known and Wilson's reputation greater "if it had not been overshadowed by the dramatic events in Virginia and North Carolina in the closing weeks of the war" (I:46).

I am deeply indebted to several libraries and historical societies for their generous assistance in providing materials for this work. The staffs of the Duke University Library, the Southern Historical Collection of the University of North Carolina, the University of Alabama Library, the Western Historical Manuscripts Collection of the University of Missouri, the Library of Congress, and the Delaware State Historical Society, Wilmington, were very helpful. The staff of the Carnegie Library, Selma, Alabama, not only provided materials but also answered numerous questions about the region and its oral history of the raid. Particularly helpful were the late Paul Spence, Manuscripts Librarian of the Illinois State Historical Society, Springfield, and the late Milo Howard, Director of the Alabama

Department of Archives and History, Montgomery. As usual, the staff of the Florida State University Library was of invaluable assistance.

A portion of the research for this book was funded by the Research Council of the Florida State University. That assistance is gratefully acknowledged.

The excellent maps of the Battle of Selma and the Battle of Columbus were done by Jim Anderson, and those of Wilson's route of march and Davis's flight by Frank Unger, both of the Florida Resource and Environmental Analysis Center of Florida State University. My thanks goes to them and to Ed Fernald, director of the center.

I would like to thank my colleague William W. Rogers, whose knowledge of the history of Alabama and Georgia is never-ending, for introducing me to the subject and for his encouragement. Encouragement and assistance also came from the late J. Leitch Wright and Joe M. Richardson of the history department, Florida State University, and from C. Peter Ripley, Black Abolitionist Papers Project, Florida State University. A debt of gratitude is also owed Kenneth Cherry, the editor of the University of Georgia Press when *Yankee Blitzkrieg* was first published, for his support and helpful suggestions, and to Malcolm Call, current director of the University of Georgia Press, who proposed reissuing *Yankee Blitzkrieg*. Malcolm and the staff of the press, especially Loris Green, were most helpful in this book's production.

All errors found in this book are unintentional but are my sole responsibility.

Yankee Blitzkrieg

CHAPTER I

"Jine the Cavalry"

Rain, rain, rain! Thirteen thousand four hundred and eighty
Union cavalrymen stood on the north bank of the Tennessee River
mounted, armed, and ready to cut a path of destruction through
the heart of Alabama and Georgia. If the rain would only stop, the
troopers could cross the river, but day after day it fell in sheets. It
was March 1865 and Maj. Gen. James Harrison Wilson ached to
hear his buglers blare "Boots and Saddles" through the camps. If
the horsemen did not ride soon, Nathan Bedford Forrest might organize an effective Confederate force out of the stragglers, deserters, and irregulars in Mississippi and Alabama. It was also possible
that continued Union victories might end the war and leave un-
tested the fine force honed to an edge by its young commander.
Piqued at the delay, Wilson wrote his friend, Adam Badeau, Gen.
Ulysses S. Grant's military secretary, "Isn't it unfortunate that the
rain cannot be controlled by General Grant."[1]

Not even the general-in-chief could halt the deluge, and Wilson
paced the floor and watched the skies and the muddy Tennessee.
By the fifteenth the rain slackened, the river began to fall, and
bugles rang. Seven days later advance units of the largest cavalry
force of the Civil War swung south. Wilson's raid had begun.

II

New Year's Day 1865 had found General Wilson at Huntsville,
Alabama. Wilson and his force of twenty-seven thousand cavalrymen had spent a cold, bleak Christmas along the Tennessee River.

Both men and horses were short of food, and the festive season passed without the holiday dinners, hot punch, and parties that were usual at home. Wilson wrote philosophically in his diary a quote he attributed to the *Atlantic Monthly:* "Backbone and grit is a good substitute when hardtack and pork fail."[2] After the war he remembered: "It was a mercy that we found 'hog and hominy' enough to keep body and soul together in that land of poor whites with neither turkeys nor chickens, and not enough girls within twenty miles for a country dance."[3]

Though the weather was cold and cheerless and stomachs were empty, Union troopers' spirits were high. Confederate armies were in retreat, and prospects of an early return home improved daily. In late December, Nashville newspapers overtook Wilson's force at Pinhook Town, on the Tennessee, and the men read accounts of Gen. William Tecumseh Sherman's march through Georgia and his capture of Savannah. When the account of Sherman's message to Lincoln with its presentation of Savannah to the president as a Christmas gift was read, the soldiers suggested that Wilson present "the city of Pinhook with all its dependencies and resources to Mr. Lincoln as a New Year's gift."[4]

By January 1865 the Confederacy was dying. Though Lee still held Petersburg, the long siege had taken its toll, and Grant continued to extend his lines, stretching the Army of Northern Virginia almost to the breaking point. Sherman's thrust through Georgia, a crushing blow to Southern morale, would shortly be followed by a campaign northward through the Carolinas. Furthermore, in Wilson's area, December had produced Gen. George H. Thomas's defeat of Gen. John B. Hood at Nashville and the subsequent flight of Hood's shattered army. In addition to these military developments, Lincoln's reelection and the tightening noose of the Union blockade seemed to make the Confederate cause increasingly hopeless.

In northern Alabama Wilson thought of ways in which his large cavalry command could add to the military problems of the Davis government. The most extensive stretch of Confederate soil largely untouched by the conflict lay between central Mississippi and central Georgia. With the exception of occasional raids, this area had seen little destruction. The possibility existed that Confederate forces in Virginia and the Carolinas might attempt to retreat into this section and, supplied by farms and factories there, prolong the war. Food supplies were adequate, and Columbus, Georgia, and Selma, Alabama, were two of the South's largest manufacturing centers. Wilson's officers were certain Davis meant to establish a "last ditch" line of defense on a line from Macon and Columbus through Montgomery, Selma, and Tuscaloosa, and on to Meridian, Mississippi.[5]

There was also the possibility of Confederate concentration in Texas. If, instead of fighting on in Alabama and Mississippi, Davis had the Trans-Mississippi in mind as a final defensive position, then his Confederates would have to pass through Alabama and Mississippi in their retreat. Wilson's strike would prevent this. Long after the war he wrote: "It is now perfectly certain that [Davis] hoped to get over into the Trans-Mississippi Department and there continue the war, and without my operations there would have been nothing in the way to prevent his success."[6]

Out of action since Nashville, Wilson's horsemen stood ready to move into the heart of the deep South. The general believed his proposed campaign would collapse Davis's "last ditch" and destroy the last hope of the rebel president.

The commander of the twenty-seven thousand blue-clad troopers poised in the Tennessee Valley was young, highly successful Maj. Gen. James Harrison Wilson. Only twenty-seven years old in 1865, Wilson, an 1860 West Point graduate, had become one of the war's best-known cavalry leaders. He was the "most distinguished" of the "boy-generals" created by the war.[7] An Illinoisan, born in Shawneetown, Wilson had entered the Military Academy in 1855 and finished five years later, ranking sixth in a class of forty-one.[8]

Wilson's first army service was in the Far West, but he was ordered east after Sumter. When the Port Royal expedition was
mounted in 1861, he went along as Gen. Thomas W. Sherman's
chief topographical engineer. In 1862 the young officer served in
Virginia and Maryland, seeing action at South Mountain and Antietam. Late in 1862 Wilson went west to join Grant's staff and
through that year and the next served as inspector general of the
Army of the Tennessee. Wilson was with the army during the
Vicksburg campaign and at Chattanooga. Around Grant's headquarters the Illinoisan was the acknowledged expert in horsemanship. He also made a reputation as a troubleshooter, and among
Grant's staff members the word was: "Better send Wilson; he be-
longs to the get-there gang, and you won't have to explain." Washington learned of Wilson's reputation from War Department official Charles A. Dana. Dana, with Grant's army, wrote Secretary of
War Edwin M. Stanton that Wilson "has remarkable talents and
uncommon executive power, and will be heard from hereafter."[9]

In January 1864, although he was the youngest brigadier in the
service, Wilson went to the War Department as chief of the Cavalry Bureau. His task was to revitalize the mounted arm, and he
worked hard to secure the best possible arms, equipment, and
mounts. The general's greatest contribution in this post was his
negotiation with the Spencer Arms Company for all the repeating
carbines it could supply to Union forces.[10]

In the spring Wilson took the field as commander of the Third
Division of Gen. Philip Sheridan's Cavalry Corps, Army of the Potomac. His first action was in the Wilderness where, failing to carry
out Gen. George Meade's instructions precisely, his performance
was lackluster. Wilson's best-known command was a 325-mile raid
south of Petersburg in June 1864, the target of which was the destruction of Lee's railroads. The Union raiders wrecked sixty miles
of track on three railroads and disrupted rebel transportation.
However, Wilson lost all of his artillery, and his wagons, and suffered thirteen hundred casualties. Many of the casualties were listed

as missing and eventually returned to Union lines. The expedition fell well short of complete success and Wilson was fortunate to extricate his force with no greater losses.[11] While serving with Sheridan, one of Wilson's fellow soldiers described him as a "slight person of a light complexion and with a rather pinched face."[12] Overall he served ably as a brigadier under Sheridan until October 1864 when Grant sent him to William Tecumseh Sherman as chief of cavalry for Sherman's Military Division of the Mississippi. On the transfer Grant wrote: "I believe Wilson will add 50 percent to the effectiveness of your cavalry."[13]

The new cavalry chief arrived in the West a stranger to the men he would serve among. A *New York Times* correspondent announced that Wilson was young and "not known here before his personal advent." The general, himself, acknowledged to Badeau: "I find that about the only thing that was known of me when I came West was that 'I had been most essentially chawed up at Ream's Station,' had lost my guns, been disgraced and ordered out West. This is rather amusing as the matter stands now but it shows how very *politic* one ought to be when brought in contact with the representatives of a free press."[14]

His command learned soon that Wilson was a tireless taskmaster who was determined to whip his horsemen to a peak of efficiency. When Sherman divided his force before he marched to the sea he sent the bulk of his cavalry, under Wilson, back to Tennessee to serve under Gen. George H. Thomas in the attempt to blunt Hood's invasion. At Franklin the cavalry battered the rebels as Gen. John M. Schofield repulsed Hood. Two weeks later at Nashville, Wilson's troopers, fighting largely on foot, contributed much to the Confederate debacle.[15]

By 1865 the young veteran commander had made an enviable reputation. "Harry" Wilson was about five feet ten inches tall but appeared taller because of his erect military bearing. Though he made no pretense of emulating the plumed "beau ideal" of the Confederacy, Jeb Stuart, Wilson's neatness led the enemy to refer to him occasionally as "Dandy Wilson."[16] The "boy-general" highly prized dignity and decorum.[17] His fellow officers regarded him as a brilliant young soldier, and a Confederate leader called him "one of the most courteous, as well as efficient, officers in the Union army."[18] Wilson was a man of strong opinions. In private, often in letters to his friend Adam Badeau, he lashed out at Union leaders. He had a high opinion of Grant, was critical of Sherman, and wrote of Thomas with both concern and exasperation. Ben Butler he thought a fool, and much of the military policy of the Union government he felt needed overhauling.[19]

Wilson was supremely confident and a keen student of strategy and tactics. He read widely and loved to discuss history and poetry. His saddlebags usually contained a book or two. The literary abilities that would eventually enable him to write numerous biographies, histories, and an eminently readable autobiography were all well developed by 1865. His letters and reports are clear and interesting, as well written as any the war produced. But by January 1865 he was first and foremost a cavalryman. He took pride in his horsemanship and boasted that he could outjump anyone in his force.

James Harrison Wilson was a complex man. He was a soldier of great energy, determination, and resourcefulness. The young officer was a hard driving commander who, unlike many of his contemporaries in both blue and gray, moved swiftly and decisively into action. Occasionally his precipitate actions caused him trouble, but more often they brought him success. His commanders knew "Harry" Wilson could be depended upon to carry out orders rapidly and forcefully. He was an intelligent man, well versed in military theory and, by the end of the Civil War, a veteran of many facets of military practice as well.

But General Wilson had personal characteristics that flawed both the man and the military chieftain. He was imperious, a person of great conceit. Often outspoken and tactless, he had an unfortunate facility for alienating people. Early in the war Wilson made command mistakes and sought to avoid responsibility for those errors. His biographer maintains that the general's "most enduring characteristic" was soaring personal ambition—an affliction shared by many of his fellow generals. Perhaps Wilson's greatest character flaw was the lack of a strong sense of humor. He took himself very seriously.[20]

Through the war, especially since the beginning of his cavalry service, Wilson had become convinced that most generals misused the mounted arm. His reading had taught him that "both Hannibal and Napoleon depended greatly upon cavalry in battle. They certainly gave great attention to its organization and use and both used it with marked effect."[21] Like Phil Sheridan, Wilson felt that horsemen should be massed into a large, highly mobile, striking force. He deplored the widespread practice of scattering cavalry among infantry. He also abhorred the idea that cavalry units were good only as messengers, escorts, foragers, scouts, or guards for supply trains. Like Confederate Gen. Nathan Bedford Forrest, the young general believed that horsemen could best serve as mounted infantry, using their horses for speed and maneuverability. Wilson was certain that a massive cavalry force could use its mounts to strike quickly, fighting dismounted in the face of fortifications or enemy lines. He held that the day of the cavalry charge—the romantic day of the *beau sabreau* and the *arme blanche*—was dead. Wilson's choice of weapons was a mass of repeating carbines used by dismounted men. But the horse was still important as a means of rapid locomotion. "The horse is the prime factor in cavalry," Wilson wrote. "Through him the cavalryman moves faster, gets there quicker, covers longer distances in less time, finds the weaker places in the enemy's lines, strikes him in flank or rear, or breaks his means of communication and supply."[22]

Through the first three years of the Civil War, horsemen had rarely been employed as shock troops. Neither side had used its mounted arm in the way developed so effectively in 1864 and 1865 by Sheridan and Wilson. Initially the Confederate superiority in cavalry was clear. Most of the experienced cavalry officers in the prewar army were Southerners. Besides the service of veteran officers, the South could fill its ranks with seasoned horsemen. Though this superiority was gradually overcome by the Union, it took three years of frustration and failure to arrive at the point reached in Wilson's command by the war's end.

From 1861 to 1864 horsemen were scattered among infantry units. Gen. Winfield Scott believed that cavalry would be " 'unimportant and secondary' against the new rifled cannons in the broken and wooded country."[23] Wilson was convinced that the aged Scott "discouraged . . . all organization of cavalry, largely on the theory that the war would be over before cavalry regiments could be organized."[24] Even a general as able as George Meade thought the cavalry's proper function was to guard wagon trains and serve as pickets.[25] For three years cavalry units had been "rather futiley used on petty defensive assignments such as outposts and patrols, as orderlies, messengers . . . as guards for slow-moving wagon convoys which infantry could have done equally well."[26]

Despite this bungling, the cavalry had made important contributions to Union arms. Most notable was General Benjamin Grierson's raid into Mississippi during the Vicksburg campaign. Grierson's horsemen proved the effectiveness of a hard riding strike behind enemy lines. His men had confused Confederate commanders, raised havoc with communications, and demonstrated an ability to live off the land as they advanced. Grierson's force, however, numbered only seventeen hundred raiders and was more a mission of reconnaissance and diversion than an invasion in force.[27] But not all Union raiders had fared so well. Col. Abel Streight had ridden into Alabama, only to be turned back and smashed by an inferior force of Confederate horsemen under Nathan Bedford Forrest. Indeed, the Union cavalry in the West had consistently emerged second best in struggles with gray-clad horsemen led by Forrest and "Fighting Joe" Wheeler. It was to redress the balance that Wilson was ordered to his new Western command in 1864. By

January 1865 his support of the mounted arm had become a mission. He wrote in his diary: "In our next war our cavalry ought to play a proper part. I desire above all things to be instrumental in bringing this about."[28]

III

After a brief disagreement with Thomas during the first week of January 1865, Wilson was ordered to move his headquarters a hundred miles west of Huntsville, concentrating along the north bank of the Tennessee River between Gravelly Springs, Alabama, and Eastport, Mississippi. Wilson had written his commanding officer several times in December that Eastport was the proper place to concentrate cavalry. Instead Thomas sent the horsemen to Huntsville. No sooner had Wilson arrived in Huntsville than "twenty minutes later came orders to go to *Eastport*."[29] The march westward through the Tennessee Valley was a hard one since the region had been scoured for supplies and little food or forage remained. By mid-month Wilson had half of his force at Gravelly Springs. The remainder, gathered from isolated garrisons in Tennessee, Kentucky, and Missouri, reached the staging area by January 25.

Wilson's chosen point of concentration, in extreme northwestern Alabama, was deemed advisable since it placed his force in a position to move into either central Alabama or into Mississippi. In addition, Eastport, Mississippi, and Waterloo, Alabama, afforded steamboat landings, the site was near the head of navigation at all stages of the river, and Wilson could get supplies from depots on and beyond the Ohio.[30] The general also found the region high and healthy with plantations suitable for cantonments and drill grounds. It was for these reasons that Wilson chose to situate his force on the north rather than the south bank of the Tennessee.

There was still some opposition in the area when Wilson arrived, and the general moved at once to clear the region of guerrillas and deserters who harassed both Union troops and already

impoverished civilians. Some of this opposition came from northeastern Mississippi, and in late January Wilson sent a heavy reconnaissance to Corinth. This column, commanded by Col. Joseph B.
Dorr of the Eighth Iowa, cleared the area with the loss of only one
man.[31] With local opposition crushed, Wilson established headquarters in "an ideal region for the work we had in hand."[32]

Wilson's "work" was the outfitting and training of a cavalry
force—the largest ever assembled in the Western Hemisphere—
which would drive deep into the interior of the Confederacy, de-
feating rebel troops, and laying waste to the countryside.[33] In January Wilson's corps was divided into seven divisons, but with two
divisions on detached duty only five were immediately available.
These units were led by Generals Eli Long, Emory Upton, Edward Hatch, Joseph F. Knipe, and Edward McCook.

Wilson was fortunate in his division commanders; they were
young, able, and energetic. Eli Long, who led the Second Division,
was accounted by Wilson "serious, deliberate, methodical, 'still as
a breeze, but dreadful as the storm.' "[34] The Kentuckian, a former
Indian fighter, gave no evidence of the show and display that were
supposed to be typical of the mounted branch. Wilson was so confident of his brigadier's abilities that he gave him little supervision
and few orders. Long was a veteran of Stones River and Chickamauga, and under his command the Second Division became
known as the "strongest and best mounted . . . of the corps."[35]

Emory Upton, commander of the Fourth Division, described by
Wilson as "an incomparable soldier," was his best-known corps
brigadier. Wilson had known Upton, a New Yorker, at West Point.
The 1860 academy graduate was twenty-five in 1865. Upton was
strong, robust, and energetic, with a reputation for personal courage and deep commitment to the Union cause. Upton was an
avowed abolitionist who had announced his hatred of slavery when
he entered West Point.[36] His wartime service had taken him to
First Bull Run, Gaines Mill, South Mountain, Antietam, Freder-
icksburg, Gettysburg, the Wilderness, Spotsylvania, and Peters-

burg. In the fall of 1864 he rode into the Shenandoah Valley with Sheridan and was seriously wounded at Winchester. His wound still troubled him slightly when Wilson asked him to join the Fourth Division, but Upton immediately accepted the command. Upton had served in both artillery and infantry and looked forward to rounding out his experiences in the cavalry. The brigadier was a keen student of organization, strategy, tactics, and logistics. But unlike many military theorists, Upton was an excellent field commander.[37]

Brig. Gen. Edward Hatch commanded the Fifth Division. In civilian life Hatch had been a sailor and a lumberman. He had volunteered and risen rapidly through the ranks with service at Island Number 10, Corinth, and on Grierson's Raid. In his early thirties, Hatch was aggressive and credited by Wilson with spearheading the cavalry advance against Hood at Nashville. Though fond of Hatch, Wilson faulted the general for saying "yes"to every suggestion regardless of logistical conditions. Wilson also described Hatch as being "talkative and somewhat given to harmless gasconade," but added that this did not affect his absolute fearlessness as a commander.[38]

Joseph F. Knipe, a Pennsylvanian, commanded the Seventh Division. Knipe had served as an enlisted man in the Mexican War and as an officer at Chancellorsville, in the Atlanta campaign, around Nashville, and in pursuit of Hood. The corps commander wrote that Knipe was "nervous, gallant, and enterprising, slight in person, cheerful in manner, and entirely subordinate in behavior."[39]

Edward M. McCook led Wilson's First Division. McCook was a member of the Union Army's most famous family, the "Fighting McCooks" of Ohio. Four of Edward McCook's brothers and ten of his first cousins served as Union officers. Six members of the two families became generals before the war ended. Edward M. McCook had a long record of distinguished service in the West at Shiloh, Perryville, and Chickamauga. Wilson found him "unusually handsome, strong, and vigorous, and while not especially a student nor learned in the military art, . . . he was always prompt and cheerful in such duties as fell to his lot."[40]

IV

By early February Wilson had his divisions situated in cantonments along the Tennessee. The divisions of Generals Long, Upton, Hatch, and Knipe were camped at Gravelly Springs. McCook's First Division was located near the steamboat landing at Waterloo. Unfortunately for Wilson's concept of massed cavalry, his force was slowly being depleted and units ordered detached to serve in other areas. Two divisions, technically a part of his command, never joined Wilson. Judson Kilpatrick's Third Division rode with Sherman to the sea, and R. W. Johnson's Sixth Division was held in central Tennessee. Wilson's most discouraging loss came in early February. On the third, Gen. Henry W. Halleck, chief of staff in Washington, ordered Thomas to instruct Wilson to send five thousand troopers to join Gen. Edward R. S. Canby's campaign against Mobile. Wilson chose Knipe's division even though it lacked equipment and mounts. Hoping that he could obtain additional horses, Wilson dismounted Hatch's division in order to ready Knipe. On the twelfth, Knipe's division sailed to New Orleans to join Canby. The departure of the Seventh left Wilson with four divisions, one of them largely dismounted. The force was cut to seventeen thousand, but five thousand horses were needed to complete the remount.[41]

Despite these losses, Wilson's plans to train and outfit a large force for an invasion of Alabama went forward. As early as October 1864 Sherman, then planning his own advance into Georgia, had suggested a cavalry invasion of Alabama. Sherman advised that this movement would have to await Hood's defeat. Wilson wholeheartedly supported the idea and kept it in mind during the Franklin-Nashville campaign.[42] When Hood was beaten and Wilson ordered to move his men into the Tennessee Valley, the cavalry general reminded his superiors of the earlier proposal. Wilson continually pressed Thomas and wrote often to Grant's headquarters in quest of orders for the campaign. At last, on February 14, Grant wrote Thomas that the time had come to unleash Wilson with a force of about five thousand men. Grant believed Wilson's three objectives would be: "First. To attack as much of the enemy's force as possible to insure success to Canby [in the Mobile campaign]. Second. To destroy the enemy's line of communications and military resources. Third. To destroy or capture their forces brought into the field." Tuscaloosa and Selma were designated by Grant as Wilson's objectives, but he added that "this . . . would not be so important as the mere fact of penetrating deep into Alabama." The general-in-chief indicated great faith in Wilson by advising Thomas that "discretion should be left with the officer commanding the expedition to go where, according to the information he may receive, he will best secure the objects named above."[43] Thomas immediately wired Grant, "I can send on the expedition you propose about 10,000 men."[44] Wilson was disappointed at the campaign Grant and Thomas envisioned. Rather than a five thousand or ten thousand-man demonstration to support Canby, he wanted to mount a full-scale invasion using his entire force. He continued to press his views on his superiors.[45]

By late February Wilson had been told by General Thomas that he could take his entire mounted command into Alabama. To secure this change in orders Wilson had devised a stratagem. When he felt his training program had progressed sufficiently, Thomas was invited to Gravelly Springs to review the corps. Thomas arrived still committed to Grant's concept of a limited expedition. Wilson hoped Thomas would be impressed by the horsemen and agree to the use of the entire force. Thomas arrived on February 23, and Wilson mustered his three mounted divisions to ride past the "Rock of Chickamauga." The review was held in a level valley two miles long and one-half mile wide. "The valley was full of

moving horsemen, companies abreast and every rider at attention.
. . . It was truly a grand sight."[46]

Thomas was impressed, and Wilson took the opportunity to con-
vince him that a mere "demonstration" would be a "useless waste
of strength." Thomas concurred, and when he left Gravelly Springs
he gave Wilson permission to move with his entire force.[47] Designated goals were Tuscaloosa, Selma, and possibly Montgomery.
Wide latitude was to be allowed Wilson when he reached these
points. He could take his force into Mississippi, or eastward toward
Columbus and Macon, or southward toward Canby at Mobile. By
March 1 Thomas and Wilson had decided on a date on which the
advance would begin. The corps would cross the Tennessee on
March 4 or 5.[48]

In the meantime men and horses had to be trained, fed, and
housed. To protect them from biting winter cold, warm cabins and
sturdy stables had to be built. The cabins, twelve feet long with a
chimney and fireplace in the rear, were made of pine logs. Each
cabin contained bunks, a table, chairs, and a variety of personal
decorations. The cantonment plan called for seventy-two cabins for
each regiment. Seventy-five yards away from the men's quarters
stood the twelve cabins of regimental headquarters. Behind each
regiment's cabins six long buildings stabled the horses.[49] Men took
pride in building their cabins and reported that they were "pretty
comfortable quarters."[50]

The units were made easily accessible to river landings, and Wilson saw to it that each regiment had an adequate water supply.
Though they complained of the taste—one journalist reported that
the men found it "exceedingly unpleasant . . . and unhealthy for
its ferrignious and lime mixture"—there was enough water during
the entire stay in the area.[51]

Water was adequate, but food was in short supply for some time.
In large part because of railroad destruction south of Nashville,
rations were short in the cantonments until mid-February. After
that time, with railroads in operation again, food arrived in plen-

tiful amounts, and the corps began to accumulate excess food and other stores for the march south.[52] Before adequate food finally came the troopers were put on short rations. This led to constant complaints and caused Wilson some of his greatest disciplinary problems. On January 28 Will Pepper of the 123rd Illinois wrote "No rations yet. All of the boys is cursing General Wilson. We live on parched corn and hominy and a little beef. This is what I call hard times and worse coming. . . . Hurrah for hard tack and sowbelly and General Wilson, you bob tail." Two days later anger over food scarcities boiled over, and Pepper reported that the Second Brigade, Second Division, was forced to "lay in line of battle all night . . . for hollering hardtack and sowbelly at him [Wilson] as he passed. The boys call him the tyrant or sowbelly at roll call."[53] On January 31 Pepper continued his complaints about food. "We got one pint of sugar for five days for seven men," he wrote. "A little sugar has to go a long ways among seven merry men." On into early February the Illinois trooper continued to protest. On the ninth he wrote that he had only cornbread and tea for dinner and added, "Nobody has any meat now."[54]

Faced by gnawing hunger, some troopers discovered a partial solution. Plenty of corn, hay, and oats for the horses came down river on steamboats and barges, and details went to the landings to unload them. Underneath the forage soldiers often found food smuggled in by sutlers "which the boys would appropriate."[55] The men might have been hungry but their mounts remained well fed. This was adherence to the old cavalry maxim, "take care of your horses before you care for yourselves." Despite the wisdom of this idea some troops saw things differently. Wilson "swore that the *horses* had to be well taken care of, if the men starved," one man commented, adding that this policy "made the whole army despise him."[56]

Foraging the countryside also supplemented the meager diet. On January 25 Sergeant Pepper wrote, "The boys got a lot of forage today such as meat, chickens and corn." With so many troops in an area where supplies were already depleted, such good fortune was only occasional, and the diet for the first month in northern Alabama was both monotonous and scanty.[57]

By the second week of February, Pepper reported that he had gone to division headquarters for eight barrels of sauerkraut and some dried apples for the hospital. Provisions were slowly arriving. With the repair of the railroad most of the men's attacks on Wilson halted. Though Pepper complained of the weather, there were no further complaints about food.[58]

Although food was in short supply and the number of mounts was inadequate, Wilson began his program of instruction for his cavalry veterans by mid-January. This was the first such systematic training program for horsemen instituted in the Union army in the West. During the pursuit of Hood after Nashville units had become separated and discipline had lapsed. "Roll calls had been neglected; and many essential military duties had been perfunctorily performed."[59] A return to rigid discipline was Wilson's first task, and by mid-February generally good order in the ranks had been established. Courts-martial were hastily summoned, and the guilty were often publicly punished. On January 29, two soldiers in the Tenth Missouri were flogged for stealing money.[60]

Despite these disputes and the enforcement of discipline, the men enjoyed the training. Constant inspections and drills gradually brought the corps to a peak of efficiency. Drill extended "from the movements of the squad to division evolutions, with the final result of establishing throughout the entire command an *esprit du corps* hitherto unknown among them."[61] One of Wilson's most important drill innovations was the change from single to double rank riding formation. The major general decided that considering the size of the force the troopers should abandon the usual single file. Riding single file, a brigade of twenty-four hundred men would string out for one and one-half miles. With six and possibly eight brigades, the mounted column would become dangerously long. From January through February and into March the corps perfected the new line of march.[62]

The general commanding was very proud of his training program. He wrote Adam Badeau, "My command is slowly increasing in discipline and organization. I hope for good things of it some day." In his autobiography Wilson boasted that the "weaklings had been weeded out," leaving "good and self-reliant soldiers, free from airs and pretensions." When he wrote his report of the Alabama-Georgia campaign on June 29, 1865, he believed "the final victory over Forrest . . . was won by patient industry and instruction while in the cantonments."[63]

In any cavalry unit the men took great pride in their horsemanship. Wilson's corps was no exception, and the general commanding set his troops an example in riding and jumping. To break the monotony of inspection and drill, Wilson encouraged his men to perfect their riding skills. Jumping their horses over fences and ditches became an enjoyable recreation, and it was a proud Sgt. James Larson of Wilson's escort, the Fourth U.S. Cavalry, who boasted that his horse could clear a rail fence just as easily as could General Wilson on his big black.[64]

While most of his men rode and jumped, many of Wilson's troopers, Hatch's division in particular, remained dismounted. The pursuit of Hood had cost many mounts, and throughout the period in camp in northern Alabama remounts were a problem. The deficit, increased by Knipe's departure, was never filled. Wilson appealed to Thomas, Sherman, and Grant, and though they sympathized, adequate remounts were not forthcoming. In early January Wilson had written Grant's headquarters: "My cavalry . . . can all be united . . . by the 15th [of January], but how a campaign of more than three days can be conducted from that point is more than I now know."[65] Many mounts in the West were being sent to Canby at New Orleans and Wilson complained: "I can't for the life of me see what General Canby can do with all the horses that are now being purchased in the West. If they will only let us get north of the Alabama River, I will agree not to make demand on the Cavalry Bureau for horses after our present wants are supplied."[66] Wilson's personal stable was giving him trouble. Waif, his favorite horse, had boils and was sent to Nashville for treatment. "My stud is . . . an infirmary for broken down cavalry horses . . . I am nearly afoot once more," wrote the general.[67]

His protests and appeals did not produce horses, and Wilson faced the probability that he would be forced to leave several thousand dismounted troopers behind when he moved south. To ensure at least three well-trained and supplied divisions, Wilson began to transfer the few remaining horses in Hatch's division to Long, Upton, and McCook.

If horses were a problem, weapons were not. After some initial difficulty caused by the rail breakdown, Wilson was able to supply almost his entire corps with the premier weapon of the day, the Spencer seven-shot repeating carbine. The Spencer had first come into use in the Union Army in 1863. Use had increased the following year, and by 1865 enough weapons were in production that Wilson's corps could be supplied. The Spencer was thirty-nine inches long, weighed eight pounds four ounces, and was well adapted for use by horsemen.

The carbine was loaded through a tubular magazine, passing through the butt of the stock, and holding 7 copper, rim-fire cartridges, which were fed forward to the breech by the action of a compressed spring inside the magazine tube. To augment rapidity of fire, these thin, detachable magazine tubes could be carried 10 in a special box, making readily available 70 rounds.[68]

Being supplied with the Spencers gave the troopers a morale boost. They realized their repeating carbine was far superior to the single-shot, muzzle and breech loaders in general use by the Confederates.[69] It was estimated that Wilson's mounted force of three divisions could fire over eighty thousand balls in one minute.[70] A trooper in the Seventh Pennsylvania wrote that he and his fellow bluecoats could load and shoot these seven-shots faster than the ordinary musket could be loaded and fired once. The story spread the Yankees could fire all week without reloading.[71] The troopers were drilled in proper use of their weapons, and at Gravelly Springs and Waterloo, "every private and corporal was expected to show at any time a Spencer carbine in perfect condition."[72]

In addition to the Spencer, the men carried a six-shot revolver and a saber. In December and January many units turned in their old, heavy dragoon sabers and were outfitted with the much lighter cavalry saber, in production since 1860. Officers also equipped themselves with this new lighter weapon. For heavier armament each division was equipped with a battery of horse artillery made up of four twelve-pounders. The firepower of Wilson's divisions was far greater than anything the Confederacy could bring against them.[73]

Wilson had served as a topographical engineer, and one look at a map of Alabama convinced him that a pontoon train was necessary. The possibility of crossing the state's many streams led to the organization of such a train. Manned by a battalion of pontoniers, the train consisted of fifty-eight wagons loaded with thirty canvas pontoon boats and lumber for the construction of a thirty-boat bridge. This equipment made it possible for Wilson to build a four-hundred-foot bridge, hopefully long enough to cross Alabama rivers over their banks from spring rains.[74]

V

With his plan formulated, his men trained, and his supplies in camp, Wilson was ready to move by early March. Then the rains came. Through late February and into March the skies deluged the Tennessee Valley. On March 2 an Alabama paper reported, "The oldest inhabitant has seldom seen heavier rains," and two weeks later advised that the Alabama River was at its highest level in forty years.[75] Camps were inundated, the Tennessee overflowed its banks, and men ready to begin their advance huddled in their tents and hoped for sunny skies. Sgt. James Larson wrote, "Although we had such good times at Gravelly Springs, the monotonous camp life became tedious and tiresome toward the beginning of March."[76] The rain increased the tedium. Will Pepper of the 123rd Illinois reported rain almost daily. On February 23 he observed, "Every little brook is at its highest ebb," and two days later the soggy landscape was further drenched by hard rain accompanied by thunder and lightning.[77] Maj. S. V. Shipman of the First Wisconsin wrote the thoughts of all: "Weather mild and raining most of the time. No drills and little more is being done than simply to exist until the rains are over."[78]

Flash flooding created hardship in some units. The men of the Seventh Kentucky were completely surrounded by water and had to swim their horses to safety. Two hundred and fifty troopers on the south bank working near Chickasaw Landing were isolated when the river rose. The men could not get back to camp and had to spend four days on the ground without cover.[79]

In spite of the rain Wilson still hoped to advance according to schedule—by March 5. On March 2 Sergeant Pepper's regiment, the 123rd Illinois, was ordered to cross the Tennessee. Rain began before light and at 10 A.M. the order was canceled. That night the soldier wrote philosophically, "My blankets are very wet but that is a soldier's luck." There was no change on the third. Pepper had to move the sick from the hospital and then move the hospital itself. He reported water two feet deep in the tents. On March 4 the Illinois soldier went down to the river. He wrote that "the river is four miles wide now . . . I seen a boat out in a cornfield. The river is higher than it has been for forty years, so the citizens say."[80]

In camps and at boat landings clothing, accouterments, and ammunition was stockpiled. When rains came the men were forced to spend much of their time moving supplies to high ground.

Some supplies were lost before the labor could be completed. At Eastport where the Tennessee overflowed quickly, Wilson lost a large supply depot.[84] Hopeful that the loss would halt Wilson's feared invasion, a Macon newspaper told its readers that "between 750 and 1,000 wagons [were] washed away . . . many soldiers [were] drowned, and the million dollars of stores [were] destroyed." This claim was a slight exaggeration, but serious damage was done. Reports of the loss spread through a number of newspapers across the deep South.[82]

Rain and increasing sickness forced Wilson to postpone the proposed advance on the fifth. The number of soldiers in hospitals was on the rise by early March. The rain and cold were largely responsible, and Henry Newhall, an Illinois private, wrote home, "There are a good many of the boys sick now, more than has been for the last two years, and I think this is about as sickly a place as we have been in for some time."[83] But the flooded Tennessee River remained Wilson's greatest barrier. On March 4 he wrote Thomas that the "Tennessee is now higher than for years and rapidly rising. It will be utterly impossible to get off tomorrow." The following day he wrote again, "It will be several days before I can begin to cross my command."[84]

VI

Stymied by the weather, Wilson was afraid of a loss of morale. His officers worked to maintain the discipline and the efficiency they had created. Wilson also continued his efforts to gain information on Confederate forces in Alabama. He knew that almost all Confederate infantry forces in the West had been moved to North Carolina to face Sherman. This left only cavalry, militia, home guards, and occasional regular infantry units in central Mississippi, Alabama, and Georgia. The region appeared vulnerable to Wilson's invaders.

As thin as Confederate defenses were, Wilson did not underestimate his opposition. He knew that Nathan Bedford Forrest, his old Nashville enemy, and long the scourge of Union horsemen, commanded the defending rebels. Wilson had great respect for Forrest and was aware that the wily Confederate had often defeated numerically superior forces. An opponent as crafty as Forrest meant that constant Union scouting was necessary. Wilson sent scouts to gather information about roads, river crossings, and troop dispositions. The Union general also used flags of truce to discover the morale of the enemy.[85]

By mid-February Wilson's scouts had funneled much important information back to corps headquarters. They discovered that the bulk of the regular Confederate cavalry, led by Gen. Philip D. Roddey, was near Tuscaloosa. Forrest was reported at Tupelo, Mississippi. Further information indicated that rebel horsemen were well mounted but disorganized and poorly supplied. Forage and food were short and rain and cold had made roads impassable. The problems that beset Wilson north of the Tennessee plagued his adversaries south of the river. Wilson's horsemen spent a great deal of time among Alabama and Mississippi civilians and reported that shortages and Confederate defeats were having a depressing effect on morale.[86]

On February 14 Wilson received some valuable intelligence from scouts sent into central Alabama. Returning riders reported that almost all of Hood's old infantry units had gone to the Carolinas, and Forrest was rounding up all the deserters and absentees he could find in Alabama and Mississippi. Estimates of Forrest's strength placed his numbers around five thousand, but only about three thousand men were mounted well enough to campaign effectively.[87]

Wilson's most direct method of securing information about his enemy was to dispatch, under a flag of truce, Captain Lewis M. Hosea to Forrest's headquarters, ostensibly to discuss prisoner exchange. Wilson sent Hosea so that "no precaution should be neglected and no information left unsought."[88] Hosea, a West Point

Gen. Nathan Bedford Forrest, C.S.A.

graduate and a regular army officer, was intelligent and observant. He selected an escort of six troopers of "fine physique," armed with sabers and the new Spencers. The captain intended to show the rebels a "fair sample of 'them Yanks up thar't the Springs.' "[89]

The Union horsemen rode into Rienzi, Mississippi, where they made contact with Forrest, then near West Point, Mississippi, by telegraph. Forrest invited Hosea and his men to come to Confederate headquarters, and they arrived on the night of February 23. The enemies met on a dark, rainy night in the living room of a rude country house lighted only by tallow candles. Hosea was most impressed by Forrest. By the light of the flickering candles he saw

a man fully six feet in height; rather waxen face; handsome; high, full forehead, and with a profusion of light gray hair thrown back from the forehead and growing down rather to a point in the middle of the same. The lines of thought and care, in an upward curve, receding, are distinctly marked and add much to the dignity of expression. The general effect is suggestive of notables of Revolutionary times.[90]

Hosea found Forrest to be a man with a quick mind and he observed, "there was about his talk and manner a certain soldierly simplicity and engaging frankness, and I was frequently lost in real admiration."[91] The closely observant captain continued his picture of one of the war's legendary figures by adding that Forrest's language "indicates a very limited education, but his impressive manner conceals many otherwise notable defects. . . . His habitual expression seemed rather subdued and thoughtful, but when his face is lighted up with a smile, which ripples all over his features, the effect is really charming."[92]

During the conversation Hosea offered, in Wilson's name, a challenge to battle. The captain reported that Forrest replied:

Jist tell General Wilson that I know the nicest little place down here . . . and whenever he is ready, I will fight with him with any number from one to ten thousand cavalry and abide the issue. Gin'ral Wilson may pick his men, and I'll pick mine. He may take his sabers and I'll take my six shooters. I don't want nary saber in my command—haven't got one. . . . I ain't no graduate of West Point; never rubbed my back up agin any college, but Wilson may take his sabers and I'll use my six shooters and agree to whup the fight with any cavalry he can bring.[93]

It was also during this meeting that Forrest was reported to have used the phrase most closely associated with him. When he admitted he knew little of strategy and tactics he added: "But I always make it a rule to get there first with the most men."[94] Hosea returned to report Forrest's words and his own impressions of what he saw inside Confederate territory. The value of the mission was slight, but both Hosea and Wilson believed the subsequent campaign was aided by what the captain learned. Forrest's acceptance of the Union challenge was a clear indication of his willingness to fight. His belligerent words may have been spoken to cover his deficiencies and indicate to his enemies that, with the Confederacy tottering, he was still willing to fight.

All of the gathered intelligence was put together, and by the time the Yanks crossed the Tennessee, Wilson felt he had a good picture of what he would face. The general wrote Sherman on March 13 that he thought the bulk of Forrest's troops were near West Point, on the Mobile and Ohio Railroad. There were other small rebel detachments along the Alabama-Mississippi border. All the rebels "have been expecting our movement all winter," wrote Wilson. He confidently added: "but once through the sterile region of North Alabama, I think I can get along pretty well."[95]

VII

Wilson was quite willing to give Forrest his fight, but the rains continued. Into the second week of March the leaden skies drenched the restive corps. On the ninth it turned very cold and snowed in the afternoon. By the following day the ground was frozen hard, hindering cavalry movement still further. Bored with the inaction, Wilson's troopers thought of home and searched for some form of amusement. Will Pepper wrote, "I am very sad this evening. I would give anything in reason for the privilege of having a good sociable chat with Miss H. or Miss B. of Illinois." Southern women were no substitute for Illinois belles. Pepper went to a nearby mill for supplies on March 11 and saw a number of women. He mused, "I haven't much for Southeran women. I would not give a snap for the best of them."[96]

The struggle to maintain discipline went on through the period of waiting. A Wisconsin officer reported almost daily court martial proceedings. He listed an occasional acquittal and a number of convictions. On one occasion a private in the Eighth Iowa Cavalry was found guilty of stealing and plundering the citizens of Corinth, Mississippi. The court sentenced him to one month's loss of pay and forced him to parade with the placard "Stealing and Marauding" in large letters on his chest. Lax discipline affected entire regiments. The Second Michigan was singled out as a unit whose men defied their officers, ran away, and made terms before they returned.[97]

If the men were anxious to break camp and march, so was their commander. Wilson was concerned for the efficiency of his force and disturbed at the loss of supplies caused by the weather. Forage was being concentrated at Chickasaw Landing and the rising river there destroyed a large quantity of grain.[98] Wilson was also concerned that his superiors might misunderstand his failure to move. Remembering Grant's impatience with Thomas before Nashville in December 1864, Wilson wanted to march before Washington thought about replacing him. He also wanted Grant to understand his problems. On March 7 he wrote his close friend Adam Badeau:

Your letters of the 16th and 19th of February are just received. I am very sorry, however, they found me here instead of on the road to Dixie as the General expects and as I hoped. This is the only time in my life I was ever ordered to start by a certain time and could not do so. My command was all ready—everything in tip top order—but the extraordinary rains and rise in the Tennessee have stopped everything. My cantonments were located on this side of the river for many reasons, all good. My command, by its present condition, clearly proves my wisdom in the matter. The Tennessee is higher than ever before known, though thank heaven it has begun to fall rapidly, and unless it rains again in three or four days I shall be able to get to river banks and begin crossing. . . . Please explain this to the general and tell him I shall not lose a moment I can possibly avoid in getting away. . . . I am most anxious, lest my delay may not be sufficiently explained, but I venture to hope the General will not lose any of his confidence in my promptitude and determination.[99]

By March 12 the rain had subsided somewhat and the river was slowly receding. Rumor swept the camps that a crossing was imminent and many troopers joined Pepper who "shaved and washed . . . put on clean clothes, and [felt] like a new man." That night he went to church in the camp of the neighboring Ninety-eighth Illinois and on his return reported, "We just have orders to march in the morning."[100] Early on the thirteenth the divisions at Gravelly Springs began the fourteen-mile march to Waterloo, reaching the landing that night. A slight drizzle held up the crossing on the fourteenth, but the following day Long's Second Division began its move to the south bank. While Pepper crossed in his hospital wagon a thunderstorm suddenly broke and the frightened Illinoisan reported, "The water ran under me. I had to get up . . . and get pine branches to put under me to get out of the water."[101]

For three days the corps was ferried across the Tennessee. Wilson had never received the horses needed to remount Hatch's division and the Fifth remained on the north bank. When the campaign ended, Wilson had second thoughts about leaving Hatch's thirty-five hundred men behind. In retrospect he decided it would have been better to march the division on foot behind the corps as a reserve. The general believed he could have mounted Hatch's men with horses captured or impressed from the enemy.[102] Even though the river had fallen slightly, continued drizzle and flooded banks made the crossing hazardous. Transports had to maneuver through shallows into what had been a field one month earlier be-

fore men and mounts could get aboard. Disembarkation was also
perilous. When the 123rd Illinois left its transport it found a deep
hole near the landing containing a drowned trooper of the Seventeenth Indiana.[103] Adding to the peril were Confederate snipers
along the south bank. Gunboats had to accompany transports to
drive sharpshooters away from the landings.[104]

Advance units set up temporary camps while the entire force
was transferred to the south bank. These camps established
around Chickasaw Landing were soggy and uncomfortable, but
the men had to remain in them until the twenty-second. Once the
corps had crossed, Wilson hoped to be able to move south on the
twentieth. Orders were issued to that effect, but Long, Upton, and
McCook reported that boats bringing forage to replace that lost
in the flood had not yet arrived.[105] Wilson's scouts had reported
that the first eighty miles were barren and devoid of food for the
mounts. The delay was maddening but the general reported confidently:

I hope we shall be off in time to do good service. My command is certainly in a magnificent condition, well armed, splendidly mounted,
perfectly clad and equipped, and will turn out a heavier fighting force
than ever before started on a similar expedition in this country. I am
personally in the best of spirits and health.[106]

By the twenty-first the forage had arrived and orders went out to
ride the following morning.

Reveille rang through camps at 3 A.M. on March 22 and the
sleepy troopers roused themselves, built fires, and cooked break-
fast. As the gray dawn broke, "Boots and Saddles" was sounded,
and 13,480 cavalrymen mounted and turned southward in ranks of
two. Most of the men still had no idea where they were going.
Wilson, concerned with security, had refused to divulge his line of
march.[107] As they rode into the heart of Alabama, Union troopers
hoped to emulate Sherman's march to the sea. They agreed with
sentiments General Upton wrote his sister: "The present cam-

paign, I trust, will seal the doom of the Confederacy. I can not see how it can be otherwise, unless great and unexpected reverses befall our arms. Peace must come soon and how welcome it will be to all."[108] They wished for an easy campaign, but a decisive one that would destroy the Confederacy's power to make war.

CHAPTER II

"Prepare to Mount"

Peach and plum blossoms waved beneath warm, sunny skies as Wilson's three divisions jogged in a southeasterly direction down parallel roads. McCook's First Division rode on the army's right, Long's Second was in the center, and Emory Upton's Fourth Division took the left. Each of Wilson's divisions was divided into two brigades. A total of twenty-three regiments, one battalion, three artillery batteries, and Wilson's escort rode into Alabama.

McCook's First Division numbered 4,069 men. The division's First Brigade was commanded by Brig. Gen. John T. Croxton of Kentucky. Croxton, a lawyer and Republican politician, was an abolitionist and a Yale graduate. The tall, twenty-eight-year-old brigadier had served with the Army of the Cumberland at Chickamauga, Atlanta, and Franklin. Wilson called him "an officer of rare discretion, coolness, and courage."[1] Croxton's brigade was made up of three cavalry regiments and one of mounted infantry. The Eighth Iowa was led by a noted Democratic editor, Col. Joseph B. Dorr. The Fourth Kentucky Mounted Infantry, led by Maj. Robert M. Kelly, the Sixth Kentucky Cavalry, commanded by Maj. William H. Fidler, and Lt. Col. Thomas W. Johnston's Second Michigan Cavalry rounded out Croxton's brigade.

The Second Brigade of the First Division rode under Col. Oscar H. LaGrange's command. LaGrange, a New Yorker, had risen from captain to colonel in the First Wisconsin. He was a tall, powerfully built officer who never expected his men to perform a duty he would not perform himself. The brigade was composed of the

Second Indiana Battalion led by Capt. Roswell S. Hill and four regiments: the Fourth Indiana under the command of Lt. Col. Horace P. Lamson; the Fourth Kentucky of Col. Wickliffe Cooper; the Seventh Kentucky led by Lt. Col. William W. Bradley; and LaGrange's old regiment, the First Wisconsin, commanded by Lt. Col. Henry Harnden. Also attached to McCook's division was the Eighteenth Indiana Artillery led by Capt. Moses M. Beck.

Brig. Gen. Eli Long's Second, with its 5,127 men, was the largest of Wilson's three divisions. The Second's First Brigade, made up entirely of Mounted Infantry, was led by Col. Abram Miller.

Miller's brigade, originally called "Wilder's Lightning Brigade," after Gen. John T. Wilder, its organizer, was composed of two Illinois and two Indiana units. The Ninety-eighth under Lt. Col. Edward Kitchell and the 123rd of Lt. Col. Jonathan Biggs, were the two Illinois Mounted Infantry regiments. The two Hoosier units were the Seventeenth led by Col. Jacob Vail, and Lt. Col. Chester G. Thomson's Seventy-second.

The Second Brigade, a cavalry unit, was commanded by Col. Robert H. G. Minty. The chief of Long's Second Brigade was the corps's most colorful officer. Col. Robert Horatio George Minty, born in Ireland, was the son of an Irishman serving as an officer in the British army. Young Minty followed his father into British service and had been stationed in the West Indies, Central America, and Africa. Minty left British service in 1853 and settled in Michigan. When the war began, Minty joined the cavalry and rose to command the Fourth Michigan. The colonel had served ably in Tennessee and Georgia, covering Thomas's retreat from Chickamauga. The blonde Irishman gave some of the *beau sabreau* image to Wilson's command. He dressed nattily and seemed debonair among the more homespun officers in the corps. With his experience, Minty often offered military advice to his less enterprising and less experienced superiors. The thirty-four-year-old colonel had won the reputation of being "headstrong" and disputatious, but Wilson lauded Minty's dash and spirit and called him a "modest and obedient officer, an excellent disciplinarian, and as good a leader as Murat himself."[2]

Minty's Second Brigade, Second Division, consisted of the Fourth Michigan, Third Ohio, Fourth Ohio, and Seventh Pennsylvania cavalry regiments. The Michigan horsemen were led by Lt. Col. Benjamin D. Pritchard; the Pennsylvanians by Col. Charles C. McCormick. The Third and Fourth Ohio were commanded by Lt. Col. Horace N. Howland and Lt. Col. George W. Dobb, respectively. The final component in Long's division was its artillery support: Capt. George Robinson's Chicago Board of Trade Battery.

Riding on the left as Wilson's corps left the Tennessee Valley was Upton's Fourth Division, composed of 3,923 soldiers. Brig. Gen. Edward F. Winslow, twenty-eight-year-old son of an old and distinguished Maine family, commanded Upton's First Brigade. Despite his age, Winslow was a veteran cavalry campaigner. He had served in the Fourth Iowa Cavalry, seeing action from Missouri to Mississippi and Tennessee. Wilson had known Winslow briefly during the Vicksburg campaign and was happy to be reunited with his acquaintance of 1863. The slight, youthful looking Winslow was an important addition to a command engaged on a mission of destruction. He had experience in railroad building, and any work of destruction or reconstruction which appeared was assigned to him.[3]

Winslow's brigade was made up of only three regiments: the Third Iowa, Col. John W. Noble commanding; the Fourth Iowa, led by Lt. Col. John H. Peters; and Lt. Col. Fred W. Benteen's Tenth Missouri.

The other brigade in Upton's division was Brig. Gen. Andrew J. Alexander's Second Brigade, Fourth Division. Alexander, a Kentuckian, had served as a first lieutenant in the prewar cavalry. With the outbreak of war Alexander went to the Army of the Potomac as a staff officer. He had served more recently as Gen. Frank

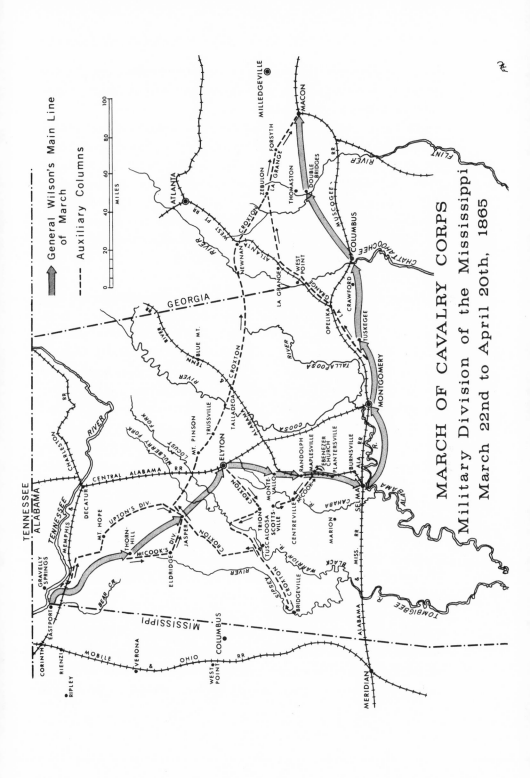

MARCH OF CAVALRY CORPS
Military Division of the Mississippi
March 22nd to April 20th, 1865

Blair's chief-of-staff in the Seventeenth Corps during the Atlanta campaign. Alexander was a vigorous and experienced officer, happy at last to be in a field command.

The Fifth Iowa and two Ohio cavalry regiments, the First and Seventh, formed Alexander's brigade. Col. J. Morris Young led the Iowans, and Col. Beroth B. Eggleston commanded the First Ohio. The Seventh Ohio was led by Col. Israel Garrard. Providing artillery support for Upton's force was Battery I, Fourth U.S. Artillery, commanded by Lt. George B. Rodney.

Wilson's escort through Alabama and Georgia was the Fourth U.S. Cavalry, a hard-riding 334-man force led by Lt. William O'Connell. Wilson also had mustered his pontoon train, hauled by fifty-six mule teams and commanded by Maj. James M. Hubbard. The pontoniers marched with Long's division in the Union center. Of the 13,480 men who moved out of Chickasaw Landing on March 22, all but about 1,500 were mounted. The dismounted men were to act as train guards and as a reserve. Hopefully, they could all be mounted when enough horses were captured.[4]

Union scouts had roamed the barrens of northwestern Alabama and returned to report to Wilson that the corps could not depend on the land for food and forage. The region was not an area of abundance in the best of times, and the war had further stripped it. Some time would be needed to cross the eighty miles of ridges and valleys, and Wilson was forced to take enough supplies to last at least five days. Troopers were instructed to carry on their mounts five days' light rations, twenty-four pounds of grain, one hundred rounds of ammunition, and one pair of extra horseshoes. The provisions were to be kept as light as possible so as not to decrease mobility.

Wilson's wagon train gave the general some concern. A train was necessary to provide many essentials, but it too might serve to decrease mobility. The train consisted of 250 wagons carrying forty-five days' coffee rations, twenty of sugar, fifteen of salt, and eighty rounds of ammunition per trooper. Pack animals loaded with five days' rations of hard bread and ten of sugar and salt plodded along behind the wagons. The Union command assumed that once the corps reached more fertile central Alabama foraging would produce the basic necessities for men and animals. Wagons were to be cut out of line and returned to Chickasaw as soon as they were emptied.

When the order to return extra wagons was issued, General Long read "majors" for "wagons." He replied to corps headquarters that he had no "extra majors" to send back. Wilson's bewildered adjutant straightened out the confusion, but Long's mistake remained a standing joke in the command.[5]

II

Innovation was a salient feature of Wilson's Alabama invasion. Nevertheless, as Union troopers rode through the northern Alabama hills, many features of cavalry campaigning remained unchanged. In fact, in many ways this group of horsemen, though a large one, behaved much like cavalrymen had since the beginning of the war.

Wilson's troopers marched on their first day at the accepted cavalry rate of three miles an hour. Five to ten minutes on the hour were allowed to rest men and mounts. Ideally a cavalry force moved thirty miles a day. Wilson had his men up at three o'clock, and he hoped to reach and perhaps exceed the thirty miles.[6] If he could not maintain this pace in the hills, he could certainly do so in the rolling land of central Alabama. As the column wound southward an occasional order "Trot, March!" was given. This change of pace was not intended to increase daily distance but rather to relieve both horses and men from the continual monotony of the walk. The trots were short, and soon the shout "Walk, March!" slowed the column again.

The troopers of Wilson's corps were veterans. Professional cavalrymen maintained that it took two years to produce a seasoned trooper, and most in the force had served longer than that.[7] Many, in fact, had been riding for four years and were experienced veterans. They remembered the wild days of 1861 and 1862 in which they tried to learn a new martial trade. Many had never ridden before, and simply remaining in the saddle and answering the commands "Trot" and "Gallop" was difficult. Even those who had ridden had to be retaught the "Army Way." When primary riding tasks were mastered, the troopers turned to bareback riding, jumping, riding in formation, and accustoming horses to firing and other noises of battle. An often difficult phase of training was the use of the saber on horseback. Dummies were used to train the inexperienced horsemen to hit the target and avoid slashing their mounts' ears or legs. Many were slow to learn, with harsh consequences for their horses. The manual of arms with pistol and carbine both on foot and in the saddle was also taught.

In the western states cavalry units had been difficult to organize in the war's first days. Farm boys from Indiana, Ohio, and Iowa had worked with horses, knew what it was to care for them, and had little desire to take them to war. At first the *beau sabreau* élan common in the Confederacy was unknown among Union horsemen, but in time the jaunty air of the mounted arm infected these farmers turned troopers.[8]

Discipline was always a serious problem in cavalry units. Because of their ability to range far and wide and because of their dashing image, cavalry units were usually more difficult to control than infantry units. Frequently the greatest task facing officers in new cavalry regiments was the maintenance of order. Troopers were occasionally forced to carry heavy saddles around camp in punishment for lapses in discipline.[9]

Carried away with their new lives as cavalrymen, 1861 recruits had provided themselves with enough equipment to break down their mounts. Around campfires four years later, Wilson's veterans joked about their early folly. When they mustered in, troopers were issued two pairs of socks, two pairs of flannel drawers, a red shirt, a blue fatigue coat, pants, boots, and an overcoat. They also acquired a saber with its four-foot metal scabbard, a pistol, a carbine, a box of cartridges, a box of percussion caps, a tin canteen, and a tin coffee cup. Added to this collection might be a saddlebag filled with extra clothing, a leather halter, an iron picket pin, a lariat, two horseshoes with extra nails, a currycomb and brush, a rubber blanket or poncho, and a pair of woolen blankets. Since there were no limitations on personal baggage, men added to this staggering accumulation everything from haversacks filled with food from home to bulletproof vests. Their mounts groaned under the burden. An Iowa cavalry veteran with Wilson remembered that

fully equipped for the field, the green cavalryman was a fearful and wonderful object. Mounted upon his charger in the midst of all the paraphernalia and adornments of war, a moving arsenal and military depot, he must have struck surprise, if not terror, into the minds of his enemies. . . . When he was on foot he moved with a great clapping and clanking of his arms and accouterments, and so constrained by the many bands crossing his body that any rapid motion was absurdly impossible. . . . When the rider was in the saddle . . . it was easy to imagine him protected from any ordinary assault. His properties rose before and behind him like fortifications, and those strung over his shoulders covered well his flanks. To the uninitiated it was a mystery how the rider got into the saddle; how could he rise to a sufficient height and how then descend upon the seat was the problem. The irreverent infantry said it was done with the aid of a derrick, or by first climbing to the top of a high fence or the fork of a tree.[10]

All of this added from 75 to 125 pounds to the mount's burden.

Active campaigning quickly decreased the equipage. Bulletproof vests and extra haversacks disappeared to be followed by extra lariats and blankets. Soon the absurd mountain of baggage was reduced to the necessary minimum. Wilson's horse soldiers carried nothing they did not need. Standard uniform was the trooper's forage cap (many officers wore the slouch hat), light blue trousers with a yellow stripe down the leg, and a short blue jacket. A wide leather belt which could take both a revolver and a saber

was worn around the waist. All of the men used the McClellan
saddle and most were armed with the Spencer carbine and Colt
pistol. Clanking at their sides was the new cavalry saber which
could be fixed to the end of the carbine and used as a bayonet.

One task the troopers had learned well by 1865 was care of their
horses. "Take care of your horse before you take care of yourself,"
was the cavalryman's creed. The men groomed and rubbed down
their mounts daily. Regulations demanded an hour's grooming
both morning and evening, and this routine was followed when
possible. They cleaned hooves and saw that horses were shod properly, relying on one of the farriers attached to the regiment. Wilson and his officers emphasized proper grooming, and the men
realized that on a campaign such as they were beginning their lives
might depend on their mount's condition. The injunction to feed
your mount before you thought of your own hunger was also ordered. If the regimental quartermaster failed to supply adequate
hay and corn the men found forage and water before they sat
down to their own meals. Early in the war, hundreds of mounts
had been lost when green troopers gave them too much water
when overheated. No longer were horses uncared for or mistreated.

The organization of a mounted arm had been a great expense
for the Union. Unlike Confederate cavalrymen who supplied their
own mounts, the Union War Department purchased horses.
Equipment of a mounted regiment at full strength of twelve hundred men cost over three hundred thousand dollars. In addition,
the pay scale for cavalrymen was higher than for infantrymen.[11]

A frequent problem for cavalry officers was interbranch hostility between cavalrymen and foot soldiers. But Wilson with an all
cavalry force was rid of that nuisance. Pay differences rankled, but
the chief aggravation was the infantry contention that while the
cavalry dashed around splattering foot soldiers with mud it did
little fighting. "Who ever saw a dead cavalryman," was a standing
joke in infantry regiments. When troopers rode by, infantry units
attempted to frighten mounts and jeered "Where's your mule?" It

was this nonfighting reputation that in part spurred Wilson to develop a new type of cavalry campaign.[12]

When Wilson led his corps into Alabama, none of its regiments was at full strength. Regulations provided that each volunteer cavalry regiment consist of twelve hundred men. A brigade at full strength should have put thirty-six hundred men in the field. Rarely, if ever, did any Union unit reach textbook numbers, so the situation was quite normal. A volunteer cavalry regiment was supposed to include twelve companies or troops with a captain, two lieutenants, eight sergeants, eight corporals, two teamsters, two farriers or blacksmiths, two musicians or buglers, one saddler, one wagoner, and seventy-eight privates. Each regiment was commanded by a colonel whose staff included one lieutenant colonel, three majors, a surgeon and assistant surgeon, one regimental commissary, a chaplain, a sergeant-major, a quartermaster-sergeant, one saddler-sergeant, two hospital stewards, and one chief farrier.[13]

From before dawn until after dark, cavalrymen responded to bugle calls. The hills rang as their notes raced up and down the line of march. Horses were tended to "Stables," and "Water Call." The order to break camp and march came to "Boots and Saddles." As they neared the enemy and closed for action, the stirring blasts of "Trot," "Gallop," and "Charge" urged them on. Reveille had roused the Yanks when they left the Tennessee Valley on March 22 and bugle notes put them to sleep that night. No sound of Confederate bugles had yet answered. Where was Forrest? How many men did he have? How soon would he appear?

III

When Hood was smashed at Nashville in December, Confederate military strength in the deep South collapsed. The defeat seriously disorganized Confederate military forces in Alabama, Mississippi, and Georgia. Morale declined, desertions increased, and the region included in the Department of Alabama, Mississippi, and

East Louisiana seemed highly vulnerable to attack. To weaken defenses further, infantry units of Hood's Army of Tennessee were gradually sent eastward to join Gen. Joseph E. Johnston's attempt to halt Sherman's drive through the Carolinas. After Nashville, Hood had been succeeded as commander of the department by Lt. Gen. Richard Taylor. Shorn of his infantry, Taylor was forced to rely chiefly on the cavalry of Maj. Gen. Nathan Bedford Forrest. If Wilson was to be stopped, Forrest's horsemen would have to do it.[14]

This situation placed a heavy burden on units badly battered by the Battle of Nashville and the struggle to protect Hood's rear in the retreat from the Tennessee capital. So great was the damage done during the retreat that Forrest's cavalry division had almost ceased to exist. In late December Forrest scattered his brigades through Mississippi, Alabama, and Tennessee in an effort to provide sufficient forage and supplies. This dispersal, it was hoped, would also make it easier for Forrest to round up deserters and stop marauding bands of Southerners from preying on their countrymen. From late December until mid-March, the Confederate commander was forced to deal almost exclusively with deserters and marauders. As late as March 18, with Wilson poised to advance, Forrest wrote the Confederate War Department that his district was alive with roving bands of "deserters and stragglers" who "exist by plunder and robbery."[15]

On New Year's Day 1865 Forrest decided to go one step beyond dispersal. In order to restore morale, effectively resupply, and crush the deserters, orders went out to furlough a substantial portion of the mounted force. While on leave the cavalrymen were to improve their equipment and clothing and scour the country for mounts. Furthermore, any trooper who returned with a deserter or a mounted recruit was to be granted an additional twenty-day leave during 1865.

Not all of Forrest's force could be sent home. Gen. Philip Roddey's cavalry was retained at its task of watching Wilson's corps. Roddey's horsemen covered the Tennessee River between Waterloo and Decatur. Brig. Gen. Lawrence S. Ross's Texas brigade, too far away from home to go on leave, remained in Corinth, Mississippi.[16]

In late January, Forrest moved his headquarters from Corinth, vulnerable to gathering Union forces, to Verona, Mississippi. Orders reached him at Verona giving him command of all cavalry in Taylor's department. The general was also named commander of the District of Mississippi, East Louisiana, and West Tennessee. Finally, Roddey's command, heretofore independent, was brought under Forrest's control. On January 28 the commander of this enlarged command was advanced to lieutenant general.[17]

It is a long climb in any army, in any war, from private to lieutenant general, but Nathan Bedford Forrest, a soldier by instinct and not by training, had made this climb. Almost forty when the Civil War began, Forrest enlisted as a private despite his age. In 1861 he was a well-to-do Memphis businessman, but it had not always been so. Through hard work Forrest had risen from poverty. At fifteen he had gone to work to help support his widowed mother and a large family, and eventually he became a dealer in cotton and real estate. He had also made much of his fortune dealing in slaves in the marts of western Tennessee. He had no time for an education, and the general remained an unlettered man with a pride in his accomplishments both civil and military. As revealed in his interview with Hosea, Forrest maintained a feeling of contempt for the well-educated. The general was six feet two inches tall, "lithe and powerful of build, with steady eyes . . . altogether a man of striking and commanding presence."[18] "One of his lieutenant colonels saw Forrest in a slightly different way: Without a uniform, . . . he looked like an old farmer. His manner was mild, his speech rather low and slow, but let him once be aroused and the whole man changed, his wrath was terrible."[19]

Forrest raised a battalion of cavalry and was commissioned its lieutenant colonel in October 1861. Trapped at Ft. Donelson, Forrest moved his command out of the fort before its surrender. Covering the Confederate retreat from Shiloh, Forrest was seriously wounded, but recovered and was named a brigadier in July 1862. He then began a series of raids through Mississippi and Tennessee that made him the terror of isolated Union garrisons. In June 1863 the new brigadier was almost killed by a pistol shot from one of his own lieutenants. Forrest was again seriously wounded, but he held the man's pistol hand, pried open his own penknife, and killed his assailant with a slash to the abdomen. Forrest recovered to command horsemen at Chickamauga, but a clash with Gen. Braxton Bragg resulted in his transfer. Then, in April 1864 Forrest was involved in the controversial Ft. Pillow massacre. Forrest's force of fifteen hundred was sent on the twelfth to attack the 557-man Union garrison at Ft. Pillow on the Mississippi. One-half of the garrison was composed of black troops, and Union authorities charged that these men were murdered after surrendering, but the Confederates denied the allegation, labeling it propaganda, although evidence of a massacre persists.[20]

When Sherman invaded Georgia in the spring of 1864 Forrest and his horsemen continued to harass Union armies in Mississippi, Alabama, and Tennessee. Time after time Union forces failed to defeat Forrest, and at Brice's Cross Roads, Mississippi, on June 10, 1864, he soundly defeated Gen. S. D. Sturgis in the battle that is his best-known victory. Through the summer and fall of 1864 he caused Sherman great concern; the Union general finally exclaiming: "That devil Forrest must be hunted down and killed if it costs ten thousand lives and bankrupts the Federal Treasury."[21] "That devil Forrest" was still at large and in the field, and his reputation was enough to cause Wilson concern. But with a dwindling force and a collapsing cause, Forrest would be hard put to defend his newly enlarged area of responsibility.

IV

In January, from Verona, Mississippi, Forrest began to organize the cavalry under his control. He labored to bring in deserters and to reorganize the widely separated units he commanded. On the day he was advanced to lieutenant general, Forrest ordered:

Strict obedience to all orders must be rigidly enforced by subordinate commanders and prompt punishment inflicted for all violations of law and orders. The rights and property of citizens must be respected and protected, and the illegal organizations of cavalry prowling through the country must be placed regularly and properly in the service or driven from the country. They are, in many instances, nothing more or less than roving bands of robbers, who consume the substance and appropriate the property of citizens without remuneration. . . . The maxim "that kindness to bad men is cruelty to the good" is peculiarly applicable to soldiers.[22]

The general's actions brought in many deserters and absentees. One method used was the appearance of a report in newspapers across Mississippi and Alabama. Houses of known deserters were to be visited and families warned: "Your . . . [kinsman] is skulking from his duty while the country is invaded—I give you one week to send them to the ranks—failing in that, your houses will be burned and you will be sent to the enemy's lines."[23] The policy rounded up many skulkers, but occasionally Forrest found it necessary to carry out the threat. The press supported Forrest and urged him to scour the country for deserters who would help "crush the vandals" who were invading the South.[24] Harsh treatment including execution was meted out, but one rebel officer believed executions had "failed to check the evil."[25]

The most controversial proposal for increasing the size of the Confederate army was that of arming Negro slaves. A debate in the Confederacy over emancipation had gone on throughout the war, and by 1864 serious talk of freeing and arming slaves was widespread.[26] The *New York Times* of February 12, 1865, reported that Forrest favored arming two hundred thousand blacks.[27] Through early 1865 Alabamans argued the proposed policy. The *Memphis Appeal*, publishing from exile in Montgomery, reported a Montgomery mass meeting which passed a resolution opposed to arming Negroes. Another Alabama journal wrote that a Mobile paper favored using Negro troops. The debate raged through the state press with arguments both pro and con. Nothing was done to implement such a policy, and the war in the deep South ended before black troops wore the gray.[28]

On March 1 Forrest transferred his headquarters to West Point, Mississippi, southeast of Verona. The general continued reorganization and created divisions made up of troops from the same state.[29] A newly formed Mississippi unit was led by Brig. Gen. James R. Chalmers. Thirty-four-year-old Chalmers was a prewar lawyer who had fought at Shiloh and Murfreesboro, and he had ridden with Forrest since Ft. Pillow. The division's three brigades were commanded by Brig. Gens. Frank C. Armstrong, Wirt Adams, and Peter B. Starke. Armstrong, only thirty, was a true cavalry veteran. Born in Indian Territory, he campaigned in the West and rode in the prewar Utah Expedition. From Wilson's Creek to 1865 his list of actions is amazing. At Pea Ridge, Corinth, Chickamauga, Atlanta, and Nashville, the general served with distinction. Wirt Adams, a Mississippian, had been an active secessionist and raised the First Mississippi Cavalry. He had experience in resisting Union raiders. In 1863 he was unsuccessful in efforts to stop Grierson's ride across Mississippi. Starke, also a Mississippian, had won his spurs at Vicksburg, Atlanta, and Nashville. The division's only artillery was the Hudson Battery, commanded by Lt. Edward S. Walton. By late March, Chalmers's unit was estimated at 3,648 men. Since Wirt Adams was shortly detached to guard the District of South Mississippi and East Louisiana, his brigade would be of little use against raiders in Alabama.[30]

Tennessee was the home of a majority of the men in a new division led by Brigadier General William H. Jackson. A West Point graduate, "Red" Jackson had served in the Vicksburg and Atlanta campaigns. He joined Forrest's corps before Nashville and covered Hood's retreat from Tennessee. Jackson's brigade leaders were to be Tyree H. Bell, Alexander W. Campbell, and Lawrence S. Ross. Like Jackson, Bell and Campbell were Tennesseans. Bell had two horses shot from under him at Shiloh and raided Union forces at Perryville and Murfreesboro. He had joined Forrest in 1863 and fought at Ft. Pillow and in several of the Confederate chieftain's other raids. Campbell was wounded at Shiloh and later became a conscript officer for Forrest. In July 1863 the new brigade commander had been captured and was not exchanged until February 1865. The last of Jackson's brigadiers was Lawrence S. "Sul" Ross. Twenty-seven-year-old Ross was a Texan who served as a Texas Ranger before the war. He enlisted in the Confederate Army as a private but like Forrest shortly became a colonel. A cavalry commander in the West for most of the war, Ross had ridden under Wheeler in the Atlanta campaign. This division's only artillery force was Lt. John W. Morton's Battery.[31]

Forrest was also attempting to organize a third division to be led by Brig. Gen. Abraham Buford, but this unit was never to be a cohesive force. When Wilson crossed the Tennessee its components either operated independently against the Federals or were denied to Forrest altogether. Buford's subordinate commanders were to be Brig. Gens. Philip B. Roddey and James H. Clanton, Col. Charles G. Armistead, leading Alabama troopers, and Col. Edward Crossland commanding his Kentuckians. Also intended for Buford's unit were troops led by Brig. Gen. Daniel W. Adams. Canby's Union strike at Mobile forced the detachment of Clanton's and Armistead's brigades. Buford, a West Pointer from Kentucky, had served on the frontier and in the Mexican War, and he had raised thoroughbreds in Kentucky until he was named a Confederate brigadier in 1862. Buford fought at Murfreesboro and joined Forrest in 1864; in December he had been wounded and was just returning to action in March. Colorful Daniel Adams was Wirt Adams's brother, who had practiced law before the war and was once acquitted after killing a man in a duel. Adams led the First Louisiana at Shiloh and was blinded in one eye. He was wounded a second time at Perryville and a third time at Chickamauga, but he had recovered by the fall of 1864 and commanded the District of Central Alabama. Philip Roddey, an Alabaman with a background like Forrest's, had worked as a tailor, sheriff, and steamboat crewman and had organized a cavalry company when hostilities began. Roddey led Bragg's escort at Shiloh and was named a brigadier in August 1863, since which time he had ridden under Wheeler and Forrest in the central South.[32]

To protect his northwestern flank Forrest created the District of West Tennessee and North Mississippi and named Brig. Gen. Marcus Wright to command. Wright, a prominent Tennessee lawyer, was an excellent choice for the detached force.[33]

On March 15 a correspondent of the *Montgomery Daily Mail*, writing from rebel camps in Mississippi, briefly characterized Confederate leaders: Armstrong "is constitutionally indefatigable"; Starke "steps lightly"; Chalmers "looks fresh and vigorous"; and Forrest "grows grey apace, his hair jet black only a few years ago, grows grey, but how erect he is, how firm his tread."[34]

Returned deserters and new recruits swelled rebel numbers somewhat, but disorganization and the scattering of units across great expanses of territory made it impossible to estimate Confederate strength accurately. Robert E. Lee was informed in early March that Forrest and Roddey led a force of about twelve thousand, but one Confederate who served with Forrest later put the figure at only five thousand, while others ranged the number up to ten thousand. Whatever the troop strength, they were so widely dispersed that an effort to concentrate against a Union invasion might mean Forrest would not arrive "first with the most men."[35]

Some Alabamans must have wondered through the winter if

Forrest would arrive at all. Greensboro's *Alabama Beacon*, in response to this speculation, assured the people:

As a large number of our readers, would like to know the whereabouts of the 'Wizard of the Saddle' we suggest to them to be quiet for a few days only, and he will bring rejoicing to every true Southern beating heart, as he is now getting ready for the move, and when he does move he will make the sound of his roaring heard among the Negroes and Yankees in the West.[36]

One of the most important by-products of Forrest's period of reorganization was the rest it gave his men. Shaking off memories of the debacle at Nashville, the men in the early months of 1865 had time to visit their homes. Forrest was correct in assuming that these furloughs would produce a physical and morale revival. Some new horses had been secured, forage had been ample, and the men had also had the opportunity to acquire new clothing and the first good food for some time. Some wrote that during the rest they had gotten "the Tennessee dirt off." Even on return to camp, rations were good and one soldier wrote, "We are drawing better rations now, peas, bacon, potatoes, and meal."[37] A trooper in the Seventh Tennessee Cavalry enjoyed the "fat horses, good clothes, and good rations." But he knew that "our quasi-holiday would be of short duration."[38] Most of those who were furloughed did return, and it was with great pride that John Young of the Seventh Tennessee wrote that every man "returned to the colors." "Some lingered by the cozy firesides . . . and were a few days late, but all came back, imbued (from association with the patriotic ladies of old Tennessee) with freshened zeal for the cause."[39]

When they returned to camp, shelter, especially during heavy rains, was a problem. Tents were in short supply, and rebel troopers collected fence rails to build "shebangs." Rubber rainclothes were used as ceilings and cornstalks covered with blankets served as flooring.[40] Weapons were also a problem. When combat began, rebel units would be unable to match Union firepower.

The morale of both the Confederate commander and his men seemed good in March 1865. Recent defeats, inferior numbers, privation, and the declining fortunes of the Confederate cause had not led to demoralization. Private Emmet Hughes, a Tennessee trooper, wrote home. "You spoke of the demoralizing situation of our troops. That is, the people thought they were demoralized; if the people that believed this could have been down here on yesterday, they would have thought quite differently."[41]

Forrest reflected this attitude. The general seemed determined to continue the fight and felt "he was in honor bound to fight to the bitter end, unless authorities should direct otherwise."[42] There was a note of fatalism in the determination to fight to the "bitter end." Among Forrest's veterans the respite had restored morale and they were fixed in their decisions to fight on. Yet the fatalism remained. A veteran horseman of the Seventh Tennessee wrote that while camped at Verona, his unit "held a mass meeting to give expression to their determination to fight to the bitter end the common enemy."[43] Chalmers's division would fight "to the end," but Lt. Col. Frank Montgomery of that unit wrote his wife: "our prospects for a successful and honorable ending of the war are gloomy, and unless the God of nations and battles interposes His almighty power or raises up friends for us abroad, I see no hope for us."[44]

While Wilson watched Forrest, the Confederates endeavored to maintain up-to-date intelligence of their enemy along the Tennessee. Philip Roddey, the former Tennessee riverman, deployed a network of scouts across northern Alabama. Aided by a friendly population, Roddey's troops supplied information as Wilson's corps trained.[45] Alabama newspapers were a reservoir of intelligence. On February 18 the *Montgomery Daily Mail* reported twenty thousand Federals in the valley who were ready to invade central Alabama. Journals often discussed such reports as mere rumor, but the *Daily Mail* believed "the report has an air of probability." Three weeks later the same paper confirmed Union move-

ments along the Tennessee from information provided by an escaped Confederate soldier.[46] Other papers, however, reported
Union troops but felt "no apprehension of a raid in force . . . this
spring."[47] Still others believed all such troop reports from the
north were a "blind" to mask the real campaign against Mobile.[48]

From various sources Forrest gathered enough information to
lead him to believe Union troops were preparing for an advance
on Selma and Tuscaloosa. Lee, commander of all Confederate
forces, was warned of such a possibility on February 25. In early
March, Alabama Governor Thomas H. Watts reported to General Taylor that twelve thousand Union troops stood ready to
march on Selma and Montgomery. Watts was so convinced of the
danger of imminent attack that he had alerted the militia and appealed to the citizens of the state to prepare to resist enemy invasion.[49] He even called on Alabama's four thousand sixteen and seventeen year olds to repel the foe. On March 3 Watts proclaimed:

Alabama is now threatened on the North, on the South and on the
West. Large numbers of vessels loaded with troops, I am advised, are
now in the outer bay of Mobile. The enemy's forces at Pensacola have
recently been increased. . . . A considerable force of the enemy is still
in North Alabama, and that threatens to come into Central and South
Alabama. . . . We must either become the slaves of Yankee masters,
degrading us to equality with the Negroes or we must with the help of
God, and our own strong arms and brave hearts, establish our freedom
and independence. Subjugation means the confiscation of your property to pay Lincoln's war debt and gratify abolition hatred.[50]

The governor's strident warning echoed alarm felt by other
Confederate leaders. Gen. Daniel Adams in the state's center was
worried about his force which he believed inadequate to resist
rumored Federal numbers in the north. He wrote Gen. Richard
Taylor of his fears, and Taylor promised to dispatch "some cavalry, and if possible some veteran infantry."[51] Taylor also advised
Adams that Wilson's advance would force Roddey's horsemen
southward and they could be linked to Adams's troops. Finally,

Taylor wrote Adams that any invasion from the north would be resisted by Forrest who would fall on Wilson's right flank.[52]

Delivering on the promise to Adams, Armstrong's brigade of Chalmers's division was sent to Pickensville, Alabama. Not satisfied by this action, the commander of the District of Central Alabama told Taylor that his own force was still small and inexperienced and he had "no confidence" in it. Adams wrote of his men: "They are untried troops, in their country, and will fall out and linger about their homes if the enemy advances." He believed three thousand men were needed to defend rail lines, and twenty-five hundred to hold both Selma and Montgomery.[53]

On March 6 Forrest began moving troops toward the suspected danger point in central Alabama. Roddey was told "to use all possible expedition" in moving to Montevallo to link up with Buford, creating a new command. This force would support Adams. On the same day James Chalmers was ordered to "prepare your command to move at once and be in readiness to move on twenty-four hours' notice."[54]

Ten days after these orders were issued the scattered Confederate generals gathered at West Point for a council of war to coordinate their defensive actions. General Taylor met with Forrest, Chalmers, Buford, and Jackson at Forrest's headquarters. The rebel leaders were convinced that any Union invasion would aim at destroying foundries and shops at Selma and Montevallo. In order to provide maximum Confederate mobility into the threatened area pontoon bridges were to be built over the Black Warrior and Cahaba rivers. Five days' rations would always be available and troops would stand ready to ride. Forrest suggested that signboards be erected to designate the best roads toward the section under attack. In addition, X's were cut on trees along the road leading to Tuscaloosa and on the route to Finch's Ferry on the Black Warrior.[55]

Suddenly the Confederate focus on Tuscaloosa, Selma, and Montevallo was switched to a new danger far to the South. Union troops under Gen. Frederick Steele, serving under Canby's command, left Pensacola and marched toward Pollard, Alabama. If this movement continued, central Alabama might be imperiled from a new quarter. On March 22, the day Wilson rode into the hills of northern Alabama, Forrest began to react to the threat from Florida. Chalmers received orders to prepare for the field, and Armstrong's brigade and the Hudson Battery were sent to follow the X's to Finch's Ferry. On the twenty-third Starke's brigade was sent after Armstrong, with Wirt Adams ordered to remain behind along the Mobile and Ohio Railroad to protect that vital artery.[56] On the same day, Buford, riding to join Roddey at Montevallo, was ordered to Selma to bolster that city's defenses against an assault from Steele.[57] One day later, the twenty-fourth, Forrest reviewed Jackson's division and the detached force of Kentuckians under Colonel Crossland as they rode by on their way eastward. They rode "all day and much of the night over muddy roads, miry swamps, and rugged hills," and as they crossed the Sipsey River just west of Tuscaloosa a grisly sight greeted the men. Rumor raced down the line of march that a drumhead court-martial had ordered the execution of two captured deserters.

As the provost guard closed up the column, it passed the dead men lying one on each side of the road with their heads against trees. Their hats had been placed over their faces, but labels written in large letters told the story: *Shot for Desertion. . . .* The affair caused a profound sensation with the rank and file and it met with pronounced condemnation.[58]

On March 26 these troopers reached Tuscaloosa, where they were cheered by the University of Alabama Corps of Cadets. The following morning the cavalrymen mounted and trotted on to the east. As late as March 27 a Mississippi officer wrote home that the invasion was coming from the South and that he and his men were riding to save central Alabama's important industries.[59]

Forrest's intelligence network had failed to inform him of Wilson's advance on the twenty-second, and for several days the Confederates were unaware that their real enemy was moving in three columns toward Jasper where the entire force would join. Only on March 26 was Forrest apprised of the threat from the north. All rebel movement was away from Wilson, and precious time was lost before Forrest could change this movement and turn to face the Union corps. If the information had been one or two days later in arriving, Confederate units might have passed south of Selma and any resistance to Wilson would have been impossible. As it was, only Jackson's division, last to move, was in position to mount an early resistance. Messengers raced across central Alabama to recall the other units to rally around Selma and Montevallo.[60]

V

While Nathan Bedford Forrest hurried to counter the Union threat up the Montgomery and Pensacola Railroad, Wilson's three divisions made their way through sparsely settled northern Alabama. Upton's division was to leave the corps' main line of march just after departure from Chickasaw Landing and ride to the east before turning south. The most eastward of Wilson's three divisions, it was to cross the Memphis and Charleston Railroad and ride through Mt. Hope on its way to Jasper, point of concentration for the corps. Long's division and the wagon train were to move through Frankfort, Russellville, and Thorn Hill on their way through the hills. McCook's First Division was to accompany Long to Thorn Hill but then leave the general line of march and bear due south to Eldridge. After passing that town McCook would swing back to the southeast and link up with Upton and Long at Jasper. This plan of troop dispersal was wise since adequate forage for the entire force could not be obtained if all thirteen thousand troops remained together. Dispersal also served to confuse the Confederates as to Wilson's objective and force defensive dispersal to protect several possibly threatened points.[61] The only risk was that Forrest might attack the divided corps. Wilson

counted on surprise and a quick passage through the barrens to
deny Forrest his opportunity to strike him while his units were
separated. The young general theorized in words that echoed his
adversary's thoughts: "As celerity of movement is the most valuable force in modern military operations, that force which moves
most rapidly can place itself in the best position for effective service."[62] Up long before dawn, the bluecoats moved to clear the hills
as rapidly as possible. The 123rd Illinois moved twenty miles on
the twenty-third, and the First Wisconsin covered eighteen, a brisk
pace given the terrain.[63] But they were in no danger. Forrest was
150 miles away at West Point and Roddey, who Wilson knew had
been ranging northern Alabama, was in the Selma area far to the
south.[64]

Union intelligence remained alert, and Wilson kept patrols
ahead of the columns to warn of the first appearance of the enemy.
From the outset, a party of twenty-five scouts led by Lt. Henry
Noyes of the Fourth U.S. Cavalry "roamed about at pleasure" well
ahead of the corps. On the twenty-fourth a Union prisoner who
had escaped from Confederates in Columbus, Mississippi, provided Wilson with detailed and accurate information on rebel dispositions in eastern Mississippi.[65] On the twenty-sixth and twenty-
seventh, captured Montgomery newspapers were brought in. The
Union command read with relief stories indicating that the enemy
was "wholly engrossed" in the operations at Mobile and Pensacola.[66]

The march through northern Alabama was made difficult by the
rugged terrain and by the residue of the rains which had deluged
the Federals for so long. The first few miles along the Tennessee
wound through fine farming country, but by March 23 the troops
found themselves in "an uncultivated, barren, and Godforsaken
land."[67] Pines and oaks covered these sandy hills and few people
lived in the region so inhospitable to farming. Although barren
and rocky, the area's natural beauty impressed German-born Capt.
Charles Hinricks. The Missouri officer described a waterfall, cas-

cading a hundred feet and filled with spring freshets. He called it
"the most beautiful spot of this kind I ever saw."[68]

Few had time to watch waterfalls. Streams and even small creeks
were over their banks and roads often had to be corduroyed. Those
men attached to wagon trains and artillery spent hours pulling
wagons and caissons out of the morass. Some were up all night
cutting new roads and building bridges across swamps flooded by
the torrents.[69] On March 26 the Tenth Missouri rose to find the
ground covered with frost, but the cold had not hardened the
ground. It was very deceptive, "looked dry on top, but horses
would sometimes mire to the belly."[70] One Iowa trooper could not
understand why Forrest had not chosen to oppose Wilson in this
area. He wrote, "An intelligent and determined campaign of resistance in this country would certainly have gained much time,
and might have been wholly victorious."[71]

Despite troop dispersal, forage and food were sometimes hard
to obtain, though foraging parties swept the flanks. The poor
farms yielded what pigs, geese, and chickens they had.[72] Regiments
vied for edibles and the Tenth Missouri complained that the
Third and Fourth Iowa had taken all the corn near camp. The
Missourians had to be content with digging for sweet potatoes. On
one occasion, though, the Missourians' supper was supplemented
by honey taken from a farmyard at the expense of several bee
stings. Yet all too often the day's efforts yielded only "poor water,
no forage."[73]

Not many people were encountered on the first five days of
march. There were several encounters with Unionists in the hills.
Sympathy for secession and the cause of the slave owners had
never been great here, and General Croxton reported a number
of "loyal" people around Eldridge. At night some Unionists
walked into Union camps and shook hands with men they seemed
to regard as liberators.[74] Others appeared, and on March 23 five
armed rebels came in and surrendered to the Tenth Missouri. The
same unit met another deserter three days later. The man sur-

rendered, was sworn into Federal service, and promised to guide his new comrades into Tuscaloosa on a back road free of pickets. But these incidents were the exceptions. More typical was a route which ran through "a complete wilderness, not a sign of civilization . . . all day, except towards night we met a man in rags, who drove a miserable herd of cattle, in a homemade cart." This was a strange land for sons of broad and fertile prairies.[75]

On March 27, as Forrest rerouted his men to face Wilson, the Union corps rode into Jasper. The small county seat of Walker County was a cluster of houses, a courthouse, and a jail. Wilson was informed at Jasper that Forrest was on the move and rebel horsemen were leaving Mississippi to concentrate on Tuscaloosa and Selma. The hills around Jasper would offer Forrest excellent defensive positions and Wilson determined to ride toward Montevallo as quickly as possible. Rapid movement, which Wilson envisioned, would be slowed by the wagon train, and he decided to leave it behind. Orders went out to march toward Montevallo by way of Elyton. About halfway between Jasper and Elyton the Black Warrior River, one of Alabama's most formidable natural barriers, had to be crossed. The train would be left on the north bank, but not before pack animals, which would proceed with the corps, had been fully loaded. Wilson reasoned that the unprotected train would be safe since Forrest could not afford to chase wagons when the state's industrial centers were in danger from thirteen thousand well-armed horsemen.[76]

Alabama rang with martial preparations. "First with the most" Forrest hurried to bring his scattered men together, and young "Harry" Wilson urged his divisions southward toward their objectives. To most, the first days of the march had been tedious and unexciting and many were saddle sore.[77] Hills and swollen streams had been the blue-clad troopers' enemies thus far, but south of the Black Warrior that sly fox of one hundred actions, Nathan Bedford Forrest, gathered a defense. Soon Confederate bugles would answer.

CHAPTER III

Getting the Bulge on Forrest

The terrain south of Jasper was not as rugged as that traversed since the twenty-second, but flooded streams still made advance arduous. This was especially true of the Mulberry and Locust Forks of the Black Warrior. Lead units struck the Mulberry Fork on the twenty-seventh and discovered a wide, rapid stream flowing down a gorge with five-hundred-foot banks in some places.[1] The men had to swim their horses across just above an area of rapids. The bottom was rocky, and as soon as a horse lost its footing the water's force swept its legs from under the animal. The men on the north bank watched as rider and mount somersaulted through the water and occasionally into the rapids. "It was indeed a hard sight," wrote Missouri Captain Hinricks.[2] In time a number of riderless horses were left standing in the river, and some horseless men clambered up the south bank. The Fourth Michigan reported the loss of one man and forty horses, and Wilson admitted that "several troopers" were "swept away and one drowned before assistance could reach him."[3] Most of the cavalry got through at no greater expense than a ducking. A small band played during the crossing, and every time a man crossed safely the band blared and his comrades cheered.[4]

The Locust Fork, deeper but not as wide or as swift, lay eight and a half miles beyond the Mulberry Fork. Union horsemen quickly crossed the barren stretch of land and easily forded the second prong of the Black Warrior on March 28.[5] With some difficulty Wilson's artillery forded both streams; horses were swum across while men carried powder on their shoulders, and ropes were used to maneuver the pieces over the streams.[6]

Once across those barriers, the line of march ran through country slightly more fertile than northern Alabama's hills. Just north of Elyton, Wilson's raiders had an opportunity to begin their basic mission—the destruction of facilities aiding the Confederate war effort. Lamson's Flour Mills were put to the torch.[7]

An army deep inside enemy country on a mission of destruction is difficult to restrain from acts of vandalism against nonmilitary targets. In the first place there is little agreement on what constitutes a "military" target. The leveling of Lamson's Mills was the first act in a long record of planned destruction, but both before and after this destruction, acts of plunder against civilians were committed. As the corps moved through the hills on the first five days, woods and fencing were burned. Maj. Stephen V. Shipman complained often of the Seventh Kentucky's penchant for shrouding the line of march in smoky haze by burning the woods.[8] This habit of woods burning would later prove perilous to Wilson's artillery, for on March 30 the Chicago Board of Trade Battery of the Second Division was forced to gallop through flaming woods where sparks scattered in the wind. "Fortunately none of our horses fell and none of the limbers were exploded," wrote the battery's historian.[9] Wisconsin's Major Shipman reported from Jasper: "All sorts of books and papers [were] scattered about the streets showing that our men had been playing the vandal. Gen. Wilson is by no means strict about foraging and plundering. It is a most dangerous practice and ought not to be tolerated. . . . One of our men got a thousand dollar Confederate bond."[10]

When the campaign began Wilson issued strict orders against burning, pillaging, and destroying private property. These orders were to be read daily to each regiment. Despite these precautions some depredations against property with no military value occurred throughout the march.[11]

As they rode along between Jasper and Elyton the troopers encountered a number of Union men. One aged Alabaman told a Union officer that he "had never before seen the flag of his country."[12] A large number of women lined the roads to gawk at the passing bluecoats; union horsemen gawked back but Captain Hinricks reported that the women were "not good looking."[13]

On the twenty-ninth Upton's division, leading the column, pushed a small party of Confederate scouts out of Elyton. The following day Long and McCook reached the village of three thousand which had become the center of a region of iron production.[14] The nascent productive facilities of the town, which Wilson remembered as "a poor insignificant Southern village," were destroyed by the raiders.[15] Near Elyton several regiments bivouacked on the plantation of William Hawkins. The plantation supplied plenty of forage and food and the Union forces reported "we live high." One Union officer found Hawkins "very cranky and insolent" but felt his behavior "will avail him little at present."[16]

By the time the Federals reached Elyton, Forrest was well aware of their presence. By the twenty-sixth Taylor had received word of Union troops in Russellville, and he told Forrest that Jackson and Crossland, moving toward Tuscaloosa, should "meet, whip, and get rid of that column of enemy as soon as possible."[17] Confederate officials in Richmond were warned a day later of Wilson's advance with Taylor's promise to "whip [the] detached column."[18] Although aware of the Union force, the departmental commander considered it a small force that could be routed easily.

But on March 28 Taylor and Forrest knew otherwise. Intelligence at last had clearly delineated the threat. Taylor telegraphed Forrest: "[General Daniel W.] Adams reports enemy camped at Jasper on the night of 26th, three divisions under Wilson, with artillery; destination Elyton and Montevallo. Roddey will be sent to impede him until you get up."[19] Forrest left West Point at once, riding after Jackson toward Tuscaloosa. He would lead a desperate attempt to concentrate as many troops as possible to defend Selma. Richard Taylor believed that with inferior numbers Forrest was the only hope: "He was a host in himself, and a dangerous adversary at any reasonable odds."[20] The people of Alabama had the same faith in Forrest. One paper heard that in Mississippi, Forrest had "organized the largest and finest army since the retreat from Tennessee. . . . Brave soldiers . . . flock to the victorious standard of such a man. . . . In his hands fifteen thousand men are equal to thirty thousand under the lead of ordinary commanders."[21] But Forrest did not have fifteen thousand men and he was not facing an "ordinary" commander. Forrest had swung into action but Wilson had been fortunate, for a combination of his own shrewdness and alacrity with the luck of Steele's diversion from Pensacola, a movement unknown to Wilson, had given the Yankees six days of unchallenged movement.[22]

On the twenty-eighth Chalmers was also made aware of the grave threat from the north. His force was near Greensboro, northwest of Selma, when its race to the south was halted. As Chalmers closed on Selma a sense of doom gripped many in Confederate ranks. One of his officers felt "the romance of the war was indeed gone, only a sense of duty sustaining the cause."[23]

Forrest and his escort passed Jackson's division, mired in the swamps near Tuscaloosa. From near Centerville, on the Cahaba River just west of Montevallo, the lieutenant general sent couriers to urge Jackson on to Centerville as quickly as possible. The Tennessean was to hold the Centerville bridge over the flooded Cahaba. That order dispatched, Forrest raced on toward Montevallo to intercept Wilson and determine where and when the Federals could be stopped north of Selma.[24]

II

Before leaving Elyton, Wilson decided to send a brigade westward to Tuscaloosa, an objective specified in Grant's orders. This force would also cover the wagon train north of the Black Warrior and serve to confuse rebel pursuit.[25] McCook was ordered to:

Detach one brigade of your division, with orders to proceed rapidly by the most direct route to Tuscaloosa to destroy the bridge, factories, mills, university (military school), and whatever else may be of benefit to the rebel cause. As soon as this work is accomplished, instruct the commanding officer to join the corps by the Centerville road. Caution him to look out for . . . [Crossland] who was expected at Tuscaloosa yesterday with a small force marching toward Montevallo. In case the bridge at Centerville is destroyed, let him cross the Cahawba, where he can do so best.[26]

McCook picked popular Gen. John T. Croxton, called a "soldier and a gentleman" by his men, to lead his brigade on the mission.[27]

Before he rode out Croxton received valuable information on enemy troop dispositions. A Judge Mudd of Elyton had been in Tuscaloosa on the twenty-eighth and he told Croxton that only militia and university cadets garrisoned the town. He further advised that no Confederate force existed in the country between Elyton and Tuscaloosa. From Wilson personally, Croxton received instructions to turn south and destroy the Alabama and Mississippi Railroad between Selma and Meridian if seizure of Tuscaloosa proved impossible. On the thirtieth Croxton's fifteen-hundred-man brigade, the Eighth Iowa, the Second Michigan, the Sixth Kentucky, and the Fourth Kentucky Mounted Infantry rode toward the university city.[28]

Croxton marched eight miles on the thirtieth before making camp. On the last day of March the brigade commander sent detachments to destroy the nearby Saunders Iron Works and stores in Jonesboro. That afternoon Croxton learned that "Red" Jackson's division, riding toward Centerville, was ahead, crossing the projected Union line of march near Trion.[29] Jackson was unaware of Croxton's detached force as he hastened to join Forrest and protect the river crossings at Centerville.[30]

Late on the thirty-first, near Trion, Croxton discovered that several Confederate forces had moved through the area in the last thirty-six hours. Jackson's division had been the most recent, and the Kentuckian decided to pursue Jackson. He pushed scouts ahead to find the rebel column, rested his main force, and sent messengers to ride to Wilson to inform the corps commander of his plans. The following day Wilson learned what Croxton intended.[31]

Unknown to Croxton, he had an opportunity to crush Jackson's artillery and train. By chance his fifteen hundred men had gotten between Jackson's cavalry and his guns and wagons, still near Tuscaloosa. But Croxton did not exploit his advantage, and Jackson turned his cavalry around before the Federals could discover their advantage and strike.[32] Jackson found the enemy in his rear and rode back toward the Union force. He assured Forrest on the thirty-first, "I am closing around him there with the view of attacking at daylight in the morning."[33]

The Tennesseans were placed so as almost to encircle Croxton's brigade. Croxton was convinced he was outnumbered and, all thought of offense gone, decided to extricate himself under cover of night. He slipped westward down the Mud Creek Road. Before his withdrawal was completed Jackson's horsemen struck. Union pickets collapsed and a number were killed and captured. Jackson's forces overran the enemy camp and pursued the retreating column for several miles. For a time the Federals retired in order, but darkness and confusion took its toll, and orderly withdrawal became flight. Part of the Eighth Iowa was cut off from the brigade, and the Iowans wandered across Alabama for several days before finding Wilson's main force.[34]

As Jackson drove Croxton down the Mud Creek Road, he realized that he was shoving the Yankees toward his virtually unprotected wagon train. He wanted to protect his train and deny the Federals entry into Tuscaloosa, but on the afternoon of April 1 he learned that the enemy to the south posed a new threat. When Croxton's scouts appeared, Jackson was riding toward Centerville to secure the vital bridge over the Cahaba at that town. Now he heard that Union troops had seized the span, and Jackson broke off his pursuit and turned again toward Centerville.[35]

The skirmish at Trion accomplished little. Croxton had been expelled from his camp, and the Union loss was variously estimated at thirty-two and forty-five killed. There is no accurate report of the supposed smaller Confederate casualty list. However, by diverting his force, Jackson had imperiled control of an important communications link. Outside of his casualties Croxton lost little in the April 1 skirmish, and he was still free to destroy the strategic property in Tuscaloosa.[36]

III

During the thirtieth and thirty-first, as Croxton's independent command approached Tuscaloosa, the balance of Wilson's corps, led by Upton, advanced on Montevallo. The men were up at 3 A.M., "Boots and Saddles" was sounded at 5 A.M., and the column moved southward through a steady drizzle. The Cahaba loomed as a formidable barrier, and a hard rain fell on the grumbling cavalrymen as they pressed toward the river and its tributaries. Wilson kept the corps moving all night of the twenty-ninth, and Upton's advance reached the river and found that rebels had felled trees into the ford, blocking passage. Fortunately a short distance downstream scouts found a railroad bridge. The structure near Hillsboro was without crossties, but the horsemen found some new ties near the bridge and, ripping them up with improvised tools, replaced the flooring destroyed by the rebels. Two thousand men waited in silence while the two-hour task was accomplished, and then they crossed in single file, carefully leading their trembling mounts.[37] When artillery crossed the span, forty feet above the water, guns were pulled by the men, and the horses, some blindfolded, were led.[38]

Upton crossed the river on the thirtieth, followed that day and the next by Long and McCook. South of the river the corps entered a land such as they had rarely seen since arriving in Alabama in January. The men found "a region abounding in forage, corn, bacon, chickens, turkeys and other comforts for hungry soldiers." In addition to fertile fields the line of march rode through gently rolling wooded hills and past the first large concentration of plantation houses the men had encountered.[39] After dark one night Upton's aide-de-camp Francis W. Morse climbed one of those hills and saw a beautiful sight, "for twenty-five miles in our rear, I could see the reflection of the thousands of camp fires."[40]

First sight by the corps' main body of the long-expected Confederate defense came on the thirtieth. Eight miles from Montevallo Philip Roddey and a small group of horsemen encountered Upton's vanguard. Upton ran Roddey's men through Montevallo but did not pursue, choosing to secure the largely deserted town. At 1 P.M. on March 31 Wilson joined Upton.[41]

Montevallo, a "pretty little town," was an important objective of Wilson's campaign.[42] The Alabama and Tennessee River Railroad ran from Selma through Montevallo before veering eastward to Talladega and into Georgia. But it was as the center of the iron and coal district of central Alabama that Montevallo was chiefly important. Capture Montevallo and destroy its foundries, mills, and collieries, and the production of the Selma-Montevallo industrial community would grind to a standstill.

Elyton's factories had been wrecked, and the greater concentration of industrial facilities between that town and Montevallo now followed. Detachments of Union horsemen worked busily to complete the destruction before Roddey, reinforced by Forrest, reappeared. At Oxmoor the Red Mountain Iron Works, capable of twenty tons of iron daily, was destroyed. As the First Wisconsin rode by these burning works Major Shipman noted large piles of pig iron that would now be useless.[43] The Cahaba Valley Rolling Mills at Irondale, producing ten tons a day, and the more productive Bibb Naval Furnace at Brierfield went up in flames. The Bibb facility was defended by a detachment from Roddey's cavalry, but Col. Fred Benteen's Tenth Missouri routed the guard and wrecked the works.[44] Ranging to the east and up the Alabama and Tennessee River Railroad, two blast furnaces and the rolling mill of the Shelby Iron Works were wrecked. Several other factories and five collieries in the area were destroyed.[45]

It is difficult to imagine a more severe blow to the economy of Alabama and the dying Confederacy than this destruction. Hundreds of laborers, black and white, were put out of work and the burgeoning coal and iron industry of Alabama was wrecked. Any hope of the region's factories' fueling continued Confederate resistance from the deep South was disappearing.

Across Alabama the press tried to keep up with the Union campaign. Information was scarce and wires from Montevallo to Selma were reported down on March 30. On the same day the *Memphis Daily Appeal* reported a "quiet" rumor-free day in Montgomery; the journal also reported McCook's force at Montevallo but told readers "unless the column is much larger than reported [5,000] no fears need be entertained of either Selma or Montgomery from this raid."[46]

IV

Shortly after Roddey's small force was driven out of Montevallo, the bulk of his command, racing from near Selma, reached Roddey just south of the captured town. Roddey believed these reinforcements gave him the strength necessary to delay Wilson and buy time for the juncture of all rebel forces in central Alabama. He dismounted his troops and set a skirmish line along a ridge two miles south of Montevallo. It was this line that Upton's scouts encountered on the morning of the thirty-first.[47] The Fourth Division's commander immediately moved a mounted force toward the rebel position holding his main force behind the town.

That was the situation when Wilson rode in at 1 P.M. The two friends rode along as Upton sketched the situation. On occasion Upton, who loved tactical theory, "annoyed" the corps commander with his constant discussion of tactics. Once Wilson said impatiently: "Damn it Upton, the tactics are good enough for this campaign. We couldn't change them if we would. In the words of the Centurion to whom one of his soldiers complained that his sword was too short, 'Get close enough to the enemy and you'll find it long enough.' "[48] On this occasion the corps commander was pleased with Upton's tactics and with his speed, and he ordered him to attack.[49]

Wilson and Upton decided to use Andrew J. Alexander's Second Brigade as spearhead of the Union charge. The First Brigade of Maine's Edward Winslow would remain in close support. Roddey's skirmish line was edging forward when Alexander's horsemen, the Fifth Iowa in the vanguard, unfurled their guidons and answered the bugle call, "Charge!" Sabers drawn, the Iowans led a classic mounted assault. The superior Union force broke the skirmish line and cut through Roddey's main force. The rebels streamed down roads leading south toward Randolph. The retreat was not precipitate, for Roddey fought from behind fence rails to slow the enemy. Both of Upton's brigades were committed and numbers and aggressiveness were too much for the defenders. Roddey fell back about three miles to Six-Mile Creek.[50]

The creek was a formidable barrier and Col. Fred Benteen's Tenth Missouri of the First Brigade halted there. Roddey was reinforced by about five hundred of Col. Edward Crossland's Kentuckians and a small number of troops under Dan Adams. The enlarged force pushed the Tenth Missouri back slightly, but John Noble's Third Iowa Cavalry rallied to support their comrades from Winslow's brigade. The Iowans assaulted the Confederates and drove Crossland back. By this time Upton's cannoneers, George Rodney's Battery of the First U.S. Artillery, bombarded

the enemy along the creek. Beyond the stream thick woods allowed the rebels to mask an orderly withdrawal. Again the dismounted Confederates fired from behind trees and fence rails.
When Crossland tried to remount, the pressing Union force captured several of the Kentuckians. Then order disintegrated; re-
calling the race southward, one Confederate veteran wrote, "I am
satisfied that . . . [Wilson] drove us fifteen miles an hour a part of
the time."[51]

As Roddey and Crossland were being driven toward Randolph,
General Forrest and his escort, after a hard ride from West Point,
reached the Montevallo-Randolph Road. Forrest was in time to
see the rear of the Union assault force and, not hesitating, the
lieutenant general rode out of the timber and closed with the bluecoats. The Union troopers repulsed Forrest, who broke off combat
and circled the enemy to ride toward Randolph. That night he
rode into the camp Roddey and Crossland had made just south of
Randolph.[52]

By nightfall on the thirty-first the Confederates had failed completely to slow down, much less halt, Wilson's raiders. In the
fourteen-mile running fight on the thirty-first, Upton had driven
the enemy before him, inflicting about a hundred casualties while
losing less than one-half that number. Wilson felt that the running
fight had given his men confidence. He wrote: "They had fairly
'got the bulge' on Forrest."[53] In his report of the campaign, he
believed that this fight had established "a moral supremacy for the
corps."[54] Evidence of this Union feeling of moral supremacy was
Capt. Charles Hinricks's boast in his diary that after a ten-minute
fight "the noses of the gents of the Confederacy were again turned
toward their dear old South."[55] Upton's division camped that night
near Randolph, and McCook and Long continued to move southward from Montevallo. Confederate dispersal remained Forrest's
most serious problem. If concentration was not achieved on April
1 or 2 there seemed little chance Selma could be defended.[56]

V

Concentration was uppermost in Forrest's mind on the night of the thirty-first. Jackson's division was across the Cahaba near Scottsville, and Taylor sent word that Chalmers was marching his division toward Plantersville, a village between Randolph and Selma. If Chalmers could join Forrest, the Confederate commander's combined force might be sufficient to slow Wilson north of Selma. Hopefully the delay would allow "Red" Jackson to move by forced march either to strike Wilson's rear, pincering him between himself and Forrest, or to join Forrest in Selma.[57] That night the lieutenant general's aide telegraphed Jackson Wilson's position and urged him to "follow down after them, taking the road behind them to Montevallo. [Forrest] does not wish you to bring on a general engagement, as he thinks their force is much stronger than yours, unless you find the balance of our forces in supporting distance of you."[58] As Forrest tried to hasten Jackson, that division chief was turning to attack Croxton and protect his wagon train.

Forrest's efforts to unite his scattered forces ran into bad luck on the morning of the first. Wilson's horsemen overhauled a messenger carrying Forrest's dispatches. From them he learned Croxton's position and was made aware of the gravity of Confederate dispersal. Wilson now knew for certain that Jackson had not yet crossed the river and that Chalmers was at least twenty miles south of Forrest. In *Under the Old Flag* Wilson wrote that with this intelligence, "if I would force the marching and the fighting with sufficient rapidity and vigor, I should have the game entirely in my hands."[59]

Vigor and rapidity describe Wilson's dispatch of Edward McCook at the head of his remaining brigade, LaGrange's Second, to ride to Centerville and seize the Cahaba bridge. In addition to controlling the span, McCook was to cross the river, march north, and attack Jackson. He would then join Croxton, who presumably would have completed his devastation of Tuscaloosa, and the united force was ordered to return to the corps at Selma. McCook was given only cavalry, leaving pack animals and wagons with Wilson.[60]

Even more vigorous was the decision to send part of the First Wisconsin racing for Centerville ahead of McCook's main body. The bluecoats sped the fifteen miles in two hours, routed Confederate defenders, capturing fifteen, and took the bridge.[61] They then barricaded the Tuscaloosa Road on the north bank of the river. McCook joined Harnden's Wisconsin horsemen about noon on the first. Leaving a bridge guard, he rode on to Scottsville where he halted for the night.[62] At Scottsville, McCook learned that Jackson had fought Croxton and shoved the Union brigade northward. That night as Union troops foraged through the dusky woods around Scottsville, they bumped into Confederates on a similar mission. The enemies agreed "to a truce while they shared such good things as the farmer had to contribute."[63]

On April 2 McCook moved the Second and Fourth Indiana toward Trion. Four miles out of Scottsville the Hoosiers ran into a barricade manned by Tyree Bell's rebel brigade. The Federals paused briefly and then the Second Indiana charged the barricade. Bell's defensive position was strong, and the Tennessean repulsed McCook's troopers. Blocked from joining Croxton, hurled back by Bell, and believing himself to be outnumbered by Jackson's division, McCook ordered abandonment of Scottsville and retired across the Cahaba.[64] As he retreated, McCook burned a cotton factory and niter works near Scottsville and, most strategically important, destroyed the Cahaba River bridge at Centerville. Maj. Stephen V. Shipman's detail in charge of destroying the bridge was forced to delay until a thirty-man force sent to scour the Cahaba's west bank for horses recrossed the span. Confederate snipers appeared and Shipman had to fight to hold the bridge, but the laggards finally appeared and raced across the structure as Shipman's crew began the destruction.[65] To increase Jackson's problems, Union scouts searched for and stove in all the boats found along the river.[66] McCook had not joined Croxton, and he had been defeated in a short but sharp engagement; nevertheless, his march had accomplished a great deal. Jackson would not unite with Forrest.

If Jackson was cut off, at least the arrival of Chalmers's division would give Forrest enough men to fight some sort of delaying action, but confusion again plagued the Confederate cavalry chief. By midday on the first Forrest found that Chalmers was moving west and away from Plantersville. The lieutenant general quickly sent couriers to Chalmers bearing orders instructing the division commander to wheel his force around and move to the Randolph-Plantersville Road. Chalmers was told to leave his artillery and train behind if necessary—speed was vital. He replied that he would move with dispatch toward Dixie Station, six miles north of Plantersville.[67] After the war Chalmers claimed flooded roads and conflicting orders had forced his delay.[68]

North of Plantersville, Bogler's Creek runs through hilly, wooded country, slashed by ravines. At Ebenezer Church, close to the creek, Forrest explored the ground and found a high position commanding the Alabama and Tennessee River Railroad and both the Randolph-Plantersville and Randolph-Maplesville roads. Such a line ran athwart Wilson's route to Selma and stood close to the point at which Chalmers's wandering division should strike the Randolph-Plantersville Road. The Confederate line ran east and west, from Mulberry Creek on the east to a wooded ridge on the western end. The right at Mulberry Creek was held by a battalion of Gen. Dan Adams's untried Alabama State Troops. The center ran along the north bank of Bogler's Creek and was defended by Roddey's cavalry, while Edward Crossland's Kentucky cavalry held the ridge on the left. On the afternoon of April 1, part of Frank Armstrong's Brigade, the advance of Chalmers's force, reached Forrest's position. The general could only hope Jackson's division and the balance of Chalmers's would arrive in time to add their numbers. The rebels set eight guns covering the two roads to support Forrest's line. To make his position more defensible, the Confederate commander ordered rail barricades erected.[69]

Estimates of the total Confederate force range from one rebel figure of fifteen hundred to a Union figure of five thousand. There is no way to determine the exact numbers, but it seems certain that Wilson's cavalrymen considerably outnumbered the defenders. A Confederate soldier later wrote: "If all the [Confederate] forces had been concentrated, as Forrest intended, somewhere between Montevallo and Selma would have been fought the cavalry battle of the ages."[70] Confederate dispersal made sure no "cavalry battle of the ages" would be fought, rather a small force's attempt to slow the relentless invader. Wilson used about nine thousand of his corps in the action at Ebenezer Church.[71]

Bugles rang through Wilson's camps before dawn on the first as the general labored to keep "the game entirely in [his] hands."[72] Wilson felt his right flank and rear were secure, and "it remained only to hurl my two splendid divisions with all possible speed against the enemy in my front, which I knew they outnumbered."[73] At daybreak the corps mounted and filed southward by twos. Upton swung his division a few miles to the east toward Maplesville. He was to reach that town and then veer southwestward and move parallel to the corps' main line of march about two miles to the west. A little south of Ebenezer Church he would return to the Randolph-Plantersville Road and ride on toward Selma on that thoroughfare. Long's big Second Division would march in the center following the Randolph-Plantersville Road. McCook was sent to Centerville to cover both right flank and rear. Wilson's Fourth U.S. Cavalry escort was detailed to burn all bridges on the Alabama and Tennessee River Railroad, which closely paralleled the corps' line of advance. Long's unit had not yet been seriously engaged and it pressed "eagerly" against the enemy.[74]

Leading Long's division was the Seventy-second Indiana Mounted Infantry, and the unit encountered Confederates about four miles south of Randolph. The Indianans advanced in the same kind of running fight Union forces had been engaged in between Montevallo and Randolph. One-half of the rebel force laid down a delaying fire while the other half set a temporary defensive line in the rear. When the Seventy-second collapsed the first line it fell back beyond the second force and established a new position, whereupon the men already set in defensive positions began to fire. The Confederates' leapfrog defense slowed Long's division all day long. By late afternoon the Confederate outriders had been shoved inside the main line along Bogler's Creek.[75]

By 4 P.M. Long had encountered the skirmish line thrown out from Forrest's massed troops near Ebenezer Church. The Second Division's chief did not yet realize how close his Indiana horsemen were to Forrest's main force. When rebel skirmishers stopped the Seventy-second Long sent word for them to dismount and fight on foot. Laying down a withering sheet of fire with their seven-shot repeaters, the Yankees advanced through the woods. Finally Forrest's skirmishers broke and ran into their lines.[76]

This withdrawal seemed like a resumption of rebel leapfrog tactics, and General Long sent four mounted companies of the Seventeenth Indiana, sabers drawn, charging the enemy. Leading the charge was Capt. Frank White, characterized by Wilson as "a berserker of the Norseman breed, broad-shouldered, deep-chested, long-limbed, . . . and 'bearded like a pard.' "[77] White's troops entered a stand of timber and disappeared from the division commander's view. The Indianans pressed the retreating skirmishers but suddenly found themselves facing vastly superior numbers. The assault force reached a Confederate battery where one trooper ran down a cannon, killing his horse and splitting a wheel of the field piece. Union Capt. James D. Taylor, like his men, found himself engaged in furious hand-to-hand combat. The young Indiana captain's adversary was Forrest. Riding King Phillip, his favorite horse, Forrest closed with Taylor, and the captain wounded the Confederate veteran with the blade of his saber. Forrest's fourth Civil War wound was not serious and the general killed Taylor with his six-shooter. Forrest said later, "If that boy had known enough to give me the point of his saber instead of its edge, I should not have been here to tell you about it."[78] Overwhelmed, the men of the Seventeenth retreated to Union lines after losing seventeen men.[79]

Long now knew that Forrest's line was held in strength. He ordered Abram Miller's brigade to dismount and face Confederate positions covering the Randolph-Plantersville Road. Miller's regimental guidons read left to right: 98th Illinois, 72nd Indiana, 123rd Illinois, and 17th Indiana. On foot the Mounted Infantry moved out toward the rebel line.[80]

As Miller struck, Upton's division galloped to his assistance. Led by Alexander's brigade, the Fourth Division riding to the east heard the firing and charged. Alexander's vanguard, Col. Israel Garrard's Seventh Ohio, led the charge, outdistanced the rest of the brigade, and suddenly rode into a clearing facing Confederate works near the Maplesville-Plantersville Road. Confederate fire quickly repulsed the eager Ohioans, and Upton sent a small force forward on foot to seize a house facing the rebel line and to act as sharpshooters until the remainder of the column arrived.[81] Then the division commander sent the Fifth Iowa and First Ohio to their relief. All of Alexander's men advanced on foot and slid to the right in an attempt to fuse with Long's division.[82]

Charging through the clearing, Alexander's men struck Gen. Dan Adams's Alabama State Troops in whom the Confederate leader had expressed "no confidence."[83] Pressure from the Union veterans had struck Forrest's line at its weakest point, and the state troops broke, crumbling the Confederate right. An immediate rout was prevented when Forrest's veteran cavalry, supporting Adams, gave way grudgingly. This stand was doomed to be short lived, for the Third and Fourth Iowa of Upton's First Brigade launched a mounted charge to support Alexander. The combined attack on foot and horseback was too powerful for the rebel cavalry to resist, and the entire Confederate right disintegrated. Forrest's center and left were no longer tenable, and the rebel force fled across Bogler's Creek and on to Plantersville and Selma.[84] The battle, called by one Union trooper "a right smart little skirmish," was over.[85]

By April 1 Wilson's raid had produced a wave of fear across Alabama. Citizens eagerly awaited word of the Federals' repulse, but press information on the battle at Ebenezer Church was conflicting. The *Montgomery Daily Mail* reported a Confederate victory, while Greensboro's *Alabama Beacon* told of Forrest's wound and the rebel retreat.[86]

At Ebenezer Church Wilson captured three hundred prisoners and three pieces of Forrest's artillery. The Confederate estimate of killed and wounded is nonexistent. Wilson's price for the victory was twelve killed and forty wounded; Wilson's wounded were treated at the church and the twelve Union dead were buried in the church graveyard.[87] The wounded were shortly moved to the village church in Plantersville where fifty-eight wounded and sick men were left when the corps moved south.[88]

After the Union dead had been interred and the wounded cared for, Wilson moved Long and Upton on to Plantersville. McCook lay at Scottsville and Centerville covering the corps' rear. The Union column had reached Alabama's fertile black belt, and its camps were surrounded by abundant food and forage. One foraging party led by Indiana Capt. Ross Hill was about to take goods from a plantation barn when a woman's voice rang out: "You, Ross Hill! How dare you rob my plantation! If you don't call your men . . . I'll go up to Indiana and make your mother whip you within an inch of your life." Turning, the officer saw a young woman who had once lived in his home town. The men were called off and the plantation's stock spared.[89]

Plantersville contained no mills or factories, but Union troopers burned the railroad depot and a cotton warehouse on the night of

April 1. It was a happy but tired corps that sat around campfires of blazing rails eating their fill.[90] For three days they had frustrated every effort of "that devil Forrest" to stop their steady advance. The Confederate defense had been inferior in numbers and weakened by confusion and division. Wilson had been marching for eleven days and now stood on the threshold of the campaign's major objective—Selma. Nineteen miles away lay that city of great strategic value to the South. If there was to be any resistance from the deep South, Selma's arsenals would have to be held. Defending those arsenals was a small, demoralized force. Not even the military magic of its veteran captain seemed capable of saving the city. Wilson did not expect Forrest to make another stand north of Selma, and the Union general seemed to have "the game entirely in [his] hands."[91]

CHAPTER IV

Wilson's Invincibles

Bedford Forrest was a resourceful commander used to "getting the bulge" on his enemies, but on the morning of April 2 all the momentum of the Civil War's last campaign in Alabama lay with James H. Wilson. It was a weak and disorganized Confederate force that had fled battlefields from Elyton to Plantersville and by the second it was inside Selma's defenses. This rebel force and its legendary leader needed time to gather reinforcements and position them inside the city's parapets, but there would be no Union delay. At 6 A.M. on the second, flags unfurled and bugles sounding, the Union raiders rode out of their camps around Plantersville. A supremely confident army, "stripped for battle," rode the last nineteen miles toward its principal objective—the industrial city of Selma.[1]

Selma stood on a bluff on the north bank of the Alabama River and was "a beautiful town with broad streets." From its fine residences Union soldiers correctly called it "a place of great wealth."[2] North of the city the country was relatively flat and it was from this direction that Selma was most vulnerable. Of the six major roads into the city, four crossed this plain. From the east the Burnsville Road ran close to the Alabama, and two avenues approached from the north. The road from Plantersville, Randolph, and Montevallo, along which Wilson had been moving, ran due north out of Selma. This road was known locally as the Range Line Road. From the northwest the Summerfield Road entered the city. Last of the four arteries was a road running west to either Marion or Cahaba. South of town a major avenue of communications was the road that crossed the Alabama River and, running just south of that stream, reached Montgomery some sixty miles to the east.

Selma was served by two railroads. Connecting the city with Elyton-Montevallo coal and iron was the Alabama and Tennessee River Railroad along which Wilson had marched and which had in large part been destroyed. The city was linked to the west by the Alabama and Mississippi Railroad which ran to Demopolis and Meridian. The Alabama River was also a vital artery of communications and commerce. Using this navigable waterway, Selma's goods could be shipped to both Montgomery and Mobile. Situated on these lines of communication and located near easily available raw materials, Selma had contributed much to the Confederate war effort. By April 1865 Selma and Columbus, Georgia, in the deep South, remained the best hopes for supplying continuing Confederate resistance.[3]

The Civil War had produced a "boom" in Selma. In 1860 Dallas County, of which Selma was the seat, had 7,785 whites. During the war an estimated ten thousand workmen were employed in the city's factories. Although the latter estimate included black laborers, evidence of considerable population increase was clear.[4] The jobs of most of the whites in this force were considered of such importance as to command exemption from military service. In late March 1865 the population of war workers was augmented by refugees. One employee of the Nitre Works was unable to find lodging so he slept on a cot in his office.[5]

In 1862 Gen. Josiah Gorgas, Confederate chief of ordnance, moved the arsenal at Mt. Vernon, Alabama, to Selma for better protection. In 1865 the huge arsenal of twenty-four buildings was commanded by Lt. Col. James L. White. When Union troops later examined the arsenal they believed its works compared favorably with those in Philadelphia and St. Louis.[6] The arsenal's value to the Southern cause was evident in the Union report of material found there in 1865. General Winslow reported: fifteen siege guns;

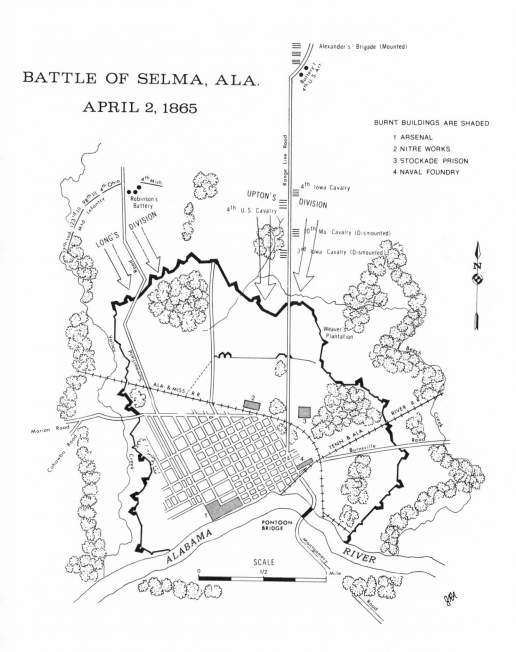

BATTLE OF SELMA, ALA.
APRIL 2, 1865

Alexander's Brigade (Mounted)

Battery I
4th U.S. Art.

BURNT BUILDINGS ARE SHADED

1 ARSENAL
2 NITRE WORKS
3 STOCKADE PRISON
4 NAVAL FOUNDRY

4th Mich.

Robinson's
Battery

UPTON'S

4th Iowa Cavalry

DIVISION

4th U.S. Cavalry

7th Ind. 123d Ill. 98th Ill. 4th Ohio
Mtd. Infantry

LONG'S   DIVISION

10th Mo. Cavalry (Dismounted)

3rd Iowa Cavalry (Dismounted)

N

Weaver
Plantation

Valley   Road

Plantation Road

Beech

ALA & MISS. R.R.

RIVER R.R.

Marion Road

Cohawba Road

Creek

Creek

TENN & ALA

Burnsville

Road

2

3

4

1

ALABAMA

PONTOON
BRIDGE

Montgomery

RIVER

Road

SCALE

0   1/2   1 Mile

JPM

ten heavy carriages; ten field pieces; sixty field carriages; ten caissons; sixty thousand rounds of artillery ammunition; and a million
rounds of small arms ammunition.[7] The complex of buildings
along the north bank of the Alabama also produced knapsacks
and clothing. Much of the latter was made by Selma's young
ladies.[8]

Also operating in Selma was Captain Catesby ap R. Jones's Selma
Naval Foundry. An estimated three thousand men made heavy
weapons in the facility. When the Naval Foundry fell into Union
hands, twenty-nine unfinished siege guns and the machinery to
produced many more were discovered.[9] The Naval Foundry also
partially armed and equipped the Confederate gunboats *Tennessee*, *Selma*, *Morgan*, and *Gaines*. Armor plate for the gunboats had
been made at the Shelby Iron Works, already wrecked by Wilson's
horsemen.[10]

Lieutenant Colonel White not only ran the arsenal; he also let
military contracts to private factories in Selma. Closely involved
in this production were the Selma Iron Works which could produce thirty tons a day, and the large eighteen-building Nitre
Works. The Powder Mill and Magazine was still another important producer. In 1865, six thousand rounds of artillery ammunition, seventy thousand rounds of small arms ammunition,
and fourteen thousand pounds of powder were stored in its buildings. In addition, ten other foundries and iron works were con-
tracted to produce the arms and ammunition needed by the Confederate Army.[11] With all of these factories in operation it is no
wonder that the claim is made that during the Civil War's last two
years, one-half of the cannon and two-thirds of the fixed ammunition used by the Confederates came from the Selma area.[12]

Guns and ammunition were only a part of Selma's production.
The area's shops produced swords, bayonets, gear for horses and
wagons, ammunition boxes, shovels, knapsacks, and every imagin-
able article of clothing.[13] Since two important railroads crossed at

Selma, the city had also become a production and repair center for locomotives and rolling stock. When Selma fell much of this material was moved westward, but Union troopers still captured five locomotives and ninety-two cars of various types. In addition, Selma contained two roundhouses and extensive railroad machinery.[14]

Along with Montgomery, Selma was also one of the food distribution centers of the fertile Alabama black belt. A large Confederate Subsistence Department had headquarters in the city. Using trains, wagons, and boats, the department gathered and shipped vast amounts of grain, meat, and fodder to Confederate troops across the South.[15]

Through most of the war one of Selma's great advantages was its distance from Union armies. In the conflict's first two years the city seemed completely secure. In 1863, with Grant in central Mississippi, Confederate authorities decided to erect a line of fortifications. Using slave labor, the city was ringed with works that had been made formidable by 1865. The main defensive line formed a semicircle around Selma. The works began west of the town near the confluence of the Alabama River and Valley Creek. They lay a short distance from Selma's western perimeter and meandered northward following the course of the creek. Crossing the Marion-Cahaba Road and the Alabama and Mississippi Railroad, this line of stockaded rifle pits paralleled the Summerfield Road for a short distance. Along this stretch of rifle pits several forts had been built to buttress the line. Near the spot at which the line veered northeast, crossing the Summerfield Road, the rifle pits became a more formidable line of continuous parapet. From just west of the Summerfield Road and across the Range Line (Plantersville) Road ran this strong parapet line. These parapets were six to eight feet tall and eight feet thick at the base. In front of the wall was a ditch five feet deep and five feet wide. East of Range Line Road, near Weaver's Plantation, the stockaded

rifle pits began again. This less formidable type of fortification
angled to the southeast, intersecting the Alabama and Tennessee
River Railroad and the road to Burnsville. It was anchored at the
Alabama River just east of Selma. The latter portion of the perimeter roughly followed the course of Beech Creek. Fields in front of
all of the works had been cleared, denying cover to an assaulting
force. At two points in the line, one to the north just west of
Range Line Road, and the other to the east near the Burnsville
Road, swampy land formed a natural defense.[16] To the south, the
broad Alabama protected the city. The Selma defense line was
close to the city on the east and west and lay about one and a half
miles from the city on the north.

If attack came, Confederate authorities seemed convinced that
the city was most vulnerable from due north. There rolling open
country with no natural barriers to delay an attacking force offered the easiest avenue of advance. For that reason the strongest
segment of the defensive position was built to stop an assault from
that quarter. It was precisely from that direction that Wilson was
approaching Selma.[17]

Strong and extensive works are of limited value if held by a
weak force. Without his entire command Forrest would have to
thin his troops in order to man the stockade and parapet. Wilson's
superior force, with the firepower advantage given them by their
seven-shot Spencers, could concentrate against one sector, while
the thinly spaced defenders, ten feet apart, could not muster
enough firepower to halt the onslaught. For the Confederates to
abandon part of their line to concentrate against a threatened sector could easily render the whole position untenable. As an added
precaution, as soon as he reached Selma Forrest ordered construction of a second and much shorter line of defense close to the city.
This line might be held by Forrest's small army, but he had no
time to complete these positions. The appearance of the Federals
halted construction and sent workmen racing for the outer wall or

into the city.[18] Forrest had little choice of plans. If reinforcements failed to arrive he would have to use the men available.

Despite preparations for defense and the approach of the enemy, much of life in Selma in late March was business as usual. The *Selma Evening Reporter* of March 28 contained little evidence of impending danger. Items for sale listed books, a mule, "a good likely House woman," and "a likely Negro girl, 16 years old." T. W. Street advertised a two-hundred-dollar reward for the return of Bob, his eighteen-year-old runaway slave, and M. J. Williams, copublisher of the newspaper, announced his candidacy for mayor. The war news that appeared outlined rebel defeats, but a Forrest letter was included that told citizens, "I am for fighting as long as there is a man left to fight with."[19]

II

After the rout at Ebenezer Church Forrest had labored through the afternoon and night of the first to rally his weary, beaten army. He rode late into the night rounding up troops separated from their commands and scattered by Wilson's raiders. The general tried to buoy their spirits as he sent them into Selma's defenses. After dark on the first, through the night, and on the morning of the second, Adams's vanquished state troops, Roddey's and Crossland's exhausted cavalrymen, and Armstrong's brigade of Chalmers's division straggled into the city.[20]

But where was Chalmers? Two days earlier the lost division had been only twenty miles from Selma. Armstrong's brigade had joined Forrest at Bogler's Creek, but the division commander, with Peter Starke's brigade and all of the division artillery, was still missing. Once again Forrest dispatched couriers to find Chalmers and rush him to Selma. Once again the messengers located the wayward general, but he never arrived. Chalmers's excuse was again that he was delayed because of swollen streams and conflicting orders.[21] The general had been caught in the morass along the Cahaba where streams at the flood had filled surrounding swamps. Wilson's rapidly advancing column, on the other hand, had the advantage of traversing the Black Warrior and Cahaba where those rivers were narrower and closer to their headwaters.

Nevertheless, Chalmers was assailed for his slowness. One Confederate soldier accused the general of saying after he received orders to race to Selma, "Let us stop and feed our horses."[22] Department commander Richard Taylor wrote of Jackson and Chalmers, both absent at Selma, "Two of Forrest's brigadiers permitted themselves to be deceived by reports of the enemy's movements toward Columbus, Mississippi, and turned west."[23] No matter where the blame should fall, Forrest would not fight Wilson "with the most."

Richard Taylor was preparing to board the Alabama and Mississippi Railroad for Meridian when Forrest rode into Selma, covered with blood from his wound at Ebenezer Church. It was noon, Sunday, April 2. The two lieutenant generals, one the son of a president, the other a self-made businessman and soldier, talked over the defense. Taylor "felt anxious" for Forrest's health, but the general assured Taylor he "was unhurt and would cut his way through."[24] In the early afternoon Taylor rode out of town on a yard locomotive.

Forrest found a city with an unusually large male population for the South of 1865. Aided by city leaders, the general hurried to form defense units out of laborers and professional men. Even "preachers of the gospel took muskets and went into the trenches."[25] Few of the men had military experience, and they were armed with a motley collection of weapons. If Dan Adams's Alabama State Troops fled before Wilson, these last minute conscripts could offer Forrest little consolation.[26] The general would have laughed if he had read the *Montgomery Daily Mail* that morning, for the paper advised the capital's residents that they were secure from

Wilson since sufficient force existed at Selma to hurl back the invader.[27]

These instant soldiers would stand in the works beside Armstrong's Mississippi veterans, Roddey's five Alabama regiments, and three veteran Kentucky regiments led by Col. Edward Crossland. Forrest's total strength at Selma is unknown. As usual, Confederate estimates are low with Union totals much higher. Three to four thousand followed Forrest according to the former, while a figure of six thousand to eight thousand faced Wilson, if the Union general and his men are to be believed.[28] The use of civilians makes an accurate count impossible. Against this mixed force Wilson would throw nine thousand horsemen fresh from a series of smashing victories.

Selma was a scene of confusion on the morning of April 2. Before Forrest arrived to achieve some order, troops wandered the streets searching for their commands. Civilians in a state of mounting excitement and fear mingled with the soldiers. Some, clutching valuables, sought escape from the city. Much of the rising crescendo of sound was due to efforts to prevent property of value from falling to the raiders. All night and through the morning cannon were dumped into the Alabama. Other goods, including cotton bales lining the river bank, were loaded on trains to be sent to Demopolis.[29] After the goods were moved by rail, Taylor ordered all remaining rolling stock, save one locomotive, to roll westward out of the Union grasp. The one engine evacuated the departmental commander.[30] While some women added to the panic, others, at the Female Institute, gathered hospital supplies and food to serve the wounded.[31] By early afternoon noise and movement had slackened. Taylor had gone, and Forrest's men were taking their positions.[32] At 2 P.M. Wilson's scouts rode across the plain north of the city and got their first look at Selma's defenses. It was a beautiful Sunday afternoon and the troops looked down on the sun "dancing in diamond flashes on the distant river winding away to the south-west. Bodies of troops in motion, with clouds of dust pierced by flashes of light from glistening bayonets, indicating the state of busy preparation within the works."[33]

III

Reveille sounded early on the second for Wilson's raiders. Every available man was taken from the pack train, and all troops crowded ammunition in every pocket.[34] Most of Long's and Upton's men had rested well and at 6 A.M. the Second Division pushed south down the Plantersville Road "like too many mad hornets."[35] Upton's Fourth followed through corn and cotton fields on a lovely spring morning. Not far out of Plantersville Long encountered rebel scouts. These Confederates offered no resistance and served only to rush word to Forrest of Wilson's advance. When Long reached a point six miles north of Selma he swung his two brigades westward and continued toward the objective down the broad yellow-clay Summerfield Road. This left the Plantersville Road (called Range Line Road as it reached Selma) to Upton. A small force from Upton was to gallop eastward to block the Burnsville Road. Finally, Wilson's escort was again given the job of destruction. The regulars were to tear up the Alabama and Tennessee River Railroad as they moved south.[36]

Throughout the campaign Wilson's intelligence, with a combination of luck and skill, had supplied the corps commander with accurate and timely information. Croxton had known troop dispositions in his front and before Plantersville; Wilson had discovered the dispersal of Forrest's forces. Now as he approached Selma, Wilson had in his hand a detailed sketch of the city's defenses. On the first a Mr. Millington, an Englishman who had helped build the Selma works, voluntarily surrendered to Upton. His ardor for the Confederate cause had waned, and he agreed to draw a sketch of the defenses.[37] With the information supplied by Millington, Wilson and Upton spent an hour conferring and decided to strike from just west of Range Line Road. There the Confederate line might be surprised by a charge through low terrain believed by the rebels to be impassable. From that quarter Upton would throw part of his division at the enemy while Long's units demonstrated in force down Summerfield Road and Upton's remaining troopers occupied the rebels east of Range Line Road.[38]

His plans made, Wilson rode along giving a word of encouragement to his division, brigade, and regimental commanders. He explained the tactics to Long, Miller, and Minty. To Miller, who led the brigade of mounted infantry, "regarded as more capable" of an attack on fortifications than cavalry, Wilson "pointed out that they were up against a heavier contract than they had ever yet carried." He gathered Miller's regimental leaders—Jonathan Biggs, "the stalwart farmer," Edward Kitchell, "the modest lawyer," and Jacob Vail, "the intrepid merchant"—and showed them Millington's sketch.[39]

By 3 P.M. Long's main force faced Confederate parapets crossing Summerfield Road. The division chief moved dismounted skirmishers forward and they engaged in sporadic fire with rebel pickets. Protected by a low ridge which shielded them from view, Long dismounted his regiments and deployed them in single assault line. From right to left Long's line read: 17th Indiana, 98th Illinois, 123rd Illinois, 4th Ohio, 7th Pennsylvania, and 4th Michigan. The Michigan unit was detailed to protect Capt. George Robinson's Chicago Board of Trade Battery positioned on Long's left and slightly east of the Summerfield Road. To secure his rear, Long detached the Seventy-second Indiana and Third Ohio from the assault line. While the division was getting set, Robinson's gunners exchanged largely ineffective rounds with the Selma defenses.[40] Long's men were impressed by the distant works. Those who had fought at Vicksburg and Atlanta thought these bastions more formidable. When the front line dismounted, their horses were sent with horse-holders to a wooded area in the rear. Then the men lay down on the ground to rest and hide themselves.[41]

Inside the works, Forrest, Armstrong, and several other officers watched the artillery exchange and thought that would be the extent of the day's fight. "None . . . thought the enemy would assault the works, exposed as they would be on the open field for some hundreds of yards." Forrest hoped for a delay and "was either cursing Chalmers for not coming up, or praying he might come in the night."[42]

About an hour after Long began positioning his men, Upton rode up on the Range Line Road. He had trees for cover as he dismounted the Third Iowa and Fred Benteen's Tenth Missouri. The Iowans were west and the Missourians east of the road. Stacked along the thoroughfare behind these two regiments were the Fourth Iowa, Fourth U.S. Cavalry, Lt. George Rodney's Battery, and farther back, Alexander's entire brigade.[43] The Union troopers, awaiting the signal to attack, were unusually quiet. Conversation lagged, and officers ordered men to make coffee, in part to take their minds off the impending charge. The Missourians lay quietly on the ground and many fell asleep.[44]

When Wilson reached the ridge north of Selma, he rode along both approaches to determine the accuracy of Millington's drawing. He saw no reason to change his plan for Upton's attack supported by Long to the west, and all units were informed that "charge" would be signaled just after dark by a single gun from Rodney's Battery.[45]

Between 4 P.M. and 5 P.M. a hitch developed in Wilson's plan; the Seventy-second Indiana and Third Ohio, guarding Long's rear, were suddenly attacked by mounted Confederates who charged out of the low ground along Valley Creek. The small attack force seems to have been a part of Chalmers's long absent division. Long's two regiments stopped the charge and counterattacked, routing the rebels. This action, however, convinced Long that he should hurl his division at the Selma works immediately.[46] Wilson praised Long for taking the initiative and called his action "fully justified."[47]

Rodney's signal had not been fired, and Long was unsure of Upton's preparedness when the order to charge was yelled down the line. Slowly the dismounted line of about fifteen hundred officers and men crested the ridge and moved at a walk toward Confederate works six hundred yards away. As they closed with the rebels, Long's men broke into a run, cheered wildly, and fired their repeaters. Confederate riflemen took their toll as the attackers were hindered by swampy ground and by a Confederate palisade. The latter, about five feet high and sharpened at the top, ran along the edge of a deep ravine in front of the works.[48] Confederate fire and these obstacles slowed Long's men, but only briefly. The blue-clad line passed the palisade, clambered through the ravine, and charged the parapet. When the attackers reached the edge of the parapet, smoke enshrouded both sides and suddenly the defenders ceased fire, saving their fusillade for those who swung onto the wall. A brief moment of eerie silence hung over the battle, then bluecoats crossed the parapet and fire blazed again.[49] Corp. John Booth of the Fourth Ohio, first to reach the works, was killed instantly, but his comrades rushed on and soon Sgt. John Morgan of the 123rd Illinois planted the stars and stripes on the Confederate works.[50]

When Union troopers jumped into Confederate lines, the enemies fought hand-to-hand with clubbed muskets. Some of the defenders were newly organized conscripts and they were overwhelmed by Federal veterans. As they retreated toward Selma, the entire Confederate parapet was exposed to fire from front and rear. Rebels in the line withdrew but for a time made a tenacious defense in a stand of heavy timber behind the breastworks. This resistance gradually sputtered out, and the dismounted mounted infantry pursued toward Selma.[51] Further defense in the area was hopeless and the Confederates scrambled back to their partially completed inner line in what the Columbus, Georgia, *Daily Sun* rather unfairly called "a disgraceful stampede."[52]

The battle along the northwestern parapet was costly to both

sides. Lt. Col. Frank Montgomery estimated that the First Mississippi lost one-fourth of its men in killed and wounded and many
more as prisoners. The colonel himself was taken by a Union sergeant who demanded his pistol and pocketbook. Montgomery
asked to keep his wife's picture, and the sergeant replied, "certainly"; then the Yankee trooper saw the officer's Confederate
money and asked if he had any other currency. When Montgomery answered in the negative, he was given back his wallet. The
sergeant saw no value in the Confederate money, and Montgomery thought sadly, "this was the 'unkindest cut of all.' "[53] There
are no casualty figures for the units of recent inductees, but they
must have been high.

Union attackers suffered casualties so heavy outside the works
that dead and wounded covered the ground.[54] As their men
charged, Long, his brigade, and regimental commanders galloped
forward on horseback. They were easy targets and Confederate
sharpshooters killed Lt. Col. George W. Dobb, commander of the
Fourth Ohio, and shot Col. Abram Miller in the leg. The Seventh
Pennsylvania's chief, Col. Charles C. McCormick, was also shot in
the leg, and the 123rd Illinois' commander, Lt. Col. Jonathan
Biggs, was severely wounded in the chest. The division commander did not escape unscathed. A Confederate ball struck General
Long in the head forcing him out of action. The wound produced
a severe concussion and paralyzed his tongue, the right side of his
face, and his right arm. It would be two weeks before Long could
speak or think clearly.[55] Long was replaced by the flamboyant
Irishman Robert Minty.[56]

To the east Upton had seen Long's advance and he lost no time
in mounting his own attack. By the time Wilson sent reliable
Capt. Lewis Hosea to urge him into action, Upton had already
moved the dismounted Third Iowa and Tenth Missouri down
Range Line Road. As the two units moved forward, several officers
galloped up and yelled, " 'Go in boys, give them hell, we have the

city, we are all right, give them hell.' From that moment there was no holding back. The men picked up the double quick."[57] The parapets ahead were lightly held, and Upton's troopers speedily crossed the line, seized the works, and waved hats in triumph.[58]

With the Fourth Division in the fight, Wilson, on his gray "Sheridan," joined Long's attackers. The general was needed to assist in reorganizing the Second Division's regiments for a new assault against Forrest's inner defenses. He also thought it was his duty to show himself in the melee with his staff, escort, and red battle flag.[59] When Wilson advanced he brought the highly mobile Chicago Board of Trade artillerymen inside the parapet to support the troopers. Rather than wait for Long's entire division to deploy, the corps commander decided to risk an advance by his mounted escort in a quick strike at Forrest's last barrier. Led by Wilson, his jacket open in the heat, the Fourth U.S. galloped down Summerfield Road waving drawn sabers.[60] Effective Confederate rifle fire against the *arme blanche* caused the Fourth's Sgt. James Larson, already unsteady on a newly broken bronc, to complain that "useless sabers" were of little assistance against a foe "firing furiously into our column from behind the embankment," but the dismounted 123rd Illinois, who watched the charge roar by, thought it "looked grand."[61] Wilson's hope for a quick and easy breach in Forrest's line was in vain, and the general himself was sent to the ground when a shot wounded his mount. But Sheridan rose, and with no other mount nearby the general rode the gray through the remainder of the battle.[62]

It was dusk when Wilson called off the regulars until he could bring up the Third Ohio and Seventeenth Indiana. Charley Brown, bugler of the Third Ohio, sounded the charge, and his regiment tore through the outer line and found Wilson and the Fourth U.S. waiting. Ths force charged the inner line and "with a shout went over the work."[63] This time the rebels broke and fled into the city. As Confederate resistance in front of Long's force evaporated, Upton's division reached Selma down the Range Line Road.[64]

As one army fled and the other pursued, pandemonium gripped Selma. A heavy cloud of dust increased confusion, and cries of women and children shattered the twilight and mingled with soldiers yelling, "Surrender! Halt!" Retreating rebels threw away guns and luggage, and many surrendered to the first Union trooper who appeared. The industrial hub of central Alabama was in Wilson's hands.[65] That night the corps commander scribbled in his diary: "Shoved everything right at the town. Carried everything before us. . . . The gallantry of the entire command splendid and that of Genl. Long's Division was magnificent."[66]

Unknown to either side, far to the northeast that same Sunday the government of Jefferson Davis had evacuated Richmond. The Confederate president, a fugitive from his own capital, began a journey that would inevitably bend westward toward Wilson, but Wilson's raiders were about to make certain that Selma would be of no further use to the fleeing Confederate government.

When resistance collapsed, Forrest and his generals left the city under cover of night. They chose the Burnsville Road to the east, where an attempt to prevent their flight was made by elements of Upton's command. Some rebel troops and four guns were captured, but the enemy commanders escaped.[67]

All over the field Union soldiers found abandoned guns, horses, and supplies. Charley Hinricks found a rebel horse in full field rig, and not knowing when the horse-holders would bring in his own mount, he captured it. He found the saddlebags contained clean clothes which "came very handy."[68] Through the night Confederate troops and civilians fled in all directions. Many were rounded up and herded back into the city. Some of the more desperate tried to swim the Alabama, and while a few reached the south shore, others drowned in the attempt.[69]

Wilson had taken twenty-seven hundred prisoners and killed

and wounded an unknown number of Forrest's men.[70] Among the slain was the pastor of the First Presbyterian Church. A legend, still current in Selma, maintains that as the minister's body passed his church a rose in full bloom dropped its petals on his bier. The rose still grows on the church and each April blooms as a living memorial.[71]

The captured rebels were confined in a stockade near the Alabama and Mississippi Railroad. The place had been built and once occupied by Union prisoners. During the Selma occupation Wilson allowed limited paroles for some captured civilians and militiamen, and some Confederate officers were permitted to leave the stockade on occasion. Inside the walls treatment was humane. Captive officers shared Union officers' mess, and nothing was said to make the rebels feel like prisoners.[72] The food was good, and wounded prisoners were cared for by the ladies of Selma. One of the few complaints from the detained Confederates came on the night of the second. Lt. Col. Montgomery disliked the Federal band's playing of "Dixie" which kept him awake and depressed.[73]

Wilson had lost forty-six killed, almost three hundred wounded, and thirteen missing, a small price to pay for so significant a victory. The corps commander wrote of the triumph: "I regard the capture of Selma the most remarkable achievement in the history of modern cavalry, and one admirably illustrative of its new powers and tendencies."[74] On April 7 an exultant Wilson issued Special Field Order No. 16 to his men:

The brevet major general commanding congratulates the officers and men of the Cavalry Corps upon their signal victory. . . . Like an avalanche the intrepid soldiers [swept through Selma]. . . . Soldiers, you have been called upon to perform long marches and endure privations, but your general relied upon and believed in your capacity and courage to undergo every task imposed upon you. Trusting in your valor, discipline and armament, he did not hesitate to attack intrenchments believed by the rebel leaders to be impregnable, and which might well

have caused double your numbers of veteran infantry to hesitate. You
have fully justified his opinions, and may justly regard yourselves invincible. Your achievements will always be considered among the most
remarkable in the annals of cavalry.[75]

The general concluded by reminding his men, "While you exult
in the success which has crowned your arms, do not forget the
memory of those who died that you might conquer."

IV

The night of April 2 was filled with confusion and disorder for
Union victors. It was a time of terror for the conquered people of
Selma. For some time after nightfall scattered combat raged through
the streets. Fifty men of the Seventh Pennsylvania battled a Confederate force shielded by cottonbale breastworks near the Selma
railroad depot.[76] Gradually the small pockets of resistance were
either crushed or melted away into the dark. Selma's authorities
had ordered the destruction of all liquor in the city, but Wilson's
rapid advance had prevented the completion of the task. That
night weary Union troopers found the alcohol and some reeled
through the streets. Sgt. Larson of the Fourth U.S. Cavalry found
a Union squad "making very free" with a wholesale liquor store.
They invited him to join them and the colorful Larson wrote, "No
soldier needs a second invitaion of that nature at the end of a campaign." When he left the store he was unable to find his company
and instead found supper and a bed in a nearby house whose only
occupants were Negroes. The slaves told Larson all the whites had
fled "when you-all started making such a racket."[77] Wilson's victory had brought "Jubilo" to the Negroes, and they joined their
liberators in drinking and plundering the city's shops and homes.[78]
The Confederate press reported clashes between Union troops and
Negroes, and such incidents were possible, but when Wilson left
Selma a large column of blacks chose to accompany the Union
horsemen.[79]

Stories of the theft of civilian property vary widely. As in the case of Sherman's Georgia and South Carolina campaigns, truth mingled with hysteria and bitterness. Wilson's men were accused of robbing dead Confederate soldiers, an act often engaged in by troops both blue and gray, and of stealing silver from Selma's homes. An Alabama governor later vowed that on the night of the second, "every house in the city was sacked, except two; every woman was robbed of her watch, her earrings, her finger rings."[80] Another report had Union troopers with a rope around an old man's neck when his slave told the vandals he would show them the buried gold and silver. The servant lured the Yankees out of the house and eventually evaded them without giving up the valuables.[81] On April 4, at Summerfield, young ladies from the Centenary Female College were reportedly attacked by soldiers trying to pilfer their watches. Supposedly an Ohio captain gave one student a six-shooter and told her to shoot anyone who came to rob.[82]

The classic example of Southern overstatement, legend, and hysteria was Sarah Ellen Phillips's report of that terrible night in Selma. Miss Phillips believed "never can we erase from memory the sounds of shot and shell." She was terrified of Wilson's raiders because their "reputation . . . had preceded them. Prison and penitentiary doors had been opened to swell the columns of the invading hosts." Bluecoats poured through the Phillips home and, according to her memoir, turned the house inside out, even threatening the girl with a raised shovel. Nearby, so Miss Phillips alleged, an old man was hung to a bedpost and burned to death.[83] Federals were even charged with destroying pianos by using them as horse troughs.[84]

The Union commander admitted some of the charges and wrote "marauders and desperadoes . . . always find a place in modern armies." Captain Hosea, however, described Wilson's immediate efforts to stop pillage. A provost guard was mounted and patrols circled the city in an attempt to contain attacks on civilians. The Union officer did perhaps overstate his case when he wrote: "The city of Selma with its conquered and helpless population, was as safely guarded within a few hours of its capture as ever by its own police."[85] Yet one Southern writer admitted that after the first night Wilson and Winslow were quick to provide protection to those requesting it.[86] The attack had caused hardship for Selma's citizens, and the general saw to it that food was distributed to the needy.[87] It is impossible to credit many of the stories of pillage. A writer who could turn clerks, farm boys, and lumbermen into a host of brutal ex-convicts could just as easily exaggerate the acts these men were charged with committing.

Sometime that night a fire broke out in downtown Selma, and two blocks along Water Street and three on Broad Street were burned. Consumed in the blaze were the Episcopal Church, a number of businesses, and several homes. Union soldiers tried to stop the fires but did not know the location of fire engines. It was midnight before the fire was under control.[88] Also blazing that night were some thirty-five thousand cotton bales fired by the Confederates when they could not be shipped westward. Five days earlier central Alabama had been warned by Gen. Dan Adams that cotton "will be burnt before it will be allowed to fall into the hands of the enemy."[89] The cotton fire destroyed all bales left in the city. In addition, Confederates fired the Central Commercial Warehouse, a conflagration which spread to an adjoining business.[90] The fires begun by Southerners led to Union charges that a great deal of the destruction of April 2 was unrelated to the invaders. Later Southern claims that the entire city was razed seem exaggerated. An Alabama newspaper reported at the time that "there was no appearance of a general conflagration. Very few of the citizens left Selma."[91] Yet in late April when two regiments from Canby's army passed through Selma on their way home they reported the people not recovered from the panic of Wilson's attack and occupation. An Illinois soldier saw a great deal of burned property and added, "this has been a very nice place but destruction makes everything look desolate."[92] But on the night of the second, as flames flickered off the city's buildings, even Wilson's war-toughened veterans found the scene disturbing, "Of all the nights of my experience, this is the most like the horrors of war—a captured city burning at night, a victorious army advancing, and a demoralized one retreating."[93] Ten miles away, as they crossed the Cahaba by ferry, Southern refugees turned to see a dull red haze in the sky.[94]

Wilson made his headquarters in the city's best hotel, the Gee House, and the city's commander, General Winslow, was headquartered at the Weaver Home. Edward Winslow, commander of Upton's First Brigade, was an engineer and railroad builder, and he was placed in charge of the destruction of Selma's strategic materials. Winslow's wreckers planned to level the Arsenal, foundries, shops, railroad facilities, and war-related goods stored in warehouses. Ammunition from the Arsenal deemed of no use to the Federals was dumped into the Alabama. On the night of April 1, one Selma family had sat on its front porch and listened for hours to the rumble of hand trucks and the splash of heavy metal as Confederates sank guns and machinery in the river. Now Union troops continued the process, and so much was thrown in the river that it eventually lay in heaps above the water.[95] When most of the explodables had been removed Winslow fired the twenty-four-building Arsenal complex. A rainy night was chosen to prevent the possible spread of the blaze. Some shells remained in the structure, and the downpour was lit by their explosions. Of assistance to Union troopers was a large force of Negroes employed to throw stores into the river. The slaves enjoyed their role in wrecking the Confederate cause.[96]

Despite Taylor's orders to remove or destroy locomotives and rolling stock, some of both were found in the captured rail junction. The city rocked as Union soldiers with prewar engineering or railroad experience got up steam in trains, set the tender's wood on fire, and "opened the throttle and let her fly at full speed." Wind spread the fire to the cars, some containing powder and ammunition, and explosions hurled debris into the air and littered the roadbed. If the fire did not spread sufficiently, then the doomed trains crashed into wrecks ahead or rolled over on curves.[97]

Large numbers of horses and mules fell into Union hands as Forrest retreated. Wilson was able to provide remounts for troopers whose animals had broken down. He adequately mounted his entire force, and when that was done the general ordered the killing of the remaining stock, about five hundred horses and five hundred mules, to deny it to the enemy. Most horses were killed and thrown into the Alabama, but enough remained in Selma to putrefy the air for days.[98]

General Winslow pronounced the city's destruction a success: "I cannot estimate in dollars the value of public property here destroyed, but all can readily see that the value in mechanical, social and war point of view is almost inestimable."[99]

In addition to mounting his command, Wilson also found enough supplies of all kinds to replenish goods lost or consumed in the first twelve days of the campaign. He was convinced that adequate supplies could be found along the line of march, and all wagons not absolutely necessary were destroyed at Selma. The army of occupation also buried the dead of both sides and established a hospital to care for sick and wounded troops and civilians. Most of the army camped on the plain north of the city, where they washed clothes, shoed their horses, cleaned their Spencers, and rested. Many not engaged in destruction or building pontoon bridges had the opportunity of going into Selma, where they wandered through the streets viewing the damage and talking to citizens. Wisconsin Major Shipman peered into the prisoner-of-war compound and drew a large crowd who bombarded him with questions and talked of taking oaths of amnesty.[100]

Word of Selma's fall rippled across the dazed state. The *Clarke County Journal* blared a banner headline, "YANKEES AT SELMA!" The paper was amazed at the rapidity of Wilson's advance, and though reports were fragmentary it believed Forrest had been routed and all government works destroyed at Selma.[101] Another journal, still unaware of Wilson's strength, tried to resassure its readers, "We can hardly think the enemy will be able to hold Selma, but will destroy all they can and then beat a retreat."[102]

V

Of great concern to Wilson as he carried out his mission of destruction was the location of Forrest's Confederates and of the two Union forces, McCook and Croxton, left to the north. When Forrest fled Selma along the Burnsville Road, he decided to bear to the north to Plantersville. The night ride northward passed bridges and depots leveled by Wilson's raiders. Occasionally Forrest's little group came close to small Union detachments, and it captured one of Wilson's troopers. From the soldier, Forrest discovered that several members of Wilson's escort, the Fourth U.S. Cavalry, were sleeping at a nearby farm. Forrest ordered an attack, but his men insisted that the general remain in the rear with rebel horseholders. This night action produced one of the most controversial incidents of Wilson's entire campaign. Union soldiers were certain that Forrest's men attacked and massacred their sleeping comrades, even though they had tried to surrender. Confederate accounts assert that the U.S. regulars fired first and that no man was injured after the force surrendered. Several prisoners were seized, but between twenty-five and thirty-five of the party were killed or wounded. Only one Confederate was wounded. It is difficult to understand how a Federal force alert enough to fire the opening shot could have suffered such heavy casualties while inflicting only one casualty on the enemy, unless an assault on sleeping men took place without warning.[103] Word of the "massacre" swept through Wilson's men, and Sergeant Larson labeled it a "repitition of Ft. Pillow." A detachment of the Fourth U.S. rode out, buried their comrades, and burned the house.[104]

When the night skirmish was over Forrest's party rode on to

Plantersville before turning west toward Marion. At Plantersville he captured the Union hospital, paroled the slightly wounded men, and left the doctors and seriously ill unmolested.[105] Gradually remnants of his command reached Forrest west of the Cahaba. It was a beaten force. A Confederate private remembered, "No weeping or wailing . . . because of the defeat of Southern hopes." For two years he said the men had contemplated the possibility of defeat and were "mentally prepared for almost anything."[106]

Wilson shortly discovered Forrest's path north and west but for a time was uncertain about McCook and Croxton.[107] On April 3 the concerned corps commander sent Upton's division to search for the missing brigades. Upton's movement had two other objectives as well: Wilson wanted to make certain all rebel forces had retreated west of the Cahaba, and Upton was to bring the remainder of the supply train back to Selma. Upton shortly found McCook, who had the supply train and for that reason had been slowed in his march to Selma. McCook had no intelligence of Croxton's whereabouts, nor was Upton able to find any information from residents of the area. On April 6 Upton rode back into Selma to inform a worried corps commander that Croxton's force was still missing.[108] McCook also arrived on the sixth. After choking on dusty roads all day the force was drenched before it could put up its tents.[109]

Upton's failure gave Wilson a new idea; perhaps the only person within easy contact who could supply information on Croxton was the Confederate commander—Forrest. Wilson sent Captain Hosea and a party to arrange a meeting between the Union commander and Forrest to discuss prisoner exchange. Talk of exchange was a cover; Wilson hoped for an inadvertent remark about the lost brigade. After delay because of the flooding, the two commanders met at the home of a Colonel Matthews on the Cahaba. After a sumptuous meal in a relaxed atmosphere with the two generals treating each other "like old acquaintances" Wilson broached the subject of exchange. During the conversation the

Federal leader mentioned Croxton, and Forrest innocently supplied the report that the brigade was safe, operating somewhere
north and west of the Black Warrior. No agreement was reached
on prisoner exchange since Forrest told Wilson he did not have
authority to make one. Forrest seemed depressed and the wound
inflicted by Captain Taylor forced him to carry his left arm in a
sling. Wilson found his opponent "loosely put together, if not
somewhat stooping and slouchy in appearance." On his return to
Selma, the Federal chief wrote in his diary that Forrest "did not
impress me as I expected—neither as large, dignified nor striking
as I expected—seemed embarrassed."[110] The old Confederate fox
said to Wilson: "Well, General, you have beaten me badly, and for
the first time I am compelled to make such an acknowledgement."
The young Federal commander replied graciously: "Our victory
was not without cost. You put up a stout fight." Forrest answered:
"If I had captured your entire force twice over it would not com-
pensate us for the blow you've inflicted upon us."

Captain Hosea, angered by the stories of Forrest's massacre of
the men of the Fourth U.S., wrote that the general "did not do
justice to my first impression of him." The captain did add that
Forrest had ridden far and was depressed by his defeats, but he believed he saw in the general "all the brutal instincts of the slave
driver." For Wilson the meeting was a success and he could make
plans to leave Selma no longer fearing for Croxton's safety.[111]

VI

Since Selma's fall Wilson had thought about and discussed with
his lieutenants the direction the campaign should take next. He
thought of supporting Canby's attack on Mobile, but he was certain the port city would fall without his assistance. Wilson did
take steps to inform Canby of his position. A trustworthy Negro,
Charles Marven, was sent by skiff down the river to Mobile. He
reached Canby and delivered word of Wilson's triumphs.[112] Wil-

son was of the opinion that "the capture of Selma having put us in possession of the enemy's greatest depot in the Southwest was a vital blow to their cause and secured to us the certainty of going in whatever direction might be found advantageous."[113] The corps commander decided it would be most advantageous to march east to Montgomery and on into Georgia by way of Columbus and Macon. After ripping up railroads and destroying supplies in his line of march, he would join Grant and Sherman to assist in crushing Lee and Johnston.[114]

Montgomery was on the south side of the Alabama, and Wilson decided to cross the river at Selma on a pontoon bridge. He would then march south of the flooded stream. The rapid current and packs of driftwood made bridge construction hazardous. Rumor circulated among Union troops that Southerners purposely floated trees down river to wreck the pontoons.[115] Against these obstacles Maj. James Hubbard and his pontoniers, including several Michigan troopers who had been lumbermen, labored for several days to put together an 870-foot-long floating bridge of thirty canvas boats, six wooden pontoons, and three large barges. Three times the span broke while the men, horses, guns, and wagons crossed.[116]

On Palm Sunday, April 9, Grant accepted Lee's surrender at Appomattox. Neither the Union horsemen who left Selma nor the citizens who watched their departure knew of this development in Virginia. On that day, one week after Selma had fallen, the first troopers crossed, and that night and the following day departure was completed. Movement after dark on the ninth was perilous and Wilson ordered several buildings along the Alabama burned to light the passage. The bridge sagged in the middle so that men and horses waded for a stretch through two feet of water. At 2 P.M. two wooden pontoons sank and the entire structure swung around in the center. Some very tired pontoniers fought on against tide and obstructions to repair the bridge. Later, with General Alexander directing men in skiffs who were guiding trees away from the bridge, a big log crashed into the general's boat and threw him into the river. As he rose to the surface he caught the bow of a pontoon and cracked three ribs.[117] When the corps had passed, the bridge was destroyed.

As the corps crossed, mounted, and rode eastward, it was accompanied by some wounded Union troops, a group of Confederate prisoners, and a column of Negroes. The wounded in wagons filled with beds and blankets were those that surgeons pronounced capable of movement. Included was still disabled Gen. Eli Long whose wagon's shades were drawn to keep out the sun. The general could not yet speak and one of his arms was useless.[118] Sixty-eight more seriously wounded troopers remained in the well-supplied hospital established in Selma and were well cared for by the women of the city.[119] The prisoners who marched with the corps were under light guard. As the days passed some were paroled and many escaped to return to their homes. There seemed to be little fight left in these Confederates.[120] A more serious problem for Wilson was the Negroes who accompanied the corps. North of Selma many slaves had abandoned plantations to join their blue-clad emancipators, and during Selma's occupation even more Negroes had fled to Union protection. Wilson like Sherman in Georgia feared for the safety of the runaways and was concerned about their effect on his progress. At Selma Wilson decided to enlist able-bodied Negroes into three regiments. A Union officer would lead each unit. One Negro regiment would be assigned to each division. When he moved eastward the Negro troops kept up the corps' pace and served ably as foragers, teamsters, train guards, and road makers. But this innovation did not stop other slaves from following in the corps' wake.[121]

By late afternoon on April 10 Selma sank below the horizon. After a week's rest, good food, and the accumulation of sturdy mounts, the Union raiders set their usual brisk pace as they jogged toward the "Cradle of the Confederacy." The people of Selma were relieved to see the backs of Wilson's men. But they were saddened as they contemplated the wreckage of their city. One month later passing Union soldiers called Selma's population the "worst whipped" rebels they had seen.[122] West of the Cahaba, Forrest was at last joined by Chalmers and Jackson, but he decided that further pursuit of Wilson was fruitless. "That devil Forrest" had been soundly defeated, and his Civil War was over.

CHAPTER V

Rocking the Cradle

Brig. Gen. Edward McCook's corps had drawn rugged duty with little chance for glory through much of the march to Selma. His First Brigade, under Croxton, wandered somewhere to the north, and the men of Col. Oscar LaGrange's Second Brigade had burned the bridge at Centerville and rounded up the wagon train while their comrades defeated Forrest at Ebenezer Church and Selma. Perhaps that was why LaGrange's troopers were given the lead as the corps rode toward Montgomery on April 10. Wilson glowed with pride as his horsemen, fresh from a rapid series of victories, passed by in their advance on the Confederacy's birthplace. There seemed to be little ahead to block his progress. Forrest was west of the Cahaba and no significant enemy army was known to be in his front. Union casualties had been light, and the corps remained strong, confident, and perhaps almost as Wilson saw them—"invincible."[1]

Lt. Col. William W. Bradley's Seventh Kentucky led the march over muddy roads on the tenth. Some of the ground seemed solid but suddenly gave way under the weight of horse and rider.[2] The day was clear, and in spite of the ground the riders made excellent progress. Occasional Confederate scouts appeared, only to ride off into the heavy forests bordering the line of march. At midday the Seventh Kentucky saw the village of Benton in the distance. Suddenly a small force of rebel pickets appeared and fired, causing the regiment to rein in. It was evident the riflemen could be shoved aside, and Lieutenant Colonel Bradley ordered a charge which ran the Confederates eastward. A detachment of the Kentuckians pursued until stopped by a heavy volley from the waiting Fourth and Seventh Alabama Cavalry regiments. The Alabamans were set along a ridge, and the Kentuckians replied and fell back to await the arrival of their comrades. Soon the entire regiment was positioned to charge, and with a shout, fired their Spencers, and broke the rebel hill line. The Confederates gave way slowly, contesting the ground. By that time Colonel LaGrange, the brigade chief, rode up and summoned Ross Hill's battalion of the Second Indiana to support the Kentuckians. The new force scattered the rebels but made the mistake of being lured into following a small detachment rather than pressing the main force. The Alabama horsemen thus avoided a debacle, but did give up Benton.[3]

LaGrange decided to keep pressure on the retreating Southerners, and the brigade commander's old regiment, the First Wisconsin, led by Lt. Col. Henry Harnden, was hurried forward. Harnden's men ran the enemy through Churchill and Big Swamp to Lowndesboro. There they seized the commissary of the Seventh Alabama, and the First Wisconsin camped for the night near Lowndesboro.[4]

Most of Wilson's troopers were unengaged on the tenth. They rode along in the spring sunshine and enjoyed the passing country. Wilson thought the area "the richest planting district of the South." Cherokee roses, a flower unknown to most of the Northerners, wound through woods along the road and were marveled at by the men. Occasional swamps had to be corduroyed, and troops expended most of their energy throwing logs and fence rails into the mire. It often took three or four logs on top of each other to keep the horses and men out of the mush.[5]

As the corps joined LaGrange's vanguard in Lowndesboro, it rode down the town's wide main street. Large oaks, roses, and jasmine lined the road and bloomed in yards of mansions belonging to affluent black belt planters, but the beauty was tempered somewhat by reports of a smallpox epidemic in the town.[6] The column stretched for miles, and while most of the men rode through

Lowndesboro early enough to see the gardens and homes, the Fourth Iowa of Upton's division did not reach the village until well after dark. Their reaction to the area's beauty was different, but no less intense.

Night was never so beautiful. . . . The very air was new and delightfully sweet. . . . [We reached] the village of Lowndesboro, long noted as the home of wealthy planters. . . . It was past midnight. No living creature appeared in the town, not a light was seen, not a sound heard except the subdued rattle of arms in the column. Even the horses' feet were hardly heard as they trod in the sandy way. . . . It was a dream world, through which the war-worn soldiers march silently in the deep shadows of the oaks.[7]

On April 11 copies of Montgomery newspapers fell into Wilson's hands, and the general read that Grant had broken the Petersburg siege and that Richmond had fallen April 2. Davis had fled to Danville, Virginia, the new Confederate capital. Wilson immediately had the news announced to the corps, and wild cheers raced from camp to camp until the fields rang with them. Wilson was certain that the conflict was about to end, and he issued new and more stringent orders against looting. No soldier could enter a house unless accompanied by a commissioned officer.[8]

LaGrange's brigade was in the vanguard once again when the corps left Lowndesboro on the eleventh. One trooper had been arrested for stealing, and to demonstrate that he meant to enforce the new regulations Wilson had the culprit flogged and then displayed to the entire corps as it rode eastward. The march on the eleventh was a resumption of the relatively peaceful cavalcade of the tenth. Rebel pickets were scarce and resistance almost nonexistent. Walking along with the Union column were Confederate prisoners. As the march progressed many lightly guarded rebels escaped. Colonel Montgomery believed that it was Wilson's plan to allow them to escape little by little so as to scatter the soldiers across the countryside. By the afternoon of the eleventh enough horses had been taken so that all officer prisoners were mounted.

The fifty that were left were watched over by Lt. Col. Frank White of the Seventeenth Indiana. White was "kind but vigilant," and the Confederate officers were well treated, but unlike their men these captives were not permitted to escape.[9]

For the second day the Union troopers became sightseers and were particularly intrigued by Spanish moss. They pulled it from trees to cushion their saddles and to sleep on that night. The black belt swarmed with slaves, "anxious to be free," who waved to the passing soldiers.[10] Talkative soldiers asked one Negro man where his master was, and the slave replied that the last he had seen of "old massa was last Monday," He continued, "Old massa headed down to Big Swamp, crying all done gone, Selma gone, Richmond gone too," to the delighted laughter of the Missouri troopers. They did not believe the slave's tale of Richmond's fall, but it was confirmed later that day.[11] That evening Wilson halted the column at Hayneville where "good looking ladies" brought food to the cavalrymen.[12] The Union troops were "living fat." Their larders were filled with eggs, sugar, coffee, molasses, butter, chickens, and "sweet potatoes to kill."[13]

No one was certain what defense the enemy could muster in front of Montgomery. Wilson was reasonably sure that no large force stood in his way, but he was prepared. Orders went out to Col. Wickliffe Cooper's Fourth Kentucky Cavalry to lead the attack on the city at daybreak. The regiment bivouacked on the night of the eleventh near Catoma Creek, only five miles from the "Cradle of the Confederacy."[14]

II

Montgomery was an important center of communications served by three railroads and the Alabama River. The city was also the site of some manufacturing and was a distributing point for black belt agricultural products. But more than these, Montgomery was Alabama's capital and it had been the first capital of the Confederate States of America. From February 4 to May 20, 1861, the city had been the first city of the South. Jefferson Davis had stepped off a train as Confederate president and the new government's Constitution had been written here. Now it was all ending. Davis was in flight and a Union army stood on the doorstep.

In addition to its symbolic place in the Confederacy, Montgomery did contain two arsenals and other concerns of importance to the rebel military. The Alabama Arms Manufacturing Company made Enfield rifles and the Montgomery Arsenal repaired weapons, and Leonard and Riddle supplied saltpeter.[15] Three railroads ran into the city. The Alabama and Florida ran to Pensacola, and the Montgomery and West Point, and Montgomery and Eufaula Railroads ran northeast and southeast out of the capital.

Through the first ten days of Wilson's march the citizens of Montgomery, like those of Selma and indeed most of Alabama, were not aware of the danger Wilson posed. In late March the *Memphis Daily Appeal*—dubbed the "moving *Appeal*" because of its many efforts to evade Union armies and keep publishing—reported the Union force near Montevallo. Yet the journal, then printing in Montgomery, advised its readers that the force was too small to be a threat.[16] On April 2, the day Selma fell, the *Daily Mail* claimed victory at Plantersville and believed that Montgomery was in no danger. Even if Wilson was not expelled from central Alabama, the *Mail*'s editor surmised, he would march south to aid Canby at Mobile.[17] On the whole reliable information was infrequent and breaks in communication together with some bravado aimed at bolstering morale account for the inaccurate reporting.

In spite of the journalistic bravado, fears and anxiety gripped the city as the Union column penetrated deeper into Alabama. The day Wilson took Selma one Montgomery resident, Miss Ellen Blue, reported that "there is so much anxiety felt about the proximity of the raiders that many people do not go to church." The following day, April 3, when word arrived of Selma's fall, Miss

Blue believed the capital was "left almost entirely at the mercy of the enemy."[18] Unlike Ellen Blue, member of an old Alabama family, Sarah Follansbee was a New Englander who had come to Montgomery just before the war. A teacher at the Home School, Sarah Follansbee was caught between her Unionism and her affection for her neighbors. No less than her neighbors was the "Yankee" schoolteacher a victim of the fears and rumors of April's first days. She described the evacuation of friends and the placing of cotton bale barricades at key cross streets near her home. She sadly gathered her school books and dismissed her girls. Believing a Unionist might not be abused by the Federals, friends sent her valuable papers and money for safekeeping.[19]

After Selma's fall Montgomery's population began to grow restive. News of the Union victory at Selma increased movement out of the city.[20] Most remained and soon small detachments of Confederate troops beaten by Wilson drifted into the capital. They were a haggard group and begged food from Montgomery's homes.[21] The *Daily Mail* reported rather disconsolately that stragglers from Selma were also passing through nearby Talladega.[22] Gen. Dan Adams, trounced twice by Wilson, was one of the retreating soldiers. Adams, still chief of the District of Alabama, took command and promised "a full defense of the city." The general told the people that since Montgomery was well fortified, all that was needed was "some additional force to garrison the works."[23] In light of the reality of the situation, which Adams surely knew, his proclamation was foolhardy and cruelly deceptive. Alabama's Governor, Thomas Watts, spoke in the same vein. On April 4, he proclaimed:

The military authorities here are determined to defend the city. With my consent the seat of government shall not be surrendered as long as there is reasonable hope of defending it. If you will come, we can save our state. Without delay the Commanders of several counties East and South of the Alabama River, will send their men to this place.[24]

Gen. Abraham Buford joined Adams in Montgomery and was given command of the city. Few volunteers came to Montgomery from surrounding counties and Adams was forced to order all the city's able-bodied men to report for duty. This force of conscripts was quartered in northeastern Montgomery near the Montgomery and West Point Railroad depot. Joining the men was a company of boys called the Watts Cadets.[25]

Adams and Buford tried to round up arms and equipment for the defense force. Relying heavily on slave labor, they also worked to strengthen Montgomery's fortifications. A third task was that of transporting cotton bales to the edge of the city, where they could be moved out of Wilson's reach or burned if necessary. Locomotives and railroad cars, steamboats, military supplies, and the records of the State of Alabama, were sent out of the city.[26] One report alleged that the Alabama Treasury was moved to a farm in Coosa County. There, according to this account, the money was both floated in a creek and buried in a field.[27]

With Wilson's men an increasing threat, Montgomery authorities began to worry about the city's stock of whiskey. Except for a reserve for personal use all alcohol was to be destroyed and all sales forbidden. As was the case at Selma the destruction was not complete when Wilson arrived, one reason being that some men consumed what they were detailed to pour into the streets.[28]

Between April 4 and April 10 the exodus from Montgomery increased daily, since "all expect a Yankee visit."[29] Columbus, Georgia, was a favorite refuge, and a rising tide of Alabamans arrived there carrying their valuables. The "moving *Appeal*" joined this flight. On April 6 the Memphis journal left for Columbus, while Montgomery's regular newspapers, the *Advertiser* and the *Daily Mail*, remained in the capital. On the fifth and sixth a momentary panic swept the city when reports were received that Wilson's force had reached Benton. People packed and prepared to flee, but a later report advised the city that the Union force was only a foraging expedition looking for food and horses. Generally those days found the city quiet and orderly.[30]

Some plan had to be made to transfer the seat of government in the event of Montgomery's capture. Eufaula was finally designated the point to which Governor Watts and the state government would flee.[31]

On April 10, word reached Montgomery that the telegraph operator at Benton had fled. This time Wilson was reported south of the Alabama, advancing on the capital in force. The *Daily Mail* called this report a "wild rumor," but Adams and Buford hurried their preparations. Their conscripts drilled, slaves piled cotton bale barricades in the streets, and women prepared facilities to care for those wounded in the capital's defense.[32]

Suddenly defense preparations stopped. Richard Taylor, the departmental commander, telegraphed Adams "to attempt no defense in Montgomery if [the] enemy moved against him in force." Instead of fighting, Adams was told to evacuate his troops and march to Columbus to join Gen. Howell Cobb's Georgia State Troops. Buford was instructed to gather all the cavalry he could find and "delay and annoy the enemy" between Montgomery and Columbus.[33] The people of the city had been promised "a full defense" and this "sudden change of program was received with stupor and no little dissatisfaction."[34]

Confusion surrounded meetings between civil and military leaders in Montgomery on the eleventh. City officials asked Adams what he intended, and he advised them that he would burn the cotton and leave the city. The *Daily Mail* claimed that Adams was opposed to giving up the city without a fight, but on April 13 the general reported that on the night of the eleventh authorities met in Montgomery, and "after a consultation . . . it was deemed advisable to evacuate the place." The *Daily Mail* also reported that when General Adams discovered that the Montgomery city government intended to ride out and surrender the city to the approaching enemy on the eleventh he threatened to arrest anyone who left the city. Sarah Follansbee presented a different view of the reaction of the citizens to proposals that the city be defended. She said that given the dearth of troops, the people thought the plan "fool hardiness."[35]

The last act of Adams's soldiers was to burn Montgomery's cotton. Between eighty and eighty-five thousand bales, worth an estimated forty million dollars in gold were fired. Bales on the outskirts were fired first, and then troops moved into the streets to light the cotton barricades. Realizing the great danger of such a blaze among the closely packed houses, Sarah Follansbee begged officers not to burn the bales at the corner near her house. They agreed, but to make certain, the plucky teacher sat on them until after midnight.[36] After citizens helped themselves, commissary stores, including sixty thousand bushels of corn, were thrown on the flames. Some troops detailed to destroy barrels of syrup found themselves "ankle deep . . . where the heads of the barrels had been knocked in."[37]

The burning cotton and stores cast a pall of smoke over the city. Despite some precautions, those who had started the fires suddenly found themselves trying to stop them. Negro firefighting companies were due considerable credit for preventing the city from being razed. Finally an eastern wind blew the flames away from Montgomery, leading one observer to comment that it was a "miracle that the city was not utterly destroyed."[38]

Governor Watts left Montgomery for Columbus before going on to Eufaula, and Adams and Buford marched their troops eastward. City officials were left to surrender. At 3 A.M. on April 12 Mayor W. L. Coleman and nine other prominent citizens rode out of the city. Near Catoma Creek the deputation entered Union lines under a flag of truce. The men reached McCook, and he summoned Wilson. The corps commander was pleasantly surprised at the proposed capitulation since he supposed Montgomery

would be "stoutly defended."[39] The Union generals agreed to protect civilians and their property, and they accepted Montgomery's
surrender.[40]

III

Before Wilson's army marched through the streets of Montgomery,
the Fourth U.S. Cavalry escort rode into the city and established
a provost guard headquarters in the executive office at the Capitol.
The regulars also formed a line in front of the Capitol. To assist
in the peaceful entry of the troops Mayor Coleman had a hastily
printed placard announcing the surrender circulated through the
streets.[41] On the morning of the twelfth Wilson reiterated his
orders against looting; straggling and stealing would not be tolerated, and the Fourth U.S. was to enforce the edict.[42] The Union
commander wanted everything orderly so that he might impress
"the people with the discipline, strength, and invincibility of the
forces under my command." Or as Captain Hinricks put it: "We
put on all the style possible and marched according to regulations."[43]

When the guard had been set, the Union band struck up, and
the corps began its parade. Four abreast, guidons flying, the horsemen in blue triumphantly trotted their mounts into the city and
past the Capitol. The Alabama Capitol stands on a hill and is visible from a great distance, and when Union troopers caught sight of
the building they cheered lustily for the United States flag waved
from the dome.[44] The column was long, and Upton's division was
last to enter. As Captain Hinricks approached the city with the
Tenth Missouri, he thought the land looked very much like his
native Germany, the only difference being the long line of gaping
Negroes strung out along the road.[45] The parade lasted nearly all
day and was without incident. Some Montgomery citizens gave
the soldiers bouquets and thousands lined the streets. One Union
trooper thought "the ladies seemed much pleased and appeared in

their Sunday attire; their bright eyes sparkling,"[46] but many watched from their windows in silence. Others like Sarah Follansbee watched the parade from behind the front yard fence. She was summoned by her servant who woke the teacher with, "Come, come, see the Yankees!" Miss Follansbee saw "host upon host of blue coats—looking brilliant with buttons and *'accouterments'* . . . fine looking men—handsomely dressed—gleaming linen . . . brass buttons, brilliant epaulets, sabres drawn and clashing, they made their entrance at full gallop. Generals Wilson and McCook at the head."

Wilson's preparations to impress the people were a huge success. Some observers estimated the force at thirty thousand, others at fifty-one thousand. One trooper stopped and asked the ladies, "What had become of all of your men when the Yankees approached?" When no one answered, the New Englander replied calmly, "They took a lesson from you at Bull Run." The trooper paused and laughing said, "Well, it was well."[47] With sabers and spurs jingling Wilson's men rode with pride and disciplined order. After the parade had been completed the troopers camped in fields on the eastern edge of the one-time Confederate capital.[48]

All of the capital's citizens did not present flowers, line the streets, or cheer the U.S. flag. Miss Ellen Blue and some friends walked down to the Alabama River on the afternoon of the thirteenth. The party passed some Union troops, and that night Ellen wrote in her diary: "Whenever I come in contact with any of the creatures especially to meet or pass them in groups, I feel humiliated and a sickening feeling comes over my heart that I cannot describe." She added, "I do not believe that the good Lord will allow us long to be so downtrodden by such people."[49]

While the corps paraded on the twelfth, Wilson pushed a scout force east of Montgomery to make certain Confederate forces were out of the area. The Seventh Kentucky and several companies of the First Wisconsin rode to Three Mile Creek on the Mt. Meigs Road, the main route to Columbus. There the force ran into Confederate pickets. Gen. Abraham Buford, ordered to "delay and annoy" the enemy, was carrying out his duty with detachments of the Fourth and Seventh Alabama Cavalry, but Buford hardly slowed the Federals. He was steadily herded eastward until nightfall found the two forces along Line Creek, about twenty miles west of Tuskegee. In the haste of their flight, Buford's men lost their Palmetto Flag brigade standard to the Seventh Kentucky. The Kentuckians also captured the garrison flag of the Montgomery True Blues.[50]

When the parade ended in Montgomery, Wilson made his headquarters at the home of a Colonel Powell "who knew how to be polite to unwelcome guests."[51] Command of the city went to General McCook, and he in turn named Colonel Cooper of the Fourth Kentucky to command the provost guard. Cooper's regiment together with a hundred picked men of the First Wisconsin under Major Shipman, and an equal force from the Third Iowa, served as provost troops, replacing the temporary guard set by the Fourth U.S.[52] When the Union occupation command was established Wilson proclaimed martial law.

> The city of Montgomery having been surrendered into the protection of United States authorities, I am assured by General McCook, commanding the United States forces in Montgomery, that all private property will be respected; so far as consistent with military operations, and that a military guard will be established for the better protection of the city and its inhabitants.
>
> The general commanding requests on the part of the people, that no citizen will attempt to leave the corporate limits.[53]

On the twelfth the post commander, General McCook, addressed an audience gathered at the Capitol for a formal flag raising. A crowd including Montgomery citizens, many Negroes, and those the *Advertiser* called "Union men of the 11th hour," listened to the brigadier. He promised protection and warned Union troops against attacks on property or persons. Eventually the stars and stripes were also raised over the courthouse, telegraph office, and McCook's headquarters in the Exchange Hotel.[54]

Alabama's capital was fortunate in avoiding the kind of destruction visited upon Selma. The city did not have Selma's strategic value and there was less to be destroyed. Probably the most important reasons for Montgomery's escape from further destruction and pillage were the coming end of the war and the brevity of Wilson's stay. From the time Wilson received word of the fall of Richmond he maintained closer rein over his men. Communications were poor and the general was not going to risk serious burning and looting after a Confederate surrender. Furthermore, he wanted to move to the east to be of possible aid in bringing the war to an end. There was no need for a lengthy rest in Montgomery and the corps only camped in the capital for two days. Will Pepper of the 123rd Illinois "had a good time," but he and his comrades were "badly fooled for we thought that we would get to stay in Montgomery awhile."[55]

Although he only had two days in the capital, the observant and ever inquisitive Captain Hinricks saw the sights. He received permission to visit the city and left camp at 11 A.M. on the thirteenth. The captain first visited a printing office to read the latest papers. There he met a discharged Confederate captain and the two drank a toast to "the Union forever." Hinricks then had a "genuine Confederate shave and [hair] cut" for which he paid fifteen dollars in Confederate money, after which he visited the hotel in which Jefferson Davis had stayed during his inauguration as Confederate president. There Hinricks ate a ten dollar dinner and smoked a one dollar cigar. Then during the afternoon he strolled through the city. One woman gave him a bouquet and a "ripe orange out of her hothouse." He saw several United States flags displayed and was told that more would be flying but for fear that "Old Forrest would arrive and hang those who showed their Unionism." When he returned to camp that afternoon, Hinricks wrote in his diary,

"I am more than ever satisfied that at an early day the Confederate bubble would burst."[56]

Generally Union soldiers behaved themselves. Colonel Cooper's provost guard patrolled the streets to preserve order, and those who petitioned for house guards received them. Except for some reported burning and looting on the outskirts, the army's stay in Montgomery was free of the worst aspects of military occupation.[57] Wilson inscribed in his diary: "Town very beautiful. . . . People delighted with our behavior."[58]

Montgomery's citizens were thankful for Wilson's precautionary measures, and "good feelings" were created between conquered and conquerer. One week later, when Union troops passing through Montgomery heard of Lincoln's assassination, it was fortunate that good relations had been established. They played a significant role in preventing an angered Union soldiery from laying waste to the city.[59]

Union troops were impressed with Montgomery's beauty. Major Shipman believed the "buildings are of good class and great taste is displayed in the grounds." He gave the city the supreme compliment a Union soldier could offer when he wrote: "I would like very much to reside here." The Wisconsin officer was asked to dinner by a citizen whose brother lived in Milwaukee.[60] Another Union trooper wrote in his journal:

Montgomery is the finest city by far we have seen in the South. The streets are wide and shaded by splendid trees; the business houses, residences, etc., show wealth, and the granite capitol building is stately with pillars, dome, etc., and beautiful for situation. The city . . . gives one the impression of sensuous, indolent ease—a lotus land, an Acadia.[61]

But the hand of destruction had come to the "lotus land," and in the two days Wilson's men garrisoned Montgomery they worked hard to destroy the city's war material. McCook supervised the destruction of the Montgomery Arsenal which contained twenty thousand stand of small arms. The by now experienced wreckers destroyed a niter works, foundries, and small shops. Carrying out their usual assault on transportation facilities, the troopers wrecked a locomotive, twenty cars, and the depots of the Montgomery and West Point and Alabama and Florida railroads. Negroes from area plantations flocked to Montgomery to greet their liberators, but they were sent home and stopped from following the column when it pushed on toward Georgia.[62]

Several small Union raiding parties ranged the countryside on the twelfth and thirteenth searching for property of military value to the Confederates. One detachment under Maj. John F. Weston of the Fourth Kentucky found three steamboats, loaded with food, sent to Cole's Station on the Tallapoosa River to ride out Wilson's occupation. The boats were sailed back to Montgomery where they were burned, "making a brilliant bonfire for the multitude which lined the shore."[63] East of the capital Union raiders tore up the Montgomery and West Point Railroad, wrecking trestles and bridges.

While they camped at Montgomery rumor made the rounds of Union tents that Forrest was outside the city demanding their surrender. That old tactic of Forrest's could now be safely derided, and Major Shipman wrote, tongue-in-cheek, that the ultimatum was "scoffed at in a very respectful manner."[64]

IV

Before he reached Montgomery Wilson had decided to march his corps through Georgia and on toward the Carolinas. The only obstacle to that plan was Canby's campaign at Mobile. But by April 14 Wilson no longer needed to concern himself with reinforcing Canby—Mobile had fallen. From Montgomery on the thirteenth the cavalry chief telegraphed General Thomas at Nashville:

The fall of Richmond and defeat of Lee have deprived rebels in this section of their last hope. If I can now destroy arsenals and supplies

at Columbus and divide their army in the southwest, they must dis-
integrate for lack of munitions. There is no force to resist me, and I
see no reasonable ground for fearing failures. My command is in magnificent condition.[65]

In his memoir Wilson wrote that he felt it was his duty to continue eastward, " 'breaking things' along the main line of Confederate communications."[66]

Looking ahead, Wilson saw one major barrier to his progress,
the Chattahoochee River. That stream flowing along the Alabama-
Georgia border was near flood stage from rains that had drenched
the Southeast. Hubbard's engineers could bridge the river with
pontoons, but the process would be slow, especially since some of
the pontoons had been destroyed at Selma. Studying his map Wilson found bridges at Columbus and West Point. The towns were
only thirty-five miles apart, and a bridge seized at either point
would cross the corps in good position to move on toward Macon
and the heart of Georgia. The general decided to divide his army
somewhere east of Montgomery, aiming a small force at West Point
and the bulk of the corps toward more heavily defended Columbus. If only one span was taken the remaining force could march
to that point with little loss of time. LaGrange's brigade was once
again given the special mission. The colonel would leave the corps
near Tuskegee and march through Auburn and Opelika on his
way to West Point, where he would secure at least one of the two
bridges so that the corps could cross if all bridges at Columbus
were impassable. Wilson would lead the main force through Tuskegee, Crawford, and Girard to Columbus.[67]

Led by LaGrange's brigade, which had the most distance to
cover, Wilson's corps left Montgomery on the morning of April
14. A number of sick and wounded were left behind. For the sake
of speed as well as the men's health, 144 troopers remained in
Montgomery.[68] Three miles out of Montgomery Confederate riflemen appeared but were scattered easily by Henry Harnden's First
Wisconsin. Soon another thin line of defenders offered sporadic

fire, and again the Wisconsin troopers sent it running. Several more times that day LaGrange's vanguard drew fire but each time routed the enemy. The Federal advance covered about forty miles on the fourteenth, pushed through Mt. Meigs, and camped near Tuskegee. Colonel LaGrange reported about a hundred prisoners taken that day.[69]

Early on the fifteenth LaGrange outflanked rebel troops and rode into Tuskegee. The town's mayor asked for protection of civilians and property, and when he received the colonel's assurance the town was surrendered. The brigade remained only briefly in Tuskegee, moving northeastward toward Opelika along the tracks of the Montgomery and West Point. Wilson, leading Upton's and Long's (now commanded by Minty) divisions, rode into Tuskegee on the afternoon of the fifteenth. Wilson set guards at schools and on street corners to continue the policy LaGrange had promised.[70]

Tuskegee drew much favorable comment from Wilson's raiders. Benjamin McGee of the Seventy-second Indiana called Tuskegee "a most beautiful place," and General Wilson found it a "beautiful" town and the "seat of education and refinement for an extensive region." Tuskegee Female College was the chief reason for the label "seat of education."[71] Major Shipman, an architect with an eye for a town's buildings, wrote of Tuskegee,

[It] is one of the finest towns I have ever met with in the South. The most exquisite taste is manifested in the ornamentation of the ample grounds around each dwelling. There is the greatest variety of evergreens and the magnolia is in great abundance. The evergreen arches through the hedges were finer than I ever saw before. The architecture of the public and private residences was quite as good if not better than at Montgomery.[72]

Some looting was charged to Wilson's troopers during their three-hour stop in Tuskegee. Carrie Hunter, a student at the Female College feared the Union approach and called it a "dread hour . . . in which we are to meet the foe face to face! The mur-

derers of our martyred brothers." She expected the marauders to
lay waste to the city's buildings and feared especially for her college. Word that General Croxton had burned the University of
Alabama at Tuscaloosa had preceded Wilson's column. Carrie expected similar devastation. She was amazed when the city was un-
harmed, and she called it a "piece of clemency quite extraordinary." However, Carrie did report that soldiers took jewels from
most of her friends in an act of "yankeefied yankeeism."[73] There
was no burning. Wilson received an appeal from the lady editor
of the *Tuskegee Press*, and the general permitted the newspaper
to continue publication so long as nothing appeared in its columns
hostile to the United States government or the Constitution.[74]

On the fifteenth Wilson received confirmation of Richmond's
fall and Grant's drive westward against Lee. Once again the corps
cheered the news. The men expressed a desire to race eastward so
as to play a role in hastening the Confederacy's demise.[75] Lt. Col.
Frank Montgomery, taken at Selma and still with the corps, was
told the news by Lt. Col. Frank White of the Seventeenth Indiana.
The Mississippian, who usually rode along with White at the head
of the regiment, doubted the news but told the Union colonel
that, if true, he hoped peace terms came to the South from soldiers,
not from stay-at-home politicians.[76]

Wilson was in complete agreement with his men's desire to be
involved in the war's climax. He did not yet know of Lee's surrender or of the direction Davis's flight had taken. He assumed a
Confederate concentration in North Carolina or "that they would
disband and endeavor to save themselves by flight." The general
added, "In either case it was clearly the duty of my command to
close in upon them on the line which it was moving, with the
greatest possible rapidity, so as to join in the final and decisive
struggle or to assist in the capture of such important persons as
might seek safety in flight."[77]

Speed had become a primary consideration, and the corps rode
out of Tuskegee at about 5 P.M. on the fifteenth. Despite efforts

to dissuade them, Negroes still flocked after Wilson's horsemen. The Seventy-second Indiana was trailed by a large group of "contrabands": "There were Negro men, women, and children on horseback, ass-back, mule-back, cow-back; in carts, wagons, wheel barrows, and every other way you could think. They seemed to have plenty to eat and were perfectly happy, thinking no doubt, that the year of jubilo had come."[78]

Infantry would have been seriously slowed by the runaways, but Wilson's cavalrymen were able to continue their brisk passage. Jingling along through the April afternoon, the main column walked and trotted the Montgomery-Columbus road while swarms of raiding parties buzzed along its flanks. These detachments were foragers who brought in food and fodder, but, despite Wilson's orders to the contrary, they also stole horses, burned farm buildings, and persuaded slaves to run away.[79] It thundered, lightninged, and drizzled that afternoon, but the foragers did their work well, and when Wilson ordered the halt on the night of April 15, the smell of fresh food hung over the campfires. That night the corps' lead units slept only about twenty-five miles from Columbus. Upton's division had taken the lead and it would move out for Columbus early on the sixteenth. Sitting in his tent Charley Hinricks, one of Upton's officers, recorded a rumor that six thousand rebels were within six miles of the Union camp. Before taps the Missouri captain described in his diary entry for the fifteenth an unusual event of the afternoon. As he rode through the thunderstorm he passed three white women "standing in the rain waving their handkerchiefs and *hurraying for Lincoln*." He was pleased as he continued, "This is the first time that this happened to us. The boys cheered them."[80]

V

While Wilson's main force paused in Tuskegee and then moved on toward Columbus, LaGrange's brigade marched along the

Montgomery and West Point toward West Point. By dark on the fifteenth the force had reached Auburn, after spending the day tearing up track and burning bridges. At first light on the sixteenth the Second and Fourth Indiana regiments broke camp and trotted northeastward, taking with them the Eighteenth Indiana Battery. The First Wisconsin and Seventh Kentucky brought up the rear and continued their mission of railroad destruction. By mid-morning the Indiana horsemen had sighted Ft. Tyler on the Alabama side of the Chattahoochee protecting the western approach to the railroad bridge. Across the river lay West Point, the line's eastern terminus.[81]

West Point contained no mills or foundries, but it was a vital rail center. The city was eastern terminus of the road from Montgomery, and western terminus of the Atlanta and West Point Railroad. Failure of the railroad builders to use standard gauge on the two lines meant that transfer of cargo and passengers was necessary. An extensive railroad yard lay at West Point, and many locomotives and cars as well as the two depots would normally have been the Union cavalrymen's chief objective. At the time, however, the bridges were uppermost in LaGrange's mind.[82]

Ft. Tyler was a thirty-five-yard-square earthwork standing on a hill on the Alabama side of the river. The structure's armament was three guns, a thirty-two-pound siege gun which covered the bridges, and two twelve-pounders. The fort had walls four and one-half feet high, surrounded by a ditch from seven to twelve feet wide and six to ten feet deep. The south wall was pierced to allow passage, and inside the fort and about ten feet from this entrance a thick eight-foot-high wall had been built. This palisade prevented an enemy from seizing the entrance and firing in on the garrison through the opening.[83]

The garrison commander was Brig. Gen. Robert C. Tyler, on crutches from a wound received at Missionary Ridge in November 1863. Tyler was a Marylander by birth who had moved to Tennessee before the war and become acquainted with the filibusterer William Walker. Tyler joined Walker's 1850 expedition to Nicaragua and, more fortunate than his leader, escaped and returned to Memphis. When war began, Tyler joined the Fifteenth Tennessee Infantry and commanded the regiment at Shiloh. He was wounded there, again at Chickamauga, and a third time at Missionary Ridge. The general was convalescing when he received word that Union raiders were closing in on West Point. Few men were available for service and Tyler gathered a "promiscuous and most voluntary force" of wounded soldiers, civilians, and hospital workers. LaGrange reported 265 men inside the fort, but one Confederate remembered less than one-half that number.[84]

The Union brigade commander did not reach Ft. Tyler until about 1:30 P.M. By the time he rode up with the First Wisconsin and Seventh Kentucky the battle had begun. Capt. Moses Beck had placed his guns on a nearby hill, and the Hoosier gunners had unlimbered and exchanged shots with Ft. Tyler. Beck's fire did little damage to the fort, but it was effective enough to drive rebel skirmishers inside the walls. While Beck bombarded the enemy the two cavalry units dismounted and formed a skirmish line.[85]

Primarily concerned about the bridges, LaGrange decided to take Lt. Col. Horace Lamson's Fourth Indiana and make a dash for the wagon bridge while the remainder of the brigade attacked Tyler's garrison. The dismounted troopers would draw Confederate fire away from his detachment and allow it to seize the span. Any attack on the fort was faced with one obvious problem—the ditch which fronted its walls. Union troopers ripped down several nearby houses to obtain long planks which would bridge the trench. The Union main line, facing the fort, remained about fifty yards away while a small group of sharpshooters crawled forward to snipe at Confederate artillerymen.[86]

With all of his men in position, LaGrange ordered the charge. The brigade commander's detachment galloped for the bridge while the dismounted regiments, First Wisconsin, Seventh Kentucky, and Ross Hill's battalion of the Second Indiana, attacked the fort. The defenders were taken by surprise, and the thirty-two-pounder was unable to stop LaGrange's race for the bridge, but its grapeshot did kill the colonel's mount. He remounted and the force raced on and reached the bridge. As they galloped across the span they found a gap in its planking where boards had been removed. The troops spurred their mounts across the gap and into West Point. They quickly repulsed a small defense force which, with turpentine and cotton, stood ready to fire the bridge, and the rail center and bridge were in Union hands. Wilson had secure passage into Georgia.[87]

In front of Ft. Tyler accurate Confederate fire stalled the assault. The ditch-spanning planks were in position but Confederate riflemen stopped the Federals from crossing. Some attacking bluecoats had jumped into the trench to continue their fire, but this position soon became untenable when defenders threw lighted shells over the parapets. The Federals extinguished some in the trench's water and tried to throw some back into the fort. Some exploded, wounding the trapped men. Union fire had also taken its toll. Eighteen Confederates, including General Tyler, lay dead, and twenty-eight more had been wounded.[88]

When LaGrange returned to the west bank the battle was still underway. The colonel ordered a concentrated bombardment by Beck's Battery which silenced the three rebel pieces. That done, LaGrange sent his line forward again. His artillery out of action, casualties high, and ammunition running low, Tyler's successor Col. James H. Fannin decided to surrender.[89] Union casualties were twenty-nine killed and wounded. Included in the list of wounded were two unit commanders. Lieutenant Colonel Harnden of the First Wisconsin was slightly wounded, and Capt. Ross Hill, intrepid leader of the Second Indiana Battalion, took a serious wound in the thigh. Hill had been shot at Selma but this wound was far more serious. The leg had to be amputated.[90]

With the Union flag flying over Ft. Tyler and West Point under control, LaGrange set guards on the bridges and turned his attention to the rail yards. They were clogged with cars filled with goods moved there to avoid Union raiders. There had not been time to transfer the food, ordnance, and clothing to the Atlanta and West Point for trans-shipment, and LaGrange's wreckers went to work. Nineteen locomotives and 340 cars were destroyed.[91]

On the night of April 16, while the smoke of burning rail yards swept down the Chattahoochee Valley, LaGrange held the bridges and waited for word from Wilson. Thirty-five miles to the south the corps was assaulting Columbus.

CHAPTER VI

"A Most Gallant Night Attack"

Newspapers were among the most prized possessions of Civil War armies. Papers from home bolstered morale and told of loved ones, but enemy journals may have been even more highly coveted. The rebel press was often the intelligence service of Union armies, giving troop movements and a gauge of popular feeling, so it was with great interest that Union troopers read Columbus papers on April 15. The journals were only one day old, and Wilson's men were informed that rebels in Columbus were "determined to give battle."[1]

At daybreak on the sixteenth "Boots and Saddles" sounded, and the line of bluecoats rode toward the promised battle. For a time no enemy showed himself, and marching was easy. Then the usual scouts were sighted and occasional road barricades had to be dragged aside. Through late morning and early afternoon the column continued to encounter Confederate scouts, but little resistance was offered. A small group was driven back at Crawford, twelve miles from Columbus, and Union troopers rode into the village to find an unusual situation. By the time the Tenth Missouri reached Crawford a plume of black smoke twisted skyward and nearby a young woman was surrounded by a crowd of Union soldiers. Charley Hinricks could not press close enough to hear the conversation so he turned aside and questioned several local women. He discovered that the flaming building was the town jail and the young woman its most recent prisoner. The captain was told that the woman, a resident of Girard, "had strongly advanced northern sentiments" and had been in jail for two years on a charge of trying to steal Negroes. When a mob in Girard threatened her life, the prisoner had been moved to Crawford. The newly freed Unionist steadfastly denied that she had ever stolen slaves; she believed that she had been jailed for her Unionism alone. Hinricks's informants believed the woman's story. When freed, the woman kissed her liberators and then fainted. The enraged men burned the jail and threatened to raze the town until the recent captive, treated well in Crawford, begged them not to. When the army moved on, the woman rode along in General Long's carriage.[2]

Six miles down the road from Crawford, at Wetumpka Creek, a group of rebel scouts appeared and burned a bridge. The harassing Confederates failed to slow the column, which forded the stream and marched on toward Columbus. The river city would be the first point in Georgia, a state already reeling from Sherman's campaign, to feel the new invader.[3]

II

Columbus, like Selma, was a certain target for Wilson. The general called the city "the key" and "the door" to Georgia.[4] The campaign aimed at destroying the Confederacy's ability to make war from the Southwest. Selma's factories had been destroyed, Columbus's equally important facilities were to meet the same fate. Columbus, on the Chattahoochee River, was a major railroad and shipping center. A spur of the Montgomery and West Point crossed the river from the west, and the Muscogee Railroad moved eastward into central Georgia. Union capture of Apalachicola, Florida, had forced wider use of the Chattahoochee after 1863. In 1865 five steamers moved goods up and down the river.[5]

Even more valuable to the Confederate war effort were the city's factories and mills. Rifles, cannon, cotton and woolen cloth, shoes and knapsacks were made there. Columbus had five large textile mills in 1865. The Eagle Mills produced two thousand yards of gray tweed and fifteen hundred yards of cotton duck daily. The Columbus Factory, north of the city, had once produced three hundred thousand yards of cotton cloth, seventy-five thousand yards of woolens, and forty thousand pounds of yarn and thread a year. Tents and shoes produced in Columbus added their value to the Confederate cause. The Columbus Factory ran a tannery worked by thirty slaves. The shop produced twelve thousand pairs of shoes a year.[6] There were also flour mills capable of producing two hundred and fifty barrels a day for transportation to Confederates in Virginia.[7]

Of more direct value to the Confederate military were the products of the factory of L. Haiman and Brother and of the Columbus Arsenal and Armory. Haiman and Brother made swords, saddles, and eventually revolvers at the Muscogee Iron Works. Confederate troops also used Haiman's belts, buckles, bayonets, and cartridge boxes. The Columbus Arsenal supplied the Confederacy with rifles and pistols. When Sherman marched into Georgia everything movable in the Atlanta Arsenal was sent to Columbus. Therefore, in the war's last year the Columbus facility's capacity had increased.[8]

Thousands of gray-clad soldiers owed what comfort they enjoyed to the Confederate Quartermaster Depot in Columbus. The principal output of the factory was uniforms and shoes. In June 1862 Richmond received fourteen railroad cars filled with uniforms from the depot. Even more significant is the estimate that more than three hundred thousand pairs of shoes were produced there. The depot also contributed saddle and harness to the Confederate cavalry.[9]

Since Columbus was a river city its works had been turned to casting cannon, building gunboats, and repairing steamboats. The Confederate Naval Iron Works cast eighty six-pound brass cannon during the war and made the boilers for a majority of the steamboats constructed in the South. Most famous products of the city's naval yards were the gunboats *Chattahoochee*, *Jackson*, and *Mus-*

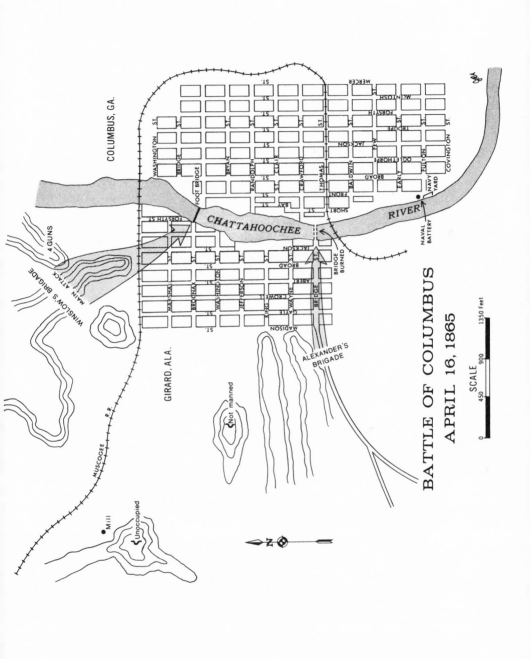

BATTLE OF COLUMBUS
APRIL 16, 1865

cogee. Union control over the river outlets had kept the gunboats out of action and the *Jackson* still lay at Columbus.[10] In addition to these more obvious aids to the Confederate cause, many specialized workshops produced smaller items for both civilian and military consumption. One Georgia historian has boasted that Columbus sent more goods to the Confederate Quartermasters Department than any city in the South except Richmond.[11] It was toward this arsenal that Wilson's horsemen trotted in the second week of April 1865.

Columbus was a city of about twelve thousand in 1865, for the population had been swollen in 1864 with refugees from Sherman. As Wilson's raiders crossed Alabama a new refugee tide rolled eastward, and the river city once again absorbed displaced persons. The fall of Montgomery brought an increase in mid-April. Among those seeking haven were the author Augustus Baldwin Longstreet, avoiding Sherman; Alabama Governor Thomas Watts, fleeing Wilson; and the *Memphis Daily Appeal.* The Memphis journal, driven out of Montgomery by Wilson, was going to try to continue publication from Columbus.[12]

When Wilson began his raid in March, Columbus showed little interest and no fear. The *Daily Sun* reported on March 31 that reports of fifteen thousand Union troopers in central Alabama were rumors and no more than "mere Northern telegraphic speculation." Besides, wrote the *Sun,* any force could be stopped because Forrest, " 'the Wizard of the Saddle,' is on the war path, and the indomitable Buford is wakeful and watchful."[13]

When word of Selma's fall reached Columbus, fear and panic began to spread. Although the "Wizard of the Saddle" and the "Watchful" Buford had been routed by Wilson, the *Daily Sun* sought to calm the populace:

Alarmists—There are in every community those who grow tremulous and excited at the remotest prospect of danger. . . . They seem to have forgotten that Sherman with his entire army was much nearer Columbus six months ago. . . . Things are somewhat different now. The city of Columbus is defended today by a much more efficient force than at any previous time, while the prospect of an attack is diminished. . . . Everything is in readiness. Let us keep cool.[14]

Even more calming was the *Sun*'s report on April 8 that Wilson would march from Selma to Mobile, not Columbus.[15]

Wilson's capture of Montgomery shattered the *Sun*'s last illusions, and the Alabama capital's refugees added to the panic in Columbus. Still the calming agent, the *Sun* reported on April 15 that it believed Wilson would not leave Montgomery "for some days to come."[16] Once again the paper's information was faulty, and on the sixteenth when scouting reports told of advancing bluecoats the *Sun* warned:

The public is hereby notified of the rapid approach of the enemy, but assured that the city of Columbus will be defended to the last. Judging from experience it is believed the city will be shelled. Notice is, therefore, given to all non-combatants to move away immediately. It is again urged upon all able bodied men of this city to report to these headquarters with whatever arms they have, to assist the commanding officer in making a resolute defense of their homes.[17]

Was Columbus prepared to make a "resolute defense"? In 1862 Columbus made its first defensive moves with the construction of fortifications in Girard, the small town on the Alabama side of the Chattahoochee, and along the river south of the city.[18] Despite these efforts, Gen. Jeremy F. Gilmer reported in 1863 that the city's defenses were inadequate and concluded: "The country around Columbus is of such a character that it is difficult to locate a line of defense works without giving a development too great for any garrison that we can hope to place there."[19] By 1864 overall command of the area had fallen to Gen. Howell Cobb, commanding Georgia State Troops. Cobb labored to improve Columbus's defenses, especially after a Union raid in July 1864 ranged eastern Alabama and appeared moving toward Columbus. That raid veered away but a more serious threat soon appeared. Sherman's Atlanta campaign switched Confederate preparations from defenses west of the city to protection for its eastern perimeter. Responding to this alarm, the Confederates constructed breastworks along Columbus's eastern fringes.

As the war's last year began local officials still endeavored to make the manufacturing center secure. Appeals in the press urged civilian cooperation and informed those who had horses that they were needed by defense forces for weekly drill.[20] Those who voluntarily loaned their mounts would be guaranteed they would not be impressed. So few were contributed that by 1865 authorities were forced to impress stock while promising owners they would be paid the standard 1865 market price. The men of Columbus were urged to join militia companies, and with Wilson on the horizon the *Daily Sun* ran an appeal pleading "delay no longer," "organize and protect your homes . . . never let it be said that Columbus fell without a struggle."[21] One week later Col. Leon von Zinken, Confederate commander at Columbus, proclaimed that enemy attack would be announced by the firing of six guns in front of post headquarters on Broad Street. This signal called for all military units to assemble with one day's rations. It also indicated the closing of all bars in the city.[22] A final, and very tardy, realization of Columbus's unpreparedness came from Georgia Governor Joseph E. Brown. On the fifteenth Brown wrote Gen. Gustavus W. Smith that Wilson's movements indicated an attack on Columbus was imminent. "To enable us to meet this successfully," wrote Brown, "you are directed to order out the militia of the State . . . to rendezvous at Columbus as fast as possible."[23]

There was no time for this assembling of state forces, and the factory center would be defended by between two and three thousand men.[24] Of this small force of defenders only a few were seasoned troops. The Seventh Alabama and part of the Clanton Battery following Buford in his "annoy and delay" mission had reached Columbus. Two regiments of the Georgia State Line were present. These units were largely untried in combat but did know the basic elements of military drill. Other units were composed of county reserves and factory workers, who, except for occasional drill, had no military experience. Many were too old or too young for regular service and some were disabled veterans. The ranking Confederate in Columbus was Gen. Howell Cobb, but field command was left to Colonel von Zinken.[25]

In order to capture Columbus, Union troopers would have to fight through Confederate lines in Girard and cross bridges into the factory city. Because of a lack of men the Confederates abandoned a line of fortifications on Girard's western fringe. This left a main line, which took advantage of the hilly terrain and covered the Fourteenth Street footbridge and the railroad bridge several blocks to the north. On the left this line began near the point at which Holland Creek empied into the Chattahoochee. It ran westward into Girard for several blocks before turning north. Running northward the works crossed the Summerville Road and then bent to the northeast. The line's right was anchored on a high hill overlooking the river. West of this main line a weaker line of rifle pits was protected by an abatis added for extra defense. A Union attack directly aimed at either bridge would have to hammer through two Confederate forces. Realizing that the two other bridges in the area could not be covered, Confederates rendered the northernmost bridge unusable and tore up plank flooring of the Dillingham Street Bridge, southernmost of the area's spans.

Within the Confederate line several forts had been built to cover roads and bridge approaches. Two forts containing twelve artillery pieces protected the Fourteenth Street Bridge while the same structure held four ten-pound Parrots to bear on roads which might be used by the enemy. These positions also contained five guns bearing on approaches to the railroad bridge. Lining these strong points were ditches eight feet wide and six feet deep. For further security part of the Seventh Alabama Cavalry was stationed north and south of Columbus on the Georgia side to guard against a flank movement from those directions.[26]

All through the morning of the sixteenth Columbus feverishly prepared for Wilson's appearance. The *Sun* had warned of the Yankees' approach, and as the morning wore on the Confederate provost marshal, Capt. Thomas E. Blanchard, rode through the city to warn of imminent attack.[27] At about 2 P.M. Union scouts surprised a gang of Negro laborers strengthening earthwork fortifications. The men retreated as the blue-clad horsemen advanced.[28]

III

Spearheading Wilson's vanguard was the First Ohio from Alexander's Brigade of General Upton's Fourth Division. As the First reached Girard, Upton rode up and asked the men, "Can you give us the bridge across the Chattahoochee?" The men shouted as they galloped by that they would try.[29] The Ohioans, led by Col. B. B. Eggleston, shoved aside rebel pickets and drove quickly through Girard to the partially destroyed Dillingham Street Bridge. For a moment Upton, standing on a hill in the rear, cried, "Columbus is ours without firing a shot."[30] At the bridge the men fired their Spencers through the structure and talked of replacing the planking. Before this could be done Confederate Capt. C. C. McGehee set fire to the bridge from the Georgia side. The bridge was now impossible to cross, and as the defenders' fire from the left swept toward them the Ohioans withdrew.[31]

Upton and Wilson rode forward to make a personal reconnaissance of rebel positions. Thick woods and jagged hills made it difficult to see any outline of enemy works, but from what they could see of the terrain, the two men decided to switch their attack from the southerly direction in which it had begun to a strike from the northwest toward the Confederate line.[32] The attack was to be mounted by the First Brigade of Upton's division commanded by Col. Edward F. Winslow. Winslow's unit, composed of the Third Iowa, Fourth Iowa, and Tenth Missouri, would move down the Summerville Road, running into Girard from the northwest.

Winslow's assault was to begin as soon as possible, but owing to confusion between division and brigade commanders Winslow's forces could not be found. Upton searched for the brigade on the wrong road, and by the time Winslow had been found the light was almost gone. Wilson and Upton considered the situation, and the corps commander, believing the men were good night fighters, talked about a strike at about 8 P.M. Wilson believed that such an attack would be a surprise and would be accomplished with less loss. Upton enthusiastically exclaimed: "Do you mean it? It will be dark as midnight by that hour and that will be a night attack indeed!" Wilson left the tactical details to Upton, who loved such things; for once the corps commander was not "annoyed" with his lieutenant's tactical discussions.[33]

While the search for Winslow went on Wilson was not idle. In late afternoon the cavalry chief sent two hundred men from the Tenth Missouri to seize the bridge at the Columbus Factory north of the city. The Tenth Missouri found the bridge partially destroyed and unusable for a crossing. This shattered Wilson's hopes that the bridge might offer a chance to avoid a head on assault against Confederate positions in Girard. That frontal attack now seemed unavoidable.[34] The delay in the Union attack proved advantageous to Wilson. During the afternoon a local citizen was found who told Wilson what he knew of Confederate dispositions. He also drew a fairly accurate rough sketch of rebel earthworks.[35] The afternoon hours were also a welcome respite for most of the hard riding horsemen, who made coffee, ate supper, and "passed an hour in absolute rest."[36]

By nightfall Confederate troops in Girard and the citizens of Columbus wondered at Wilson's delay in attacking. Since two o'clock Yankee troopers had been visible on the hills around the Alabama town. Some Confederate batteries shelled visible Federals, but the firing was ineffective. Rumors flew through Columbus. Many citizens believed that Wilson was waiting for his artillery which would bombard the city after dark.[37]

IV

By 8 P.M. on a clear, dark night Wilson had Winslow's brigade in position. Leading the assault were six dismounted companies of Col. John W. Noble's Third Iowa. This three-hundred-man force, guided through the dark by the white line of the Summerville Road, would strike the outer Confederate defensive positions before it encountered the rebel main line. Lieutenant Colonel Benteen's Tenth Missouri and Lt. Col. John H. Peters's Fourth Iowa, both units mounted, were in reserve and ready to ride to support Noble's lead troops.[38]

Just as Noble's Iowans launched their attack, Confederate muskets opened a heavy fire joined by artillery. The aim was high and little damage was done. Not deterred by the bombardment, the Third Iowa charged, sliced through the outer line's abatis and pushed the defenders back. Winslow and Upton, riding close to the advancing men, believed the Confederates' main line had been breached, and Upton ordered the Tenth Missouri in columns of fours to ride for the bridge. The Missourians charged through the night, and two companies led by Capt. B. M. McGlasson rode down the road and through the entire Confederate defensive position. Riding with the Tenth Missouri was German-American Captain Hinricks who vividly described the charge:

We layed low until after dark, then mounted without the bugle sound. . . . We were ordered to be quiet, not to speak aloud and all noisy things such as tin baskets and pans were ordered to be thrown away. We halted and awaited for the signal. It got as dark as pitch, not a sound could be heard anywhere, some of the men had dismounted and fallen asleep. All of a sudden there was a shot, another, and in a second 10,000 more. The whole country seemed to be alive with demons . . . the next second brought the balls of the enemy by thousands over our heads and the shells hurried their way in every direction, leaving a fiery streak behind them. This was the first time that I ever saw shelling during night time, it is a beautiful but awful spectacle. The order came for us to charge. A sweet thing I can tell you, to charge the enemy's works, when it is dark as pitch and you don't know where they are. Particularly sweet when every second your eyes are blinded by the blue light of the shells exploding all around you and passing within four or five feet of the ground across the road you have to travel, not speaking of the grape, cannister and small bullets which however likely you cannot see, but only hear whistling by, or striking trees, or something else.[39]

In the dark and confusing woods McGlasson's troopers were either unseen or mistaken for retreating Confederates. Passing within "ten steps" of General Cobb, the Missourians reached the footbridge. Briefly they controlled the span before counterattacking rebels from Columbus dislodged them.[40]

The early action revealed to Wilson, Upton, and Winslow that the greatest concentration of rebels lay to their left. The flashes puncturing the dark indicated Confederate strongpoints, and it was toward these points that the remainder of the Third Iowa and Tenth Missouri as well as the Fourth Iowa were directed. Through the April night Upton personally led the advance, crying "Charge 'em!" The troopers replied yelling, "Selma, Selma, Go for the bridge!"[41] They had to descend a ravine and charge through thick woods where some confusion ensued. Captain Hinricks heard someone yell, "here is no road," others yelled, "go to the right," still others advised, "go to the left." Thoroughly bewildered, Hinricks remembered that part of his company "got tangled up." He continued: "I turned to where the most went, to the right. The company in my rear charged in on me, we all got tangled up."[42] The Union veterans finally managed to bring order out of the jumble in the woods and pressed the Confederate forts. Disorder in Union ranks was more than matched by the tumult among the poorly trained Confederates, many of whom were under fire for the first time. The bluecoats collapsed the enemy line and fire slackened. Some Confederate officers told their men it was every man for himself as their forces fled. As suddenly as it had begun the battle was over.

Inexperience, fear, and the dark produced a complete Confederate rout. Troops fled the field, and both armies raced for the bridge. The span was a scene of chaos as "horsemen and footmen, artillery wagons and ambulances were crowded and jammed together in the narrow avenue, which was 'dark as Egypt' . . . for that bridge had no gas fixtures and was never lighted. How it was that many were not crushed to death in the tumultuous transit of the Chattahoochee, seem incomprehensible."[43] Part of Peters's Fourth Iowa reached the covered wooden structure and in the dark passed many retreating Southerners before they knew it. The Iowans could smell turpentine and knew the enemy planned to fire the bridge. Yet the rebels were reluctant to start a fire that might kill their own troops. One Confederate did strike a match but he was struck down by men of Company K, Fourth Iowa.[44] The Iowans got across in the confusion and after a "sharp fight" for a Confederate battery scattered what defense remained and saved the bridge.[45] General Wilson crossed the Chattahoochee shortly after 11 P.M., just after "all firing had ceased."[46] Later that night he ended his brief diary entry for the sixteenth with, "Magnificent achievement."[47]

Only Upton's Fourth Division had been engaged. Minty's Second Division had camped west of Girard and followed the battle by sound. Major Shipman wrote: "At about 8 o'clock the cannonading was very heavy and brisk on both sides, and our men charged with a shout when the firing became very heavy." These Federals did not doubt a victory, but it was not until 1 A.M. that they knew the outcome for certain. At 1 A.M. general call was sounded and Minty's men were told Columbus had fallen. Confederate prisoners listened to the same sounds, and Lieutenant Colonel Montgomery thought Wilson was being checked. He and his fellow officer prisoners did not join in the cheers following the battle report.[48]

V

Panic gripped Columbus, and the confused sound of flight rumbled through the night. Cobb and von Zinken were not able to lead an orderly withdrawal, and troops fled in all directions. Civilians as well as soldiers streamed out roads east of the fallen city. One man reported "a perfect panic" and cries of "the Yankees are coming" along roads to the east. He added "at one place the women and children were running through the streets like people deranged, and men, with mules and wagons, driving in every direction."[49] Captain Hinricks's company rode all the way through the city and camped on the road to Macon. He posted videttes and entered a neighboring house. There he found a wounded man who alleged "that he had been shot by the rebels in the morning because he refused to take arms." The man added, "two men were killed because they refused to fight."[50] About six hundred Confederate troops escaped. General Cobb managed to avoid capture and fled to Macon, where he would soon face Wilson's raiders again.[51]

By the following morning Wilson knew that the "most gallant night attack" had taken prisoner over a thousand officers and men.[52] One Confederate colonel and his regimental adjutant were brought in by Pvt. Robert C. Wood of the Fourth Iowa. Only a few hours earlier their roles had been reversed, when Wood, reconnoitering the shadowy Confederate works with Upton and a small party, got too close and was captured. During the Union assault Wood escaped, joined the attackers, and captured his late captors. For his adventures the private received a special citation for bravery from Wilson.[53] The Columbus captives were marched to Macon and paroled when Wilson discovered Johnston's capitulation to Sherman. But Columbus was the end of the road for those rebel officers who had ridden with the corps since the fall of Selma; paroled and allowed to keep their horses, they began their sad march back home.[54]

Casualties on both sides in the struggle for Columbus are impossible to determine. Estimates of Union dead run from Wilson's report of twenty-five to other figures of only five or six. The disorder in Confederate ranks allowed for no accurate reporting. Only nine listed dead are known, and eight of those listed died on the Georgia side. On the afternoon of the seventeenth Captain Hinricks revisited the Girard battlefield and his observations indicated the inaccuracy of Confederate figures. He wrote "our dead had already been gathered but the rebels were yet laying about in the woods and they were at work gathering the wounded."[55] Among the Confederate dead were Col. C. A. L. Lamar of Cobb's staff, *Enquirer* editor J. J. Jones, and Capt. S. Isidore Guillet, aide to Colonel von Zinken.[56]

On the west bank Captain Hinricks encountered a number of women and children terrified by the battle, hungry and afraid of the resumption of the violence. They had been told that Forrest would attack on the night of the seventeenth, and they were seeking refuge in the country. The Missourian advised them there was no danger of a Forrest attack and persuaded them to return to their homes. When he found that they had no food, the captain found a dozen Negroes, carrying rations given them in Columbus by Union authorities, and he forced the blacks to give their supplies to Southern whites.[57]

When Wilson entered Columbus he gave Gen. Winslow command of the city and charged him with destroying all property deemed of use to the rebels in what the major general regarded as the last great Confederate storehouse.[58] The corps commander established his headquarters in the home of Col. Randolph L. Mott, an opponent of secession who reportedly had flown the Union flag from his home throughout the war. Mott boasted that his home was the only spot in Georgia that had never seceded. Wilson remembered that Mott had flown the flag but kept it "inside but substantially over the part of the house used as a dwelling."[59]

Wilson wrote in his memoirs, "I resolved to destroy everything within reach that could be made useful for further continuance of

the Rebellion."[60] Under Winslow's supervision the seventeenth
was a day of doom for the Georgia factory city. Explosions rocked
Columbus, and a pall of smoke hung in the air. The gunboat *Jackson* was destroyed along with L. Haiman and Brother, the Arsenal,
and the Confederate Naval Iron Works. The Confederate Quartermaster Depot, a paper mill, and all textile and flour mills in the
city were put to the torch. When the rest of Wilson's corps had
crossed the Chattahoochee both remaining bridges were destroyed.
All the railroad rolling stock, including fifteen locomotives and
about two hundred cars, was wrecked. New explosions rocked the
city as five thousand rounds of ammunition and seventy-four cannon went up. Newspapers fared badly. The *Sun* and the *Columbus
Times* were wrecked, and the *Memphis Appeal* ended its wanderings as its presses were destroyed. Only the *Columbus Daily Enquirer*'s presses remained intact, but Wilson forced the paper to
cease publication.[61]

One item on the list for destruction by every Union raider was
cotton. Wilson sought out cotton, which he wrote after the war
"was the only product of the South that would sell for gold, and
it was at that time worth over a dollar a pound."[62] He later defended his cotton burning when he wrote a citizen of Columbus:
"As it was the policy . . . of the Confederate authorities from the
time my command left the Tennessee River till it reached Macon
to destroy cotton and warehouses apparently without reference to
whether they were public or private, it was my policy and practice
to help them in their insensate work so long as they continued
it."[63] In Columbus bales and warehouses burned brightly as Wilson fired an estimated hundred thousand bales. Some Georgians
challenged the figure. Their estimate was only about one-half Wilson's count,[64] but whatever the figure the monetary loss to the area
was staggering.

On the seventeenth the bulk of Wilson's Second Division, unengaged on the sixteenth, arrived. As they approached Columbus
the men of the Seventy-second Indiana thought "sure that a terri-

ble battle was raging." Loud explosions were constant and "vast columns of smoke, black and sulphurous" hung over the city. There should have been little confusion, however, in the minds of most of the reinforcement. These men had seen similar clouds rise over Selma two weeks before. The Hoosiers marched through the streets to "Hail Columbia," which "was appropriate" but somewhat ironical since "we had given Columbus hail."[65] One of Wilson's troopers observed, "The fire at Selma was small compared to this."[66]

Wisconsin's Major Shipman, out of action on the sixteenth, rode into Columbus at 7 A.M. on the seventeenth. As he looked around at the destruction he thought, "The arsenal and government manufacturies were numerous and of a high order of mechanical skill. . . . It must be a very severe loss to the Confederates."[67]

The Union officers' reports listed destruction of goods of use to the Confederate military and of a small number of private dwellings.[68] Wilson summed up: "The value . . . of property destroyed cannot be estimated."[69] Georgians who have written since the event present a picture of much wider devastation of civilian property. One report had Union troopers stealing sugar, molasses, and peanuts from homes. The account continued: "The Yankees even took the dresses of the young ladies who were living with us and tied them together to feed the horses in. . . . Some of the prettiest ones they gave to the servants, and they gave the horses and carriages we had, and those that belonged to our friends, to the Negroes, too."[70]

All charges of destruction cannot be made against Union cavalrymen. The burning of factories meant unemployment for thousands of citizens, and mobs ranged the city. Hinricks reported "the poor citizens were helping themselves freely to everything in the stores."[71] In addition, the city's Negroes hailed their liberators and engaged in plundering grocery and clothing stores along Broad Street.[72] One Union soldier reported a scene of pillage involving an almost complete cross section of Columbus society:

It is a strange scene, and it is interesting to watch the free play of human nature. Soldiers are going for the substantials, women for apparel, and the niggers for anything red. There is evident demoralization among the females. They frantically join and jostle in the chaos, and seem crazy for plunder. There are well-dressed ladies in the throng.[73]

Before Wilson left the city he ordered an issue of rations to Columbus's needy citizens. Negroes were not only given rations, but were also given goods of all kinds taken from factories burned by Winslow. Confederate uniforms, shoes, shirts, pants, kitchen equipment, and tools were distributed.[74]

VI

By the evening of April 17 much of Columbus lay in ashes. Through that night shells still exploded and occasionally "a magazine was blown up and made the earth tremble for miles." The thriving factory would be of little use to the dying Confederacy. Wilson was ready to ride. On the seventeenth he received word that Col. Oliver LaGrange's Second Brigade had taken West Point. The two forces would join in Macon, and the corps commander wanted to waste no more time than necessary in Columbus. He felt that his command was "in magnificent condition," as he led it on toward Macon.[75] Local tradition maintained that Wilson left the city in a carriage seated between two gaudily dressed ex-slaves. There are no Union reports of such a scene, and Major Shipman and Captain Hinricks, alive to stories of the kind, would surely have mentioned something of the sort. Besides, all knowledge of the young, businesslike cavalry chieftain who greatly prized "dignity and decorum" tends to discredit the story.[76]

Wilson's force had fought its last battle. Although Wilson did not know it, and would not know it until the nineteenth, Lee had surrendered one week before the night fight at Columbus. By the time he reached Macon, Lincoln was dead and Johnston and Sherman had signed an armistice in North Carolina. Some have called the fight for Columbus the Civil War's last battle. Others have found subsequent actions in the West and qualify the claim. To those writers Columbus is the war's last battle east of the Mississippi.[77]

The Union victory at Columbus was a further indication of the abilities of both officers and men of Wilson's raiding force, even though the battle was fought against untrained defenders. The battle for Columbus and the city's destruction were tragic events. Better communications might have saved lives, and with Grant victorious and Sherman negotiating with Johnston, the devastation of the area might have been prevented. Neither Wilson nor Confederate defenders knew of the events in Virginia and North Carolina. Fifty years later Wilson wrote: "Had we but known what had taken place in Virginia . . . we should certainly not have . . . participated in the injury which was inflicted upon [Columbus's] industries."[78] An undetermined number of soldiers and the people of Columbus had to pay the price for being engaged in one of the Civil War's last battles, a battle of no real military consequence in a dying conflict.

CHAPTER VII

The Lost Brigade

As Wilson pushed Forrest back at Ebenezer Church, took Selma, and moved eastward, miles to the west the Lost Brigade fought its own campaign. Brig. Gen. John T. Croxton, the Yale-educated abolitionist, spent a hectic April 1. His brigade, fifteen hundred strong, ordered by Wilson to leave the corps and ride to Tuscaloosa to destroy "whatever . . . may be of benefit to the rebel cause," had run into an aggressive rebel.[1] "Red" Jackson on his way to seize and secure the bridge over the Cahaba at Centerville had discovered Croxton near Trion. The forces clashed on the morning of the first with Jackson's rebels chasing the Federals out of their camp and shoving them northward. But in mid-afternoon Jackson received word of Union troops to the south at the bridge he was supposed to control, and the Confederate leader called off the pursuit and wheeled southward.[2] Jackson was convinced Tuscaloosa had been saved and sent a dispatch to the town advising the people that Croxton's brigade "is scattered in the mountains, and cannot again be collected." He added, "Assure the fair ladies of Tuscaloosa, that the tread of the Vandal hordes shall not pollute the streets of their beautiful city."[3]

The flight on the first was across flooded streams and through hilly terrain. Although Croxton's men could not have known, the day was a harbinger of many days to come. Yet the general kept his men together and by nightfall assumed that Jackson had turned south to join Forrest against Wilson. The brigade's retreat, however, was moving it away from the corps as well as away from Tuscaloosa. Continuing their northward movement, Croxton's men by sundown reached Johnson's Ferry on the Black Warrior River.

The command had ridden forty miles that day, and that night stood forty miles north of its objective—Tuscaloosa.[4]

It was a tired brigade that reached Johnson's Ferry that night. The tall brigadier Wilson called "an officer of rare discretion" needed just that trait to decide the next move. He talked over his plans with his regimental commanders: Col. Joseph Dorr of the Eighth Iowa, Col. Thomas Johnston of the Second Michigan, Maj. William Fidler of the Sixth Kentucky and the Fourth Kentucky Mounted Infantry's leader, Col. Robert Kelly. Croxton decided to cross the Black Warrior at Johnson's Ferry and approach Tuscaloosa from the north and from west of the river. Although the town was on the eastern bank, as was his command at that time, there seemed several excellent reasons for the plan. In the first place, an attack east of the river might be blocked by Jackson. Croxton believed Jackson's force greatly superior to his own, and he had no idea exactly where the Confederate forces were located. A second consideration was the element of surprise. Surely Jackson must have warned Tuscaloosa of the nearness of Union raiders east of the Black Warrior. An attack from west of the river and north of the university city would then be unexpected. Finally, the road along the western bank seemed the best avenue of advance.[5] For these reasons Croxton began crossing his men on the night of April 1.

As he made his decision, Croxton did not know that Wilson had moved McCook to Centerville to link up with his brigade. That night McCook was north of the Cahaba near Scottsville camped on the road to Tuscaloosa. But Croxton was not depending on reinforcements, he intended to use his brigade alone to carry out Wilson's orders.[6]

II

The badly fatigued brigade got little rest on the night of the first. Only one flatboat and a "few miserable dugouts" were available to cross the command. Through the night and into the morning of April 2 men and wagons were ferried across the Black Warrior while the horses swam. A Michigan trooper remembered the crossing as "a very hazardous undertaking but very laborious and exciting."[7] By the afternoon of the second the First Brigade assembled on the west bank.[8]

Once across, Croxton rested his men in preparation for a forty-mile ride toward Tuscaloosa, and early on April 3 they moved out down Watermelon Road toward Northport, the small town across the Black Warrior from their objective. The brigadier urged all possible speed since he wanted to reach Northport by dark. Croxton, called "an artful dodger" by one Southerner, was interested in maximum surprise for his attack, and he sent advance outriders to hold all Confederate scouts and citizens found along the line of march.[9] The policy of seizing Confederate scouts yielded an unexpected dividend on the afternoon of the third. Twelve miles from the bridge Croxton's pickets apprehended an "important" Confederate scout. The general questioned the man, who revealed some information concerning defenses in Northport and Tuscaloosa. Chief among the intelligence gained was the positioning of rebel patrols at Northport and at the vital bridge over the Black Warrior. Without this information Croxton's attack might have been very different and much less successful.[10]

Armed with his new information Croxton had decided to move his brigade to the bridge that night. He would then take a force of dismounted troopers, creep to within sight of the span, and strike at dawn. While the dismounted attack seized the bridge, the balance of the brigade would race on horseback into Tuscaloosa and take the city before a defense could be mustered. Security had paid off earlier that day and Croxton continued to move cautiously as he reached Northport; he even sent scouts ahead to place straw on bridges crossed by the command. The cushion would muffle hoofbeats and give no advance warning to rebel sentinels.[11]

At about 9 P.M. on April 3 Croxton's advance reached Northport. The general stopped the brigade in a cedar grove and, hiding most of his men, picked 150 troopers from the Second Michigan for a stealthy approach to the bridge. Negroes were found who volunteered to guide Croxton and the Michigan troopers. Through the still night the force moved forward, but as it neared the bridge loud noises near the structure gripped their attention. The disturbance was quickly identified as Confederate troops ripping up the bridge's flooring. Croxton immediately abandoned his earlier plan and decided to attack at once. The force on the bridge was small, and the general could only hope that damage was not too great and that his Michigan detachment could shove the wreckers aside. Although a trooper from the Eighth Iowa wrote, "We of Croxton's cavalry were exceptionally well drilled in sabre tactics," the general preferred an attack that depended on the seven-shot Spencers.[12] Croxton sent Lt. Col. Thomas W. Johnston and his 150 men racing for the bridge.[13]

The Confederate bridge guards, surprised and outnumbered, could not hold the span. The men engaged in destroying the planking fled down the structure where they joined a small group behind a cotton bale barricade. Never pausing, the Michigan troopers poured a withering fire on the beleaguered defenders, routing them.[14] Entry into Tuscaloosa was secure.

Hardly pausing to survey their conquest, Colonel Johnston sent fifty of his raiders after two six-pound Confederate cannons kept in a nearby stable. In his report of the operation Croxton did not indicate his source of the information of the location of the enemy guns. He wrote only that he sent the party to seize the guns "of which I had learned."[15] Another source maintains that Federal spies in Tuscaloosa had discovered the location and informed the attacking force, but there is a paucity of information on the spies. Who they were and how and when they reached the city remains unexplained. One account mentioned spies in a hospital and a Presbyterian Church wheedling information out of unsuspecting Southerners, but the men remain hazy and unidentified.[16] At any rate, the two pieces were soon returned to the bridge. Tuscaloosa's defenders would fight without artillery support. While the artillery was being taken, Croxton's men replaced the twenty destroyed feet of the bridge's planking and the general brought up the remainder of the brigade. The Sixth Kentucky, the Eighth Iowa and the rest of Johnston's Michigan unit were dismounted and quickly sent across the Black Warrior.[17]

Not only had the bridge guard been taken unaware, but also the entire defense force had to react out of surprise in the middle of the night. The bridge fight alerted citizens who rushed to Col. James Murfee and Dr. Landon C. Garland with the news. Murfee was the commandant of the University of Alabama Cadets, and Garland was president of the institution. Since 1861 the University of Alabama had maintained a corps of cadets. As a body it had no military experience, but individual members had graduated and gone on to Confederate service. Union authorities held the university to be a "military school," and Wilson's orders dispatching Croxton's brigade had emphasized destruction of the "military school" as well as other facilities in Tuscaloosa.[18] The neat cadets were often the butt of jokes from rebel veterans, and the student-soldiers were called "Katydids" because the veterans saw a resemblance between the cadets in full uniform and the insect.[19] Now the sleeping "Katydids" heard the long roll and rumbled out of bed to resist the Union raiders. The cadets were eager for action as they followed Murfee and Garland and some of their professors toward the enemy.[20]

When they reached River Hill in Tuscaloosa, Colonel Murfee sent a small force to get the two six-pounders. While they waited, the cadets were joined by a few local militiamen. Soon the detachment returned to tell a shocked Murfee that the Federals had seized their artillery.[21]

Despite this setback, the "Katydids" fired toward Croxton's men at the bridge. The shots did little damage, but after firing a return volley the raiders retired toward the river. The brief action and information from citizens convinced Dr. Garland that he faced a vastly superior force, one that his students could not hope to defeat. The cadets were ordered to return to the campus and did so without being pursued. Dr. Garland was not yet satisfied, and he ordered the cadets to prepare for a forced march. He did not intend to see his students decimated nor did he intend to see them captured. The cadets supplied themselves as well as possible with food and ammunition and, destroying ammunition remaining at the university, marched out of town.[22]

With the flight of the "Katydids" all resistance ended. At 1 A.M. on the fourth, Capt. Aaron Hardcastle, the city's ranking military officer, and the mayor capitulated to Croxton. The Union brigade lost twenty-three men killed and wounded while losses of the Confederate defenders were not accurately reported. Croxton took between sixty and seventy prisoners.[23]

When Union troops began scouring the city for Confederate soldiers, a squad of troopers located a house in which a wedding supper was in progress. Several of the soldiers entered the house to arrest the Confederate officers present. Pleas of the women did not stop the removal of the wedding guests to Croxton's tent. The groom, Capt. James A. Carpenter, one of those arrested, asked to see the general, and fortunately for him the two had known each other in Kentucky before the war. Croxton listened to the Confederate officer's request to be paroled so that the marriage might go on. He agreed to the parole and returned the officer to his bride, the former Miss Emily Leach.[24]

III

Croxton's mission to Tuscaloosa was one of destruction, and the brigade commander wanted to complete that job at once and be gone. The evacuating Confederates had already fired a warehouse containing tax-in-kind stores, and soon joining that blaze was one set by Union cavalrymen in a hat factory. As the factory, supplier of hats for Confederate troops, blazed, Negroes poured into the building and took hats.[25]

The next morning Croxton sent a detachment to the University of Alabama "military school" to destroy the institution. Washington, Jefferson, Franklin, and Madison Halls were fired. Despite protests of the school's librarian, Croxton's wreckers insensately burned the Rotunda which contained the university library. The university's powder magazine was a "military" target, and the Union detachment poured a trail of powder leading away from the building and ignited the magazine in a deafening explosion heard for miles. The detonating powder hurled stones and burning debris into the air, and some of it started fires in adjacent homes. The fires were visible for twelve miles out into the country. Not all of the university's buildings were burned. The president's home and the observatory, among others, were left standing.[26]

On through the fourth and fifth, dry days when burning was easy, Croxton's raiders carried out their devastation. The Leach and Avery Foundry, two cotton warehouses, and the Black Warrior Cotton Factory went up in flames as did a tannery, niter works, and a corn-filled warehouse.[27] At Tannehill in Tuscaloosa County, the Roupes Valley Iron Works had forged cannon balls, gun barrels, and household implements. Croxton wrecked the foundry and burned as much of the rest of the complex as time allowed.[28] A great deal of Tuscaloosa's cotton, however, avoided the torch, for much of it was hidden in the county when word of Wilson's raid was first received.[29]

As Croxton destroyed much of Tuscaloosa, he seized goods his brigade might need for the resumption of his campaign. He was a great distance from the corps and would have to supply his force's needs from the country through which it passed. Before warehouses were burned troopers loaded themselves with all the food and forage they could carry. All sound horses and mules in the county were rounded up and impressed by the Federals. One of Croxton's prisoners, John L. Hunnicutt, a young militiaman, graphically discovered the pressing needs of the Yankee troopers. A Union lieutenant approached Hunnicutt and said, "that looks like a dandy good hat you have on there." The officer tried it on, found it a good fit, and traded, giving the Southerner his old hat full of holes. Then they sat down and traded boots as well.[30] When the brigade's needs had been satisfied, Croxton distributed supplies to the large number of destitute Negroes in the city. He then put the torch to the remainder of the goods. Also in Tuscaloosa, Union troopers found the office of Confederate States Depositor and took a million dollars in Confederate currency and twice as much in vouchers.[31]

As usual, controversy surrounds reported Union attacks on non-military targets. Capt. William A. Sutherland, assistant adjutant-general of Croxton's command, stated in his report that "all private property was respected, and the soldiers were not permitted to enter the houses." Confederates claim some of Croxton's men, a group of renegade whites and a collection of Negroes, looted both homes and stores. One Southern commentator reported attacks on civilians and maintained that Croxton came "with the intent to destroy and to humiliate . . . to break the morale of the people. It was to be the final body-blow, the backbone must be broken." And yet the same Southerner believed that "Tuscaloosa did not suffer greatly from the looters."[32]

Not all personal contact was hostile. In addition to Croxton's permission for a marriage to continue there was other social contact between the invaders and the people. A. S. Ruby of the Eighth Iowa dined with a Methodist minister who berated him for coming "to kill us all." Ruby replied that the soldiers "did not come to kill, but were serving from an honest sense of duty, to try to preserve the Union."[33]

During Croxton's short stay in Tuscaloosa desertion was a problem for one of his regiments. On the fourth, Pvt. John Rose of the Eighth Iowa, stole a Spencer and two revolvers before leaving camp. As they prepared to leave the area on the fifth, three more cavalrymen disappeared. One of the latter, Pvt. James Craighead of the Eighth, deserted but was later reported killed by an Alabama sheriff who caught the renegade stealing horses.[34]

IV

By the morning of April 5 Croxton had carried out Wilson's order to lay waste to Tuscaloosa's war potential. The general was prepared to leave the city, but he was unsure in which direction he should ride. For six days he had received no word from Wilson. Croxton had no knowledge of the Battle of Ebenezer Church or of the fall of Selma, on the second. The corps commander's orders of March 30 instructed Croxton to cross the Cahaba bridge at Centerville and link up with the corps at Selma. Jackson's presence in that area was still reported, and Croxton felt the road southeastward was closed to him. When he left Elyton on the thirtieth, Wilson had ordered Croxton to break up the Alabama and Mississippi Railroad west of Selma if he found an assault on Tuscaloosa impossible. The brigadier now decided to ride to the southwest and destroy the railroad between Demopolis and Meridian. Croxton believed that he could defeat any force of equal size Forrest might send against him. Furthermore, he would simply run to avoid contact with any vastly superior Confederate force he encountered. His fifteen hundred horsemen crossed the Black Warrior and burned the bridge between Tuscaloosa and Northport.[35]

When the Yankees left Tuscaloosa, some townspeople gathered "around the flag pole on the old drill ground, and with a few soldiers they danced around the pole, singing 'Dixie' and the 'Bonny Blue Flag,' and indulging in a general rejoicing that the hated bluecoats had at last departed."[36]

Croxton's brigade was twenty-five miles west of Tuscaloosa when it camped on the night of the fifth. It had moved all day down the road to Columbus, Mississippi, while a scout force from the Sixth Kentucky ranged the countryside in search of information. The scouts, led by Capt. Sutherland, were to rejoin Croxton when both units had crossed the Sipsey River.[37]

Next morning the brigade broke camp and rode toward Lanier's Mill on the Sipsey, near Bridgeville. Just after he reached the river Croxton heard that a force of three thousand Confederate cavalry was near Pickensville and controlled the bridge over the swollen Tombigbee River. This would effectively block Croxton from moving on to the southwest against the railroad. At the same time, he received his first definitive word of Wilson's position. Croxton learned that the corps had taken Selma and that Forrest had fled west of the Cahaba and was presently situated at Marion. Jackson, it was also learned, was west of the Cahaba, somewhere between Centerville and Tuscaloosa. After looting and burning Lanier's Mill, Croxton's men reversed direction and moved down the road toward Tuscaloosa.[38]

The report of a Confederate force at Pickensville was accurate. Wirt Adams's brigade of Chalmers's division had recently been moved to the town, a crossing point on the Tombigbee. Richard Taylor had ordered Adams to march out of Columbus, where he had guarded the Mobile and Ohio Railroad, on through Pickensville and to Marion where he would join Forrest. On April 5 Adams had left Columbus, but Taylor telegraphed Forrest that the rebel force might be delayed by the Union brigade operating around Tuscaloosa. When he crossed the Tombigbee, Adams was informed of Croxton's general position, and the Confederates moved in pursuit. Although Croxton variously estimated Adams's strength at three thousand and twenty-eight hundred, the Confederate brigade actually numbered only fifteen hundred.[39]

Around 10 A.M. on the sixth Croxton halted his force to feed men and animals. Two hours later Croxton mustered the brigade and resumed the ride toward Tuscaloosa. The Sixth Kentucky was placed last in line as rear guard, and the march had just been sounded when Adams's force slammed into the Kentuckians. A

Michigan trooper believed the men of the Sixth were "lacking in self-reliance," but whatever the reason, the regiment collapsed, many falling into enemy hands. The Sixth Kentucky was shoved into the brigade train, and the retreat became disorderly. The Confederates seized part of the train, including an ambulance wagon carrying Croxton's personal effects.[40]

Retreating Federals and their pursuers were strung out for miles along the road to Tuscaloosa, and Adams's men became more disorganized in their advance than Croxton's were in their flight. Adams had difficulty in pouring in needed reinforcements, while Croxton sent the Second Michigan to bolster the Kentuckians. The Second was positioned across the road to delay Confederate attackers. The retreating Kentuckians passed through an opening made by the Second Michigan, an opening that closed immediately to block the attacking rebels.[41] At the time Adams's men struck the Michigan regiment, the bluecoats had taken position behind fence rails, trees, and mounds of supplies taken from Lanier's Mill that morning. Furthermore, their line was on the edge of a wide, cleared field across which the enemy would have to charge. Their Spencers poured a heavy fire at the attack line and allowed a more orderly withdrawal. Until dark, and through a heavy downpour, the Union brigade moved toward Northport with Wirt Adams's men close behind. That night the two weary, sodden forces camped near Romulus, not far from Northport. The action of April 6 had cost Croxton thirty-four casualties and part of his train. Most serious was the loss of Maj. William Fidler, commander of the badly battered Sixth Kentucky. Fidler and two troopers were cut off during the running fight and eventually wandered to the home of John D. Horton, a farmer with sons in the Confederate Army. Horton set his hounds on the fleeing Kentuckians, captured them, and sent them to prison at Eutaw for the few days left in the war. Capt. Edmund Penn led the Sixth Kentucky for the rest of Croxton's march.[42] Confederate casualties, as usual, are unknown. Although the Federals retreated all afternoon, the withdrawal itself was in no sense a Union loss. Croxton was moving in the direction he had planned. It was this action on the sixth that Wilson learned about in his interview with Forrest.[43]

On April 7 Adams sent out scouts to discover Croxton's position, but the rebel brigade did not attack. Adams seems to have feared that Croxton would suddenly move westward toward Columbus to cut the Mobile and Ohio Railroad. When his patrols reported that afternoon that Croxton was "making forced marches on Columbus," Adams swung his brigade around to defend his base and the railroad. On April 8 the Confederates marched into Columbus to discover they had been chasing phantoms. The information of the Confederate scouts was faulty; there was no threat to the west, and Croxton was still moving toward Tuscaloosa. Once Adams reached Mississippi, Taylor ordered his brigadier to remain there to defend the railroad.[44]

Croxton was back in Northport by dark on April 7, but Adams had disappeared, and no enemy was found in the neighborhood. Croxton had a multitude of problems nevertheless. Capt. William Sutherland and his company of scouts from the Sixth Kentucky had been gone for two days, and no word of their whereabouts was forthcoming on the night of the seventh. More important still was Wilson's position. Croxton did not know if the corps was still in Selma or, if it had departed, the direction of its new advance. It was a frustrating and perplexing time for the brigade. The Northport area had been cleaned of supplies by their first appearance, and food and fodder were difficult to obtain. Croxton had to move his men out of town so that horses could be grazed in the fields. For four days the "lost brigade" bivouacked in the Northport-Tuscaloosa area hoping Sutherland would ride in and that word from the corps could be obtained. For four days Croxton heard nothing. Unknown to the brigade commander, Sutherland's detachment had been cut off from the brigade during the running fight with Adams. It could not ascertain Croxton's new location

and finally rode northward to Union lines along the Tennessee
River.[45]

Lack of information on Wilson's movements finally led Croxton
to his map and to speculation. He reasoned that the corps could
only have moved south to join Canby at Mobile or eastward to
Montgomery. An attack westward on Demopolis or Marion would
have permitted contact between the corps and its missing brigade.
A movement northward would accomplish nothing. After considering these factors, Croxton decided to march toward Elyton where
he would have a better chance of opening communications with
Wilson.[46]

V

Tuscaloosa County saw the last of the bothersome brigade on
April 11. The raiders had so stripped the country that one Confederate militiaman wrote, "We had to commence life at the very bottom."[47] The Union line of march wound northward away from
the Black Warrior and aimed toward Jasper, the corps' point of
concentration on March 27. Croxton camped his men in Walker
County, not far from Jasper, on the night of the eleventh. The
next morning the troopers turned eastward through Jasper on a
line of march broken by numerous rivers and creeks. For the next
week the "lost brigade" spent much of its time and energy crossing
flooded streams. Many bridges had been destroyed. Those with
only partially wrecked spans could be repaired and used. Much of
the time, however, the waterways had to be crossed either by swim-
ming or by ferry boat or canoe. Supplies were also a problem since
Croxton's route lay well north of the black belt and through hilly
country with few farms. In this manner the men crossed both forks
of the Black Warrior and reached Mt. Pinson, where Croxton at
last learned Wilson's location. Confederate deserters informed
Croxton that Wilson had gone eastward toward Montgomery. The
general decided to move in the same direction.[48]

On April 19 Croxton camped at Mt. Pinson where his men destroyed a foundry and niter works. The following morning the brigade rode eastward toward Trussville and Talladega, reaching the latter by sundown on the twenty-second. Croxton bivouacked at Talladega after routing a small defense force. There he was informed that Confederate Brig. Gen. Benjamin J. Hill and a force of several hundred men were situated a few miles to the north guarding a supply depot at Blue Mountain Station.

Hill's force was a hodgepodge of local militiamen and convalescents, outnumbered about three-to-one by Croxton's veterans, but the Union troopers were apprehensive lest their supply of ammunition be exhausted.[49] By the time the two units met many of Hill's men had disappeared into the woods, and only a handful remained to be routed by Croxton. The Union horsemen followed up their victory by riding into nearby Oxford and burning the Oxford Iron Company Furnace. Continuing on toward Blue Mountain Station, the raiders destroyed Alabama and Tennessee River Railroad bridges. At the station Croxton had his men rip up rails, and burn the depot, rolling stock, and ammunition and stores. Ironically, much of this material had been evacuated from Selma and run north as Wilson approached.[50]

With Oxford and Blue Mountain Station in flames, Croxton moved his force eastward. He burned a cotton factory at Daviston and arrived late on April 24 at Blue Ridge on the Tallapoosa River. As he rode through eastern Alabama, Croxton learned at last that Wilson had marched into Georgia after leaving Montgomery. Croxton tracked the corps eastward and crossed into Georgia, bivouacking near Carrollton on April 25. By the time the brigade reached Georgia its men knew the war was almost over and they would soon join the corps. For days they had passed parolees from Lee's Army of Northern Virginia making their way home. They also found papers that told of Appomattox and the Sherman-Johnston armistice.[51] Their anxious wanderings were over. Yet the men of Croxton's brigade were proud of what they had done:

Held in an open trap this small resolute band of seasoned troops, known to history as the Lost Brigade, fought a superior force by day, marched all night, swam swollen streams. . . . The boys called the campaign, "Croxton's Naval Expedition". . . . How we ever did succeed in holding out until the final surrender . . . is yet an enigma to those of us who went through it.[52]

After almost a month on its own the "lost brigade" had only an easy ride to Macon before juncture with Wilson and the corps.[53]

CHAPTER VIII

Macon, Davis, and Peace

Destroying the Confederacy's ability to rally around Jefferson Davis and fight on was on Wilson's mind as the corps left Columbus. The Union horsemen had already smashed most of the facilities a reeling Confederate government needed to continue the fight, but they were not yet through "breaking things."[1] It was only a little less than one hundred miles from Columbus to Macon, but the route chosen by the major general would not be the most direct one. It would be the route along which lay the largest number of textile factories and railroads.

The Union line of march bent northeastward toward Thomaston. Between Columbus and Thomaston loomed another river obstacle. Fifty-four miles from Columbus the Flint River crossed Wilson's projected line of march at a place called Double Bridges. The name derived from the fact that an island lay in the stream, making it necessary to build two bridges to span the Flint. Thus far rivers had hardly slowed much less stopped the Yankee cavalrymen. Wilson acted swiftly to make certain the Flint would be no more difficult to cross than the Black Warrior, Cahaba, Alabama, or Chattahoochee. While Columbus was being destroyed Wilson ordered Robert Minty, commanding the Second Division, to race troops to Double Bridges to surprise and brush aside any defenders.[2]

Late on the seventeenth, the Fourth Michigan and Third Ohio left Columbus under orders to ride all night and seize the spans the next morning. The two regiments forced their mounts to exhaustion and reached the strategic crossing shortly after dawn. The Double Bridges offered the rebels several excellent points to position a defense, but the hard-riding Federals exploited the element of surprise so completely that defense was impossible. Fifty Confederate guards rose on the eighteenth unaware that a powerful enemy force was ready to strike, so when a battalion of the Fourth Michigan burst out of the trees and charged the defenders, they could only muster scattered shots before disappearing north of the Flint. Benjamin Pritchard's Michigan troopers captured five field guns and the bridges. The Michigan and Ohio regiments set a line of defense and waited for the corps.[3]

Along the dark red clay roads north of Columbus Wilson's advancing cavalry corps passed equipment lining ditches and thrown into fields by rebels who had fled the river city. The Federals could have taken scores of captives, but the line was already encumbered enough and fleeing Southerners were largely left alone. When the troopers discovered they were headed for Macon they speculated about their next objective. "Another hard nut," wrote Charley Hinricks, "I hope not too hard." The Missouri captain thought the country "fine," but not so rich as the Alabama black belt. The corps rode through the little towns of Fairview and Pleasant Hill which Hinricks thought were "remarkable only about their names, Fairview has no fair view at all, and Pleasant Hill is all but a pleasant hill."[4] Not far out of Columbus the troopers began encountering occasional Confederate soldiers making their way home from Virginia. Many of these veterans were barefooted, carried arms in slings, and limped in what a Pennsylvania trooper called "the funeral march of the 'lost cause.' "[5] Rumors spread through the corps that Lee had surrendered to Grant, but not everyone believed what the haggard rebels told them, and reliable news remained sketchy.[6]

After the corps crossed Double Bridges on the eighteenth and nineteenth, raiding parties fanned out from the column wrecking bridges. At Thomaston the Second Division destroyed three textile factories and a train filled with Confederate stores. Late on the nineteenth an unsuspecting train from Macon reached Thomaston only to be seized by Wilson's raiders. On the new arrival, Union troopers found newspapers whose news sent cheers roaring through the city. Bluecoats read that Lee had indeed surrendered to Grant.[7]

From Thomaston on the nineteenth, Wilson sent small bands of raiders northward. One unit reached Griffin where it burned railroad facilities. The troops in Griffin also fired a warehouse filled with stores, after liberally distributing its contents to Negroes and poor whites. Kate Cumming, a Confederate nurse in Griffin, reported hostility between Negroes and Union troopers. The soldiers, she charged, beat and knocked down some of the Negroes who, the people of Griffin were allegedly informed, were "the worst behaved Negroes they [the Union troops] had met anywhere."[8]

Miss Cumming, bitterly anti-Federal, admitted after the troopers had passed that "they have done little or no damage to the place." The fiery Southerner mentioned an incident in which a Union officer refrained from burning a part of the railroad depot when a "Mrs. Rawlings implored [him] not to do so, as her house would be burned too. He told her if it would benefit the United States government ten thousand dollars, and destroy ten cents worth of private property, it should not be burned." The skeptical nurse added, "So much goodness looks suspicious."[9]

These were Upton's troops who had ranged northward, and on April 20 Wilson ordered them to turn south following the Macon and Western Railroad to Macon. By dark on the twentieth, they had reached Forsyth after ripping up rails all day long. By that afternoon men and beasts had taken on a strange aspect: "The soil is of a red colour and as the sun was scorching hot and no breeze stirring, the dust was almost suffocating. We looked red from top to bottom, horses, clothes, and all, Negroes and white men all looked like Indians."[10] Upton's horsemen had also met LaGrange's brigade. The latter, moving eastward after its victory at West Point, had marched through LaGrange and Griffin before meeting the Fourth Division.[11]

Also on the twentieth Wilson sent Minty's Second Division eastward from Thomaston toward Society Hill and Macon. Led by Frank White's experienced Seventeenth Indiana, the division ran into a small force of rebels at Society Hill, twenty-one miles from Macon. Both there and a little farther on at Montpelier Springs, White's Hoosiers drove the defenders out of their positions, and at Montpelier Springs a number of retreating Confederates were taken prisoner. Moving on toward Macon, the Seventeenth Indiana trotted toward a bridge over Tobesofkee Creek. At the stream the Union column encountered another Confederate force, this one in the process of burning the bridge. White immediately ordered the charge and his horsemen clattered onto the span. The advance suddenly reined in and warned their comrades that planks were missing and horses could not cross. The force was quickly dismounted and continued the charge on foot. The defenders were routed, whereupon the Seventeenth extinguished the flames and saved the bridge.[12]

II

After the fall of Columbus, Macon, the state capital since Milledgeville's fall to Sherman, feverishly prepared to resist Wilson's advance. For weeks the *Macon Daily Telegraph and Confederate* had assured its readers there was no danger of Union attack from the west since "General Forrest can take care of everything in that quarter."[13] With Wilson east of the Chattahoochee the journal pleaded with all able-bodied Georgians to join the militia. The city had filled with refugees from the four points of the compass. Officers and men alike had been separated from their commands, and Gen. William W. Mackall, commander of the Confederate garrison at Macon, ordered all these men to join active units.[14]

Emotion not reason guided the hand of the author of "Fall In," a front page article in the April 18 issue of the *Daily Telegraph and Confederate.* Despite Lee's surrender, crumbling Confederate resistance across the South, and Wilson's victorious march, the author urged any man "interested in the safety of his home, and the honor of his State" to join the army. Shame and fear were his weapons as the journalist warned Macon's citizens that "if by their supineness and inactivity they permit this city to fall into the hands of their foe . . . their homes will be desolated, their property stolen, their wives and daughters outraged and insulted." Furthermore, the newspaper believed the city could be successfully defended. "As certain as the sun shines we can whip the enemy," wrote the *Daily Telegraph and Confederate.* It was a misleading boast that concluded Wilson "would not dare attack such a force, as can be concentrated here in the next three days." Apparently rebel confidence was based on rumors that Forrest, at the head of a large force, was at Wilson's heels pushing the Federals across Georgia. In addition, the Macon press believed Wilson's corps was a force of only three or four thousand. In a real flight of fancy, the paper boasted, "It is confidently expected that the entire force of raiders will be captured."[15]

Many Georgians were not deceived by such bombast; they felt little hope. George Mercer wrote from Macon on the sixteenth: "Our vindictive enemies seem successful on every hand, and God appears to smile on their cause. . . . [They] are penetrating every part of our land." One day later Fanny Andrews reached the city and wrote in her diary, "We are told that the city is to be defended, but if that is so, the Lord only knows where the men are to come from."[16] On April 19 Howell Cobb reached Macon from Columbus and the citizens learned what Miss Andrews feared. The promised Confederate troops were phantoms; "such a force" did not exist. There would be no Confederate concentration at Macon.[17]

Confederate recruiting efforts in Macon had enlisted only three new companies of militia. These untrained soldiers joined the small local garrison, the Columbus refugees, a few companies of reserves and a pitiful force of convalescents. From these sources the defense could muster only about twenty-five hundred men, but military and civil authorities seemed determined to resist. General Cobb, the former Speaker of the U.S. House of Representatives, ordered whisky destroyed and cotton bale barricades erected across city streets.[18]

Not all those in Macon prepared to fight, and on the eighteenth a train left the city loaded with refugees. As it neared Barnesville rumors that the road ahead had been destroyed led to a decision to return to Macon. The following day the Southwestern Depot was filled with rolling stock ready to evacuate citizens from Wilson's path. Fanny Andrews saw a haggard Sidney Lanier as well as Robert Toombs and Joseph E. Brown board the train. All through the night of the eighteenth the tramp of men and horses and the rumble of wagons could be heard leaving Macon. Miss Andrews, a spirited fire-eater, felt the encircling doom: "The demoralization is complete. We are whipped, there is no doubt about it. Everybody feels it, and there is no use for the men to try to fight any longer."[19]

Late on the day he rode into Macon Cobb received a stunning if not altogether unexpected message from his superior, Gen. P. G. T. Beauregard:

Inform General commanding enemy's forces in your front that a truce for the purpose of a final settlement was agreed upon yesterday between Generals Johnston and Sherman, applicable to all forces under their commands. A message to that effect from General Sherman will be sent to him as soon as practicable. The contending forces are to occupy their present position, forty-eight hours, warning being given in the event of the resumption of hostilities.[20]

Cobb moved with haste to put the order into effect. He sent Gen. Felix Robertson, a West Point classmate of Wilson's, to ride out under a flag of truce to meet the Union advance. At the same time Robertson was dispatched, Cobb began pulling his troops out of

Macon's fortifications. He also informed his militiamen of the situation and began sending them home.[21]

III

After taking the bridge over Tobesofkee Creek, Wilson's vanguard, Lt. Col. Frank White's Seventeenth Indiana, proceeded on toward Macon. About thirteen miles from the city White's men met General Robertson and the rebel flag of truce. White halted his troops, met the Confederate general, and sent the truce communication to his division commander Minty. Minty sent the communication on to Wilson, but the Irish officer, not waiting for the corps commander's reply, told White to accept Robertson's unconditional surrender. If these terms were not acceptable the enemy was to be given five minutes to clear the road before the Seventeenth Indiana rode on against Macon. Robertson refused the terms and his party retired toward the city.[22]

White waited the five minutes and then moved his command forward. It was not long before the Seventeenth overhauled the Confederate truce party and, certain the party intended to slow their progress, the Union troopers charged. A short battle developed with the retreating Southerners firing at White's men. The Indianans shoved the small rebel body across Rocky Creek and into the Macon fortifications. Cobb had informed his troops of the Sherman-Johnston armistice and no resistance was offered the Federals.[23]

White and the Seventeenth Indiana rode on into Macon and were soon met by a second truce party from General Cobb. The armistice terms were reiterated and White was told that Cobb had ordered his forces to disband. The Union lieutenant colonel was also told that under the armistice terms he should withdraw to the point at which Robertson had first presented the Sherman-Johnston convention. White refused. He told Cobb's emissaries that he could not receive orders through them, and he demanded the immediate surrender of all forces at Macon. Cobb was angry with the reply, but well aware of the futility of resistance, he surrendered under protest at 6 P.M. on April 20. White accepted the capitulation and rode into the courthouse square. He established patrols to maintain order and waited for the corps.[24]

As the Seventeenth Indiana rode into Macon, Wilson, some distance to the rear, received word of Cobb's request that the corps halt and all fighting cease. The major general raced to the head of the column to talk to the truce party. He was too late to stop White, and by the time Wilson overtook the Indianans, Cobb had surrendered the city. When Wilson rode into Macon he talked to White and rode off to confer with the "proud and imperious" Cobb.[25] The Confederate chief demanded that Wilson retire to the point at which Robertson and White first met. The Union commander upheld the actions of his subordinates. He advised Cobb that his officers had no authority to halt without his order to do so. Wilson continued his dissent from Cobb's view by taking the position, already advanced by Lt. Col. White, that a Union corps could not recognize an armistice presented through the enemy. He considered Macon's capture valid and informed Cobb that he would be bound only by prior orders until direct contact with Sherman told him differently.[26]

Gen. Cobb continued to protest but his cries were in vain. Wilson had taken two thousand Confederate troops, sixty pieces of artillery, about three thousand stand of arms, and large amounts of stores. In addition to Cobb, Wilson's raiders had corralled four other general officers. Brig. Gens. Gustavus W. Smith, William W. Mackall, Hugh W. Mercer, and Robertson, all for some time connected with the unsuccessful defense of Georgia, had fallen into Union hands.[27]

On the twentieth the *Daily Telegraph and Confederate* published its last issue under the editorship of rebel patriot H. R. Flash. This issue carried advertisements for Charles, Harrison, and Elias, three runaway slaves. They were the last such notices ever to appear in the city. When the paper reappeared on May 4, *Confederate* had disappeared from the masthead and new publishers were listed.[28]

On April 21 Wilson at last established communications with Sherman. The Confederate telegraph was used to verify the armistice, and Wilson's commander ordered him to "abstain from acts of war and devastation." Wilson was further ordered to begin paying for needed supplies and to arrange with the Confederates for parole of all captives.[29]

Tragic news also reached Wilson on the twenty-first. He was informed by Sherman of Lincoln's assassination. At its moment of triumph, the corps grieved deeply for the president.[30] At first the men refused to believe the report. The joy of their victory seemed tarnished and threats of revenge were common. Officers watched the men closely in fear that "distressing results might have followed any indiscreet word or act on the part of a Southerner."[31] Fortunately no incidents occurred to mar the calm of peace.

On the twenty-second Wilson took time to write his friend Adam Badeau: "I rejoice with all my heart at the great victory General Grant has won both for the country and himself. The effects are just meeting us—and everybody in my command rejoices at the early prospect of peace." Wilson told Grant's aide that he was "anxious" to find out more about the situation in the east. "Peace or no peace," he wrote, "I will agree to *pacify* the entire country between the Savannah River and the Mississippi with my corps." The exultant cavalry leader boasted, "My health is splendid, and I have the best cavalry and the best cavalry officers in America to keep me in good spirits." He gave the letter to Hosea and sent the captain riding east with messages for both Sherman and Grant.[32]

One week later Adam Badeau replied, informing Wilson, "Your glorious successes have been duly chronicled, and made the country glad even in this hour of her deepest mourning. Your friends are of course particularly rejoiced at so complete a vindication of their hopes for you."[33]

Far to the rear, and one day behind the Second Division, the men of Upton's division were unaware of the surrender as they closed on Macon. Negroes told them the city had fallen, but since they passed barricades, dead horses, and broken guns, they refused to believe the slaves. When they reached the outskirts, Upton's troopers learned the "glad news," and "formed up and put on all the style possible," as they passed through the city. The inquisitive Hinricks stopped in the city and asked for a late paper. Some Macon ladies obliged, and the captain read of the Sherman-Johnston armistice. He wrote in his diary that night: "How I felt, I cannot describe, for you know what I always said, that an armistice was peace. Should golden peace really be so near—God grant it!"[34]

Once hostilities were ended, Cobb and Wilson cooperated to provide for both soldiers and civilians. The Confederate leader directed Wilson to areas in which food and forage could readily be obtained. He worked hard to ease the condition of Macon's population and was lauded by Wilson as a "man of austere manners and great dignity, who scorned to ask favors for himself, but did his utmost to ameliorate the condition of his fellow citizens."[35] Wilson made his headquarters at the Lanier House, and for his role in Macon's fall Frank White was given command of the city. He set a provost guard which was largely successful in preserving order and protecting civilians. Some acts of vandalism were committed despite Union efforts. Houses were broken into and robbed and on April 22 two blocks of the city burned.[36] Despite these incidents, Wilson wrote in his diary on the twenty-second, "getting along nicely—town quiet."[37]

Nine days after Macon was captured, and almost two months after leaving the corps at Elyton, Croxton's "Lost Brigade" rode into Wilson's camps. After leaving Carrollton, his point of entry into Georgia, Croxton had marched through Newnan, Barnesville, and Forsyth. At Carrollton Croxton's men had first learned of Lee's surrender and of the Sherman-Johnston negotiations. As the brigade crossed Georgia it met large numbers of Lee's paroled soldiers and a Michigan trooper reported at Barnesville, "the town [was] filled with Johnnies."[38] Croxton's arrival reunited the entire corps and ended Wilson's active military campaigning. On April 30 the corps commander was informed of the surrender of all Confederate forces east of the Chattahoochee River.[39]

IV

With hostilities at an end Wilson's veterans "sat about fires, or lay down, in silence. If they spoke it was in subdued tones. . . . Officers and men alike seemed to have forgotten their smaller duties. All were absorbed in their thoughts and hopes."[40] For the most part, troops used to hard riding, enemy fire, fording streams, and days of destroying railroads and factories had suddenly become an occupation force with few duties and growing boredom. But for some of Wilson's raiders active service was not over. As Wilson had long ago anticipated, the area into which his troops had ridden was the land toward which most of the Confederacy's leaders would flee. Jefferson Davis, Alexander H. Stephens, Judah P. Benjamin, and a legion of lesser figures were rumored making for Georgia, on their way to escape through Florida or to continue resistance in Texas. Patrols were organized, and many of Wilson's raiders scattered across the state to pursue the fugitives. Wilson also dispatched forces in all directions to accept the surrender of isolated Confederate garrisons and begin the transition from war to peace.

The corps' principal duty remained the capture of Jefferson Davis. On April 23 Wilson learned that Davis had been seen at Charlotte, North Carolina, and was making his way to the deep South. The Union commander did not trust the southern telegraph, so he dispatched units to cover all paths into north Georgia. On the twenty-seventh Upton was sent with a small force to Augusta. Alexander's brigade followed to reinforce Upton, and Wins-

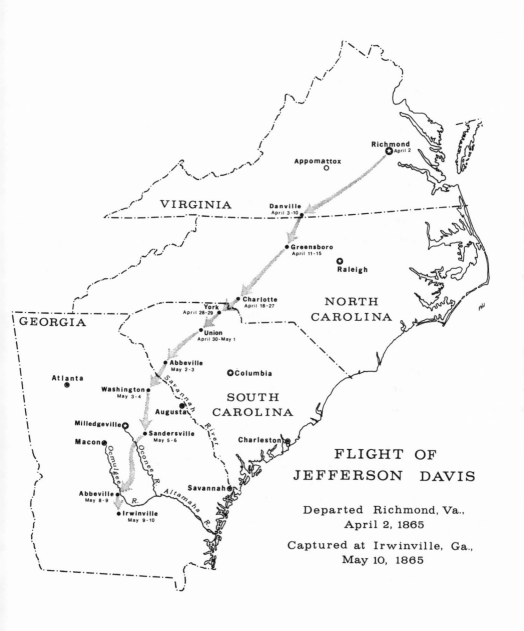

Richmond
April 2

Appomattox
O

VIRGINIA

Danville
April 3-10

Greensboro
April 11-15

Raleigh

Charlotte
April 18-27

York
April 28-29

NORTH
CAROLINA

GEORGIA

Union
April 30-May 1

Abbeville
May 2-3

Columbia

Atlanta

Washington
May 3-4

Augusta

SOUTH
CAROLINA

Milledgeville

Sandersville
May 5-6

Macon

Charleston

Abbeville
May 8-9

Savannah

Savannah River

Ocmulgee R.

Oconee R.

Altamaha R.

Irwinville
May 9-10

FLIGHT OF
JEFFERSON DAVIS

Departed Richmond, Va.,
April 2, 1865

Captured at Irwinville, Ga.,
May 10, 1865

low's brigade was moved to Atlanta. "Every officer and man was anxious to assist in the capture of Davis."[41]

To urge the troops on in their quest, Wilson offered a $500,000 reward for Davis's capture. The reward, originally suggested by Upton, was to be paid from the Confederate treasury, believed to be carried by the fleeing president. This reward was posted before the official offer of $100,000 was telegraphed from Stanton. None of Wilson's pursuing units had heard of Stanton's reward until after Davis's apprehension.[42]

As Alexander rode toward Augusta he was ordered to send out a scouting party disguised as rebels. Lt. Joseph A. O. Yeoman and twenty troopers soon made their way into South Carolina and joined the Davis party near Abbeville. There were men from so many different Confederate units with Davis that it was relatively simple for Yeoman's scouts to ride with the enemy column. The fleeing president crossed the Savannah River on pontoons and arrived in Washington, Georgia, on May 3. Three days later Wilson learned, through a Yeoman courier, that Davis was in Washington. After Washington, Yeoman lost sight of Davis and so informed search headquarters in Macon.[43]

Wilson was convinced that the rebel fugitives would make their way through the pine forests of southwestern Georgia. He ordered guards placed on ferries on the Ocmulgee River and prepared to dispatch fresh troops toward the area Davis was believed to be traversing. On May 6 Croxton and Minty were ordered to send their best regiments toward Dublin and the Ocmulgee. Croxton picked Henry Harnden's First Wisconsin and Minty Benjamin Pritchard's Fourth Michigan. The corps commander had set a network of Union troops over the entire state. Upton was at Augusta and Winslow at Atlanta. Alexander had veered northward from Augusta and was ranging into extreme north Georgia. Small detachments were fixed at Columbus and West Point, and McCook was ordered to lead a force due South to Albany and on toward Thomasville and Tallahassee to look for fugitives. With the de-

parture of the First Wisconsin and Fourth Michigan only a frac-
tion of the corps remained at Wilson's Macon headquarters.[44]

While he rested in Washington, Davis learned of the presence
of Upton's men in Augusta. He decided to dismiss the bulk of his
accompanying troops and ride on southward with a small escort.
Of great concern to the harried president was the safety of his wife
and children, traveling just ahead of his own group. Shortly after
leaving Washington he caught up with Mrs. Davis's party. Slowed
by poor roads and concern for his family, Davis covered about 150
miles in the four days after his departure from Washington.

The slowness of the fugitives' progress meant that by the time
Colonel Harnden's First Wisconsin reached Dublin the Union
officer found that a party had just crossed the ferry and "gone
south on the river road."[45] Further information was difficult to
obtain from the area swarming with Joe Johnston's disbanded
rebel soldiers. Harnden's men had ridden for twenty-four hours
and he ordered them to turn in, but hardly had the colonel retired when his Negro servant roused him and presented an old
Negro who identified the party moving "south on the river road"
as that of President Davis. Reckoning that his quarry had a twelve-
hour lead, Harnden mounted his troops and rode in pursuit. In
the darkness the unit made poor progress, and at dawn it was
slowed by a partially destroyed bridge at Turkey Creek. While
they repaired the span they found that a party had passed the previous evening. One of its members had dropped a scrap from a
Richmond newspaper and another traveler was addressed as "Mr.
President."

This intelligence led Harnden to press his pursuit, but rain
washed out the Confederates' wagon tracks and slowed the Yankee
troopers. On the afternoon of the eighth, Harnden found a Georgian who was forced to guide the Union party to the plantation at
which Davis had rested the night before. While the men foraged
their horses, Harnden found a man to guide them across a nearby
swamp. The ride was arduous, and at dark a tired, hungry party

lay down and tried to rest and dry out only to be drenched most of the night by a heavy storm. Up on the ninth, they pushed on to the Ocmulgee River which they crossed on a dilapidated flatboat. While they crossed the stream Harnden received new information that convinced him he was catching up to the rebel fugitives. The colonel and his men rode into Abbeville and received confirmation that Davis was just ahead, moving down a road to Irwinville. Harnden decided not to close on the Davis party until after dark, and at Abbeville he fed and rested his column.

Just as he rode out of Abbeville, Harnden met four soldiers from Col. Pritchard's Fourth Michigan. Pritchard had marched from Macon, leaving detachments at key river crossings. Harnden sent his men on toward Davis while he rode back to see Pritchard. The Wisconsin colonel told Pritchard all he knew of Davis's whereabouts, declined reinforcements, and rode back to his regiment. The Wisconsin horsemen soon found the smoldering ashes of the Davis party's midday campfire and pressed on till nightfall.

When Harnden left him, Pritchard continued down the river road. He soon found a Negro who confirmed Davis's presence nearby. When the two Union colonels conferred on May 9, they agreed that Harnden would continue his pursuit along the direct road toward Davis while Pritchard "would follow the river indefinitely or till he found something further to justify his leaving it. This was the condition when the latter [Pritchard] got the Negro's information."[46] Both blue-clad units were converging on Davis whose party had reached the vicinity of Irwinville. Darkness closed on the dusky woods as the two Union units, unaware of each other's position, approached their quarry. Wilson believed Pritchard should have sent a courier to Harnden informing the Wisconsin unit of his change of plans, but the Michigan officer failed to do so. But the major general wrote: "I have never thought that Pritchard's conduct was censurable for the reason that it was probably an oversight which might have occurred to any vigorous and zealous officer while in the heat and anxiety of the hour."[47]

It was about 4 P.M. when Pritchard changed his route and pressed for Irwinville. He reached the sleeping village in the early hours of May 10, and although the column attempted to remain silent, it aroused the citizens. The colonel told the townspeople he was the rear guard of the Davis party, and he was directed to the president's camp one and a half miles north of town on the Abbeville Road. The troopers quickly rode toward the enemy camp and positioned themselves to strike at first light.

While Pritchard moved into position, Col. Harnden rested his men. They were roused just before dawn and moved at daylight toward Davis's camp. After a short march the Wisconsin troopers encountered a detachment which opened fire. Harnden immediately assumed he had struck Davis's escort, and he dismounted the bulk of his men to fight on foot. A small force was sent on horseback to prevent the fugitives' escape. A sharp skirmish rolled through the pines. Two men were killed and one officer and three men were wounded before it was discovered that the combatants were the two Union units. Pritchard left his men posted on the edge of the Davis camp to ride toward the sound of firing and there encountered Harnden, riding from the opposite direction. The two commanders quickly discovered the truth and brought the tragic melee between friends to an end.

The noise of Union firing aroused Davis and his party. The Confederate president, fully clothed in a gray suit, jumped up, at first convinced the attackers were Southern marauders rumored to have been along the party's flanks for several days.[48] Davis opened the tent flaps and saw Pritchard's blue-clad troops swarming over the camp. Mrs. Davis urged immediate flight, but Davis, fearing for his family, hesitated a few minutes. Finally, grabbing his wife's waterproof, he left the tent. At the last moment, Mrs. Davis took off her shawl and put it about her husband's shoulders.

Davis had not moved far when troopers commanded by Lt. Julian Dickinson, adjutant of the Fourth Michigan, ordered him to halt and surrender. Instead of surrendering, Davis advanced toward a mounted trooper, intending to hurl him out of the saddle and vault into the saddle and escape. It was an old Indian trick known to Davis since his early days as a frontier lieutenant. As he advanced, the cavalryman lowered his carbine, and Mrs. Davis, fearing for her husband's life, rushed forward and embraced him. The act probably saved the president's life, but it surely doomed his escape attempt. "God's will be done," was all he could say as he sat down under guard.[49]

Soon Pritchard and Harnden rode into the rebel camp. The first man they saw was John Reagan, Confederate Postmaster General, who pointed to the captured president. When asked if he were the Confederate chieftain the prisoner replied, "Yes, I am President Davis."[50] The two colonels counted their captives and discovered they held Davis, Reagan, Cols. Burton Harrison, Preston Johnston, and F. R. Lubbock, four junior officers, and thirteen enlisted men. In addition, Mrs. Davis, her sister Margaret Howell, four children, and several Negro servants and teamsters had been taken.

On May 11 Pritchard sent a dispatch to Minty reporting Davis's capture. The note was brief, with few details. One day later the division commander received Pritchard's welcome news and reported it to Wilson. The corps commander at once wired Stanton, Grant, and Thomas. In his diary, Wilson duly noted the apprehension of the Davis party. He also mentioned, without comment, the skirmish between his two units.[51] That night he wrote Adam Badeau a private letter informing Grant's secretary: "The zeal and activity displayed by my entire force have been heightened by the general belief that the murder of Mr. Lincoln was concocted by Davis and his confederates."[52]

On the thirteenth reports of Davis's apprehension underwent a significant alteration. No new dispatch from Pritchard or Harnden seems to account for the change in the story. Perhaps it was circulated orally by Davis's Union escort which reached Macon on the thirteenth and turned the ex-president over to Wilson. Both the major general's dispatch to Stanton and his letter to Badeau, sent on the thirteenth, contained Wilson's first reference to Davis's attempt to flee disguised as a woman. The War Secretary was informed that Davis "put on one of Mrs. Davis's dresses and started for the woods, closely pursued by our men." He reported the tale to Badeau and added that Mrs. Davis and her sister had attempted to pass Davis off as their mother.[53]

In *Under the Old Flag* Wilson, confusing the date, wrote that on May 12 General Minty broke into his quarters with the news: "We have captured Jeff Davis and, by jingo, we got him in his wife's clothes." Wilson added he was afraid Minty's words might indicate a hoax and he said, "I trust there is no mistake about it." Minty at once saw Wilson's concern and assured him, "It's all right, General; here is Pritchard's dispatch by a special courier."[54] Wilson said his report to Washington was based upon Pritchard's dispatch, and yet the colonel's only dispatch on the capture of Davis in the *Official Records* said nothing about Davis's dress.[55] The general defended himself from charges that he lied about the conditions of the Confederate leader's capture. He pointed out that Davis was "literally" in his wife's clothes. Furthermore, added Wilson, as the report flashed around the world writers and artists embellished the story to the point of the absurd.

Yet there is no doubt Wilson played a major role in disseminating the distortion. Perhaps the general saw a chance for increased publicity for himself. By June, Wilson's story of the capture was carried in most national newspapers and magazines. *Harper's Weekly* published the general's remarks which tantalizingly boasted: "The story of Davis's ignoble attempt at flight is even more ignoble than I told it."[56] It was unfortunate that the former Confederate chief executive was subjected to such demeaning fabrications. And it is unfortunate that Union officers played a role in adding to further distortion of the fabrications. The timing of Davis's capture accounted in part for the relish with which the tale was greeted. The glory and satisfaction of victory had been partially snatched from the Federals by Lincoln's assassination. Many believed the rebel leader had a hand in the assassination plot, indeed the reward signed by Stanton contained that charge. Why not heap scorn on the man many regarded as the architect of four years of suffering as well as their more recent bereavement?

The Davis family rode in an ambulance while their Confederate escort rode their horses under the watchful eyes of the Michigan and Wisconsin troopers. As they passed Union camps, bands blared "Yankee Doodle," and soldiers jeered at their late enemy. When Col. Pritchard discovered the hundred-thousand-dollar reward poster with its charge against Davis he showed the handbill to the accused. The ex-president was scornful of the charges and saw in them an attempt to build up enough hatred to lead to his murder.[57]

On the afternoon of May 13 the party reached Macon. As it moved through the streets large crowds gathered and troops had to clear a path, but there were no cheers of greeting from the Georgians, nor were there shouts or "tokens of exultation" from Federal troops.[58] "A really brave man rejoices not over a fallen foe," wrote a member of the Eighth Iowa.[59] The ex-president and his family were housed in the Lanier House and were sent a sumptuous meal by Wilson. As he entered the hotel Davis walked between two lines of Wilson's cavalrymen who faced inward and snapped to present arms. It was a salute to a fallen foe and the last salute to Jefferson Davis as president of the Confederacy. After his dinner Davis and the Union general had a "friendly interview" of about one hour.[60] Wilson remembered that Davis "looked bronzed and somewhat careworn, but hardy and vigorous, and during the conversation behaved with perfect self-possession and dignity." Davis recalled that Wilson "manifested a courteous, obliging temper."[61] The two men talked of West Point and of Civil War generals on both sides. The former Confederate chief praised Bragg, Hardee, and Taylor and "spoke feelingly of Lee's character and deeds." He criticized Joe Johnston for "timidity and insubordination," Beauregard for "military pedantry," and Hood for "heroic rashness." Davis expressed surprise at Grant's "skill and persistency," and praised Thomas and Sherman. He spoke of Lincoln's death in "terms of respect and kindness." Of the charge against him of complicity in the assassination, Davis expressed surprise and pain, but the charge did not trouble him. He told the general: "I have no doubt, General, the Government of the United States will bring a much more serious charge against me." Finally, Davis could not conceal his dislike for Andrew Johnson. He believed Lincoln's successor "would be governed by a vindictive and unforgiving temper toward the Southern people."[62]

At the end of the meeting Davis introduced his little son Jeff to the general, and the two men talked of the manner of the ex-president's transportation northward. Since he was accompanied by women and children, Davis asked for the easier water route. Wilson agreed to the route as well as to Davis's request that Colonel Pritchard be sent as his guard. At 5 P.M. on the thirteenth Davis and his party, under heavy guard, left Macon by rail for Augusta, Savannah, and the sea. As Davis moved toward his chains, Wilson reflected on his command's role in the pursuit and capture: "Our task was done and done well."[63]

V

Jefferson Davis was not the only fleeing rebel to fall to Wilson's command. The network of scouts spread across Georgia and Florida seized several other Confederate leaders. Former Vice President Alexander H. Stephens was taken at his plantation, "Liberty Hall," in Crawfordville, Georgia, by a detachment of the Fourth Iowa and formally surrendered to General Upton. "Little Aleck" was eventually to join the Davis party at Augusta and sail to prison with the man he had come to despise.[64]

Company H of the Fourth Iowa took Confederate Secretary of the Navy Stephen R. Mallory and Georgia Sen. Benjamin H. Hill

at LaGrange. Another Georgia senator, Herschel Johnson, fell to
Company I of the Fourth Iowa. Sen. Clement C. Clay of Alabama,
accused in Stanton's charge of complicity in Lincoln's murder,
sought out Union authorities and surrendered at LaGrange so that
he might clear himself. Clay could easily have escaped since few,
if any, in Wilson's command knew him on sight.[65] Georgia Governor Joseph E. Brown and Confederate Cavalry General "Fighting Joe" Wheeler were also taken by troops of Wilson's command.[66] The Union dragnet was not complete; Judah P. Benjamin
and Robert Toombs evaded Wilson and escaped. In spite of these
occasional escapes, Wilson was proud of his men's capture of Davis,
"the arch rebel," Stephens, and the others. "I think I drew a net
around Mr. Davis that would have reflected credit upon a de-
tective policeman," wrote the general.[67]

Capt. Henry E. Noyes of Wilson's escort, the Fourth U.S., was
sent to secure Andersonville Prison. The captives had been evacuated, but he found the ailing commandant, Henry Wirz, and
placed him under arrest. Noyes also seized all prison records and
took them to the major general who forwarded them to the U.S.
Adjutant General.[68]

It was also the duty of Wilson's command to parole rebel forces
in Georgia, Florida, and parts of the Carolinas. Union detachments spread across the four states and paroled fifty-nine thousand
defeated Confederates.[69]

As Wilson's men crossed the deep South they carried not only
paroles, but the flag and authority of the United States as well.
Cities which had never seen blue-clad invaders now watched as
Union cavalrymen rode in and took possession of public facilities.
On May 8 Gen. Emory Upton took possession of the United States
Arsenal at Augusta. In the flag raising ceremony he said to his
command and some assembled citizens:

Four years ago the Governor of Georgia, at the head of an armed
force, hauled down the American flag at this arsenal. The President of

the United States called the nation to arms to repossess the forts and arsenals which had been seized. After four years of sanguinary war and conflict we execute the order of the great preserver of union and liberty, and to-day we again hoist the stars and stripes over the United States Arsenal at Augusta. Majestically, triumphantly she rises![70]

Edward McCook's arrival in Tallahassee, Florida on May 10 brought the last Confederate state capital east of the Mississippi under Federal control. McCook was ordered by Wilson to enforce the law, suppress marauders, and parole all rebel troops he could find.[71] The Ohio general, at the head of about five hundred troopers, "made a very modest entrance, respecting the humiliation of our people," wrote one Florida observer. She added, "The General was very properly received by representative men of the place, and the courtesies due him were gracefully extended."[72] McCook wired Wilson that "only the most entire spirit of submission to my authority, and in the majority of instances an apparent cheerful acquiescence to the present order of things," existed in the state. A Jacksonville newspaper praised McCook's handling of the situation and reported "Yankees and Rebels now mingle with each other as friendly as though they had never been arrayed against each other in hostile attitude."[73] Ten days after the Yanks' arrival a ceremony was held raising the national banner over the Florida state capitol.

From Macon, Wilson directed not only the search for fugitives but also the last problems of war and the first problems of peace. On May 3 he communicated the Sherman-Johnston surrender convention to Gov. Brown. This included provisions for paroling officers and men and for surrender of all miltary stores. Brown informed Wilson of his state's destitution and of the "loss and woe" resulting from the "fortunes of war." The Georgia leader also asked Union authorities to allow him, together with other state leaders, to play a significant role in the postwar restoration of order and prosperity. Wilson passed the request on to Secretary of War

Stanton and to the President. On the fifth Brown, who Wilson discovered had called the Georgia Legislature into session. arrived in
Macon. The cagey Georgian sent the general a note informing him
that he would "receive" him at 8:30 P.M. Wilson replied, "If he
desires an interview with me he can have it by calling at my headquarters."[74] The two men met at Union headquarters on the sixth
in a stormy session. The "haughty and officious" Brown was told the
legislature would not meet. Furthermore, Wilson presented a demand that all state troops be surrendered, and that Brown as "commander in chief" sign a personal statement of pardon. The governor was "very much exercised" by this, and he told the young
general that signing would "compromise" him, wrecking his political prospects. An angry Wilson roared, "My God! Governor, is
it possible that you imagine, in the face of the part you have taken
against the United States for the last four years, you have any prospect in this country but to be hanged?" The chastened Brown
signed the paper.[75] On May 9 Wilson transmitted Washington's
reply to the request for instructions on Brown's role in the postwar period. Brown was told that all of the state's problems had
been caused by "treason, insurrection, and rebellion against the
laws of the United States," and the "fortunes of war" were the
"just penalty of their crimes of treason and rebellion." Furthermore, the task of restoring order could never be left to traitors.
Wilson was also directed to place Brown under arrest and send
him to Washington.[76]

The daily task of feeding his men and animals vexed Wilson.
Forage and stores had to be purchased, and fortunately General
Cobb continued to be of assistance to his captors in supplying necessities. Macon's citizens returned to their usual occupations and,
as Wilson observed, "perceiving that we were not barbarians . . .
gradually softened in their behavior, and some even went so far as
to speak of us as fellow countrymen."[77] To the north, at Milledgeville, Dr. Henry K. Green of the state asylum appealed to Wilson
for food for his patients. The general immediately sent rations and

his "restraint, tact, and good judgement left a favorable impression upon the people of Georgia."[78]

Newly freed blacks migrated widely in the first days of peace, but Wilson noted no serious contraband problem in Macon. Notice was circulated to both blacks and whites to remain at home, and it was generally observed during the corps' stay in the city. Wilson agreed to let Union soldiers assist Macon authorities in "clearing" the city of "strange Negroes."[79] The military commander also issued orders indicating that while freedmen would be forced to respect civil and criminal law, their former masters were legally bound to respect the newfound legal rights of their former chattels.[80] Blacks who did reach Macon found a hostile reception from many Union troopers, especially those from Kentucky and Missouri, whose racism was not erased by their blue uniforms.[81]

For a time the greatest problem of migration continued to be Confederates from Lee's and Johnston's armies walking home. Capt. Hinricks often fraternized with these men, sharing coffee and "Confederate whiskey." The Missouri officer believed that men who had fought the war would live harmoniously together in peace. "I should not wonder at all to see those politicians and 'War to the knife and knife to the hilt' men at home get a sound thrashing from both parties when the boys come home," wrote Hinricks.[82]

Stories of robbery and plunder against Macon citizens were recorded in the memoirs of Georgians. Kate Cumming, in Griffin, told of instances of Macon residents coming to Griffin to remain until the troops had departed.[83] Maj. Shipman reported depredations by incendiaries leading to the burning of several buildings. Capt. Hinricks saw troops exploding Confederate shells on the city's edge. But both officers found Macon's residents ready for peace and a restoration of the Union. The townspeople were kind and helpful to their captors.[84] Wilson decreed a tolerant policy toward the enemy: "Rather than insist that townspeople immediately vow their love and undying devotion to the federal government, he allowed them time to recover from their bitterness."[85] By mid-May much about the city had the appearance of antebellum peace. *Macbeth* was performed before a large audience, and W. E. Cocke's restaurant on Mulberry Street advertised mint juleps and turtle soup "in abundance."[86]

In late May and early June the Cavalry Corps, Military Division of the Mississippi, began to break up. Unit by unit, Wilson's command moved northward to be mustered out. As regiments left Macon their leave taking seemed to bode well for national reunion: "Numbers [of Union troops] have expressed to us the warmest sentiments of friendship towards the citizens of Macon. . . . The conduct of the troops generally has been of the most unexceptionable character, and their intercourse with our people always pleasant. It is universally acknowledged that the city has not enjoyed so quiet a season for years."[87] Regiments marched to Atlanta and Chattanooga and went home by rail from the latter. By the end of June the war's largest cavalry force had almost ceased to exist.[88] Its men had returned to their homes bearing with them the pride of having been a part of a brilliantly successful campaign. The commander of each unit issued a farewell to his men. Typical was Col. Fred Benteen's adieu to the men of the Tenth Missouri. He regretted the "sundering of ties that have bound us together during the past five months." He reviewed the victories on the "glorious fields" of Montevallo, Ebenezer Church, Selma, and Columbus, and concluded: "The memory of that campaign shall ever remain fresh and bright in all our hearts."[89] On July 2 Wilson issued a final order to his men telling them, "Your corps has ceased to exist." He sent them home to peace with the injunction: "Having discharged every military duty honestly and faithfully, return to your homes with the noble sentiment of your martyr President deeply impressed upon every heart, 'With malice against none, and charity for all, strive to do the right as God gives you to see the right.' "[90]

VI

While the memory of their campaign remained "fresh and bright" for Wilson, his officers, and men, its memory had never really been created for many Americans. As the cavalry corps crossed Alabama and Georgia, the Confederacy collapsed. Appomattox, Johnston's capitulation, and Lincoln's death claimed the headlines. In addition, the mission was so dangerous that no correspondents went along. The raid was denied the journalistic coverage that might have given it lasting fame. Only Wilson's capture of Jefferson Davis thrust the superb cavalry force into the notice of the nation.

When he wrote his report on June 29, Wilson outlined the accomplishments of the campaign. In slightly less than two months his horsemen had marched 525 miles. They had completely outmarched and twice outfought the rebel "wizard" Nathan Bedford Forrest. Victories could be counted at Montevallo, Ebenezer Church, Selma, Tuscaloosa, West Point, and Columbus. The symbolically important "Cradle of the Confederacy" had been taken as had the president and vice-president of the fallen government. Wilson's force took 6,820 prisoners and counted over 1,000 enemy killed and wounded. The cost in Union ranks was 99 killed, 598 wounded, and 28 missing.[91]

The greatest blow to the dying Confederate cause was the trail of destruction through this Southern heartland, hardly touched by war. Wilson seized 288 pieces of artillery and almost a hundred thousand stand of small arms. He wrecked seven iron works, seven foundries, seven machine shops, two rolling mills, five collieries, thirteen factories, four niter works, three arsenals, one navy yard, one powder magazine, and five steamboats. Thirty-five locomotives, 565 railway cars, miles of track, and huge quantities of quartermaster, commissary, and ordnance stores were destroyed.[92] Robert C. Black, historian of Confederate railroads, has called Wilson's destructive scythe, "the *coup de grace*" of the deep South's railroad

network. He believed the raid "practically destroyed the last Southern ability to carry on the conflict east of the Mississippi." There
was no way Taylor and Forrest could follow Wilson by rail, so badly
damaged were Alabama's rail lines.[93] Historians of the Alabama
iron industry have called the "efficiency" of Wilson's destruction
"unique." Every facility for iron manufacture in Alabama except
the one in Lamar County was wrecked.[94] The major general advised his superiors: "The destruction of iron-works, foundries, arsenals, supplies, ammunition, and provisions in Alabama and
Georgia, as well as the means of transporting the same to both the
armies under Taylor and Johnston, was an irreparable blow to the
rebel cause."[95]

"Irreparable blow" it was. Confederate leaders had long talked
about fighting to the "last ditch," and President Davis continued
to the end to urge prolonged resistance from the deep South. Indeed, his flight was aimed at putting himself at the head of Taylor's troops who, supplied by the farms and factories of the deep
South, would carry on the struggle.[96] The young Union cavalry
chief was determined to render Davis's "last ditch" untenable.

Contemporary Southerners and some Civil War historians have
seen the campaign as useless and brutal. One of the latter, in an
outburst of emotional inaccuracy has written that Wilson "was ravaging the countryside like a Tartar horde." The same author con-
demned the general for burning cotton and thus impoverishing
Southern families. And yet he made no reference to the cotton
burning ordered by state and Confederate governments which Wilson encountered in Alabama and Georgia.[97]

Charges of brutality and unnecessary destruction against Wilson
and his men should be shared with the governors of Alabama and
Georgia and Confederate military leaders in the region who imperiled cities with their cotton bale fires and urged the enlistment
of seventeen-year-olds to defend cities against overwhelming numbers of veteran soldiers. A share of the responsibility for the de-

struction should also be borne by the president of a defeated government, whose rhetoric tried to carry on a war hopelessly lost.

Wilson believed that his objective was to destroy the power of the Confederacy to carry on the war from the deep South. His men were trained wreckers who carried out with efficiency their mission of the destruction of anything of use to the Confederate war effort. Yet, there is no denying that from Jasper to Macon property of no use to the rebel military was put to the torch. The extent of this nonmilitary destruction is controversial; even Southern accounts differ in their assessment. Yet no city along Wilson's path met with the devastation Sherman's campaigns visited upon Atlanta and Columbia. The cavalry corps was far smaller than Sherman's army, and discipline was easier to maintain. Besides, Wilson's horsemen moved too rapidly to linger and plunder. Sherman's "bummers" have virtually no parallel in the corps. And clearly when peace came to the theater in which Wilson served, all systematic destruction was halted.

Almost half a century after the war Wilson best summed up his view of his mission in a letter to a Union veteran. The general believed his command's "services were unusual if not extraordinary." He further thought: "we should have had a period of unrest, unhappiness and possibly of war or guerrilla warfare, at least, had Selma, West Point, Columbus, and Macon not been captured and had Davis and his cabinet succeeded in getting away to the Trans-Mississippi Department."[98] The general reiterated this theme in several letters to Charles Francis Adams. It was "certain that Davis intended to carry on the war" in the Trans-Mississippi and "without my operations there would have been nothing in the way to prevent his success." As a factor in bringing a swift peace Wilson wrote, "I feel that my part in the capture of the Rebel chieftain was quite as influential as Lee's part in failing to declare in favor of guerrilla warfare."[99]

Wilson's raid has been praised as the Civil War's best example of the proper use of cavalry. Maj. A. R. Chaffee, a later American cavalryman, lauded Wilson for his ability to use and care for horses in mass. Chaffee believed that Wilson "knew the great value of firepower and how to combine it with rapid movement, and with mounted assault when practicable. . . . [Wilson] thoroughly visualized the employment of large bodies of cavalry, and knew that only in that way could it be employed effectively," wrote Chaffee, who hoped Wilson would remain a model for the U.S. mounted arm.[100] Even old enemies praised the corps commander. Richard Taylor wrote that Wilson's "soldierly qualities are entitled to respect," and added that of all Union expeditions "his was the best conducted."[101] Union contemporaries heaped plaudits on the march through Alabama and Georgia. Sherman called the corps the best cavalry force ever under his command, and Grant joined in the accolades.[102]

The distinguished British military theorist-historian Maj. G. F. R. Henderson praised the Civil War's mounted rifleman. "No troops could have been better adapted to the country over which they fought than the American mounted rifleman. . . . On their own ground they would probably have defeated any European cavalry of the period," wrote the Englishman. He continued, "Our brethren in arms across the Atlantic teach us what may be done by a mounted force that is not much inferior to good infantry and at the same time has all the mobility of cavalry." Henderson's detailed illustration of this Civil War lesson was Wilson's Raid.[103]

Twentieth-century historians have also found James H. Wilson among the war's ablest cavalry leaders.[104] Wilson's raid has been seen as "more than a raid—it was an invasion by an army of cavalry, a preview of a blitzkrieg." The blue-clad force was "true mechanized infantry, in the modern sense, except that their means of locomotion consumed hay and grain rather than gasoline."[105] The corps commander's biographer calls him "a general whose contributions to military science were not restricted to application during his own era but which have significant application for modern-day warfare."[106]

Wilson's fine, mobile striking force utilized the best in cavalry theory formulated during the war. By 1865 a fortuitous combination of theory and practice put a well-organized, well-armed force under the command of young officers determined to use the mounted army properly. The "Yankee Blitzkrieg" was not only the largest Civil War cavalry campaign, it was also the most successful. The greatest test of its success was the closing of the "last ditch" and the surrender of all Confederate forces in the deep South.

Notes

PREFACE

1. James Harrison Wilson, *Under the Old Flag* (New York, 1912), II:241–242.

CHAPTER I

1. James H. Wilson to Adam Badeau, March 20, 1865, James H. Wilson Mss., Library of Congress, Washington. Wilson is hereafter cited as JHW.

2. James H. Wilson Diary, January 2, 1865, James H. Wilson Mss., Delaware State Historical Society, Wilmington.

3. Wilson, *Old Flag*, II:161.

4. Ibid.

5. Lewis M. Hosea, "The Campaign of Selma," *Sketches of War History, 1861–1865, Papers Read before the Ohio Commandery of the Military Order of the Loyal Legion of the United States* (Cincinnati, 1888), I:81; William F. Scott, *The Story of a Cavalry Regiment: The Career of the Fourth Iowa Veteran Volunteers, from Kansas to Georgia, 1861–1865* (New York, 1893), p. 417.

6. JHW to Charles Francis Adams, February 22, 1908, Wilson Mss., Library of Congress.

7. Edward G. Longacre, *From Union Stars to Top Hat: A Biography of the Extraordinary General James Harrison Wilson* (Harrisburg, Pa., 1972), p. 13.

8. Wilson's West Point class was the only one in the Academy's history to have a five year term. The innovation was made by U.S. Secretary of War Jefferson Davis.

9. Longacre, *Union Stars*, pp. 75, 84, 95.

10. JHW to Sir Thomas Fraser, September 22, 1910; JHW to Smith

D. Atkins, October 11, 1909, Wilson Mss., Library of Congress; Long-acre, *Union Stars*, p. 102.

11. Longacre, *Union Stars*, pp. 117–144.

12. James R. Johnson and Alfred H. Bill, *Horsemen, Blue and Gray* (New York, 1960), p. 157.

13. U.S. War Department, *The War of the Rebellion: A Compila-tion of the Official Records of the Union and Confederate Armies* (Washington, 1880–1901), ser. 1, vol. xxxix, pt. 3, p. 64. Hereafter cited as *OR*.

14. *New York Times*, March 30, 1865; JHW to Adam Badeau, Janu-ary 26, 1865, Wilson Mss., Library of Congress. Between June 22 and July 1, 1864 Wilson raided Lee's railroad network with one action at Ream's Station, Virginia (*OR*, ser. 1, vol. xxxix, pt. 2, p. 442).

15. Longacre, *Union Stars*, p. 192; See also: Stanley F. Horn, *The Decisive Battle of Nashville* (Baton Rouge, 1956).

16. Benjamin F. McGee, *History of the 72nd Indiana Volunteer In-fantry of the Mounted Lightning Brigade* (Lafayette, Ind., 1882), p. 265; Wilson, *Old Flag*, 11:1.

17. Longacre, *Union Stars*, p. 34.

18. Richard Taylor, *Destruction and Reconstruction: Personal Ex-periences of the Late War*, Richard B. Harwell, ed. (New York, 1955), p. 311.

19. In his recent biography of Wilson, Edward G. Longacre main-tains that Wilson: "had long admired Thomas's soldierly ways . . . and his sympathy was particularly drawn by Thomas's interest in cavalry warfare. By this time too, [1865] Wilson's once idol-like worship of Grant may have diminished" (Longacre, *Union Stars*, p. 179). Long-acre gives no specific evidence to support this contention. In his cor-respondence with Badeau, Wilson labeled Thomas "selfish," and wrote of Grant: "with General Grant nothing is done from improper motives, everything is for the good of the service." He added: "Grant is *sui generis*, has no equal, no successful imitator among his lieutenants in unselfish, true-hearted devotion to duty. He excels them all in magna-nimity and truthfulness. You must not look for the same virtues every-where" (JHW to Adam Badeau, January 26, 1865, Wilson Mss., Li-brary of Congress).

20. Longacre, *Union Stars*, pp. 14–15, 33, 52, 153, 155–156.

21. Wilson Diary, February 4, 1865, Wilson Mss., D.S.H.S.

22. JHW to Joseph T. Dickman, June 16, 1913, Wilson Mss., Library of Congress.

23. John K. Herr and Edward S. Wallace, *The Story of the U.S. Cavalry, 1755–1942* (Boston, 1953), p. 124.

24. JHW to Charles Francis Adams, February 11, 1908, Wilson Mss., Library of Congress.

25. Fairfax Downey, *Clash of Cavalry: The Battle of Brandy Station, June 9, 1863* (New York, 1959), p. 151.

26. Herr and Wallace, *U.S. Cavalry*, p. 18.

27. Dee Alexander Brown, *Grierson's Raid* (Urbana, Ill., 1954) is an excellent study of this raid.

28. Wilson Diary, February 6, 1865, Wilson Mss., D.S.H.S.

29. JHW to Adam Badeau, January 2, 1865, Wilson Mss., Library of Congress.

30. Wilson, *Old Flag*, II:164.

31. Ms. of Lecture Delivered by Col. E. B. Beaumont at West Point, in Wilson Mss., Library of Congress; Homer Mead, *The Eighth Iowa Cavalry in the Civil War* (Carthage, Ill., n.d.), p. 15.

32. Wilson, *Old Flag*, II:164.

33. Johnson and Bill, *Horsemen*, p. 202; Herr and Wallace, *U.S. Cavalry*, p. 124; Longacre, *Union Stars*, p. 14.

34. Wilson, *Old Flag*, II:170.

35. Ibid., p. 171.

36. JWH to Charles Francis Adams, December 14, 1911, Wilson Mss., Library of Congress; Peter S. Michie, ed., *The Life and Letters of Emory Upton* (New York, 1885), p. xi.

37. Wilson, *Old Flag*, II:174; Michie, *Upton*, p. 131.

38. Wilson, *Old Flag*, II:174.

39. Ibid., p. 176.

40. Ibid., p. 168.

41. *OR*, ser. 1, vol. XLIX, pt. 1, pp. 342, 354.

42. Wilson, *Old Flag*, II:181.

43. *OR*, ser. 1, vol. XLIX, pt. 1, p. 708.

44. Ibid., p. 709.

45. Ibid., p. 354.

46. Edward Smith Atkins, "Wilson's Famous Raid," *The National Tribune*, Washington, D.C., June 2, 1910, p. 7. The review is also described by E. N. Gilpin in "The Last Campaign—A Cavalryman's Journal," *Journal of the United States Cavalry Association*, XIII (April, 1908). Gilpin, used to more grandeur at such occasions, reported no ladies, correspondents or Congressmen present, p. 619.

47. *OR*, ser. 1, vol. XLIX, pt. 1, p. 355; Wilson, *Old Flag*, II: 179–180.

48. *OR*, ser. 1, vol. XLIX, pt. 1, pp. 342, 356, 806.

49. See U.S. War Department, *Atlas to Accompany the War of the Rebellion: A Compilation of the Official Records of the Union and Confederate Armies* (Washington, 1891–1895), Plate LXVIII, no. 9.

50. Atkins, "Wilson's Famous Raid," p. 7; Henry M. Newhall to Sister, February 25, 1865, Newhall Mss., Illinois State Historical Library, Springfield.

51. *New York Times*, April 4, 1865; *OR*, ser. 1, vol. XLIX, pt. 1, p. 354; Scott, *Fourth Iowa*, p. 419.

52. Mead, *8th Iowa*, p. 17; Joseph G. Vale, *Minty and the Cavalry: A History of Cavalry Campaigns in the Western Armies* (Harrisburg, Pa., 1886), p. 422.

53. William Pepper Diary, January 28–30, 1865, Pepper Mss., Illinois State Historical Library, Springfield. This story is also mentioned in Atkins, "Wilson's Famous Raid," *National Tribune*, p. 7.

54. Pepper Diary, January 31–February 9, 1865, Pepper Mss.

55. Atkins, "Wilson's Famous Raid," p. 7.

56. Longacre, *Union Stars*, p. 165.

57. Pepper Diary, January 25, 1865, Pepper Mss.

58. Ibid., February 14, 1865. See Diary for February 14–March 22, 1865.

59. Michie, *Upton*, p. 134.

60. Charles F. Hinricks Diary, January 29, 1865, Hinricks Mss., Western Historical Manuscripts Collection, University of Missouri, Columbia.

61. Hosea, "Campaign of Selma," p. 80.

62. C. C. Andrews, *History of the Campaign of Mobile, Including the Cooperative Operations of General Wilson's Cavalry in Alabama* (New York, 1867), p. 243; R. C. Rankin, *History of the 7th Ohio Volunteer Cavalry* (Ripley, Ohio, 1881), p. 26; Scott, *Fourth Iowa*, p. 427.

63. JHW to Adam Badeau, January 26, 1865, Wilson Mss., Library of Congress; Wilson, *Old Flag*, II: 179; *OR*, ser. 1, vol. XLIX, pt. 1, p. 355.

64. Scott, *Fourth Iowa*, pp. 426–427; James Larson, *Sergeant Larson, 4th Cavalry* (San Antonio, Tex., 1935), p. 289.

65. JHW to Adam Badeau, January 2, 1865, Wilson Mss., Library of Congress.

66. *OR*, ser. 1, vol. XLIX, pt. 1, p. 689.

67. JHW to Adam Badeau, January 4, 1865, Wilson Mss., Library of Congress.

68. Arcadi Gluckman, *United States Muskets, Rifles and Carbines* (Buffalo, N.Y., 1948), pp. 438–439. Spencers were made by the Spencer Repeating Rifle Company of Boston. Up to December 31, 1865, 77,181 Spencers had been procured by the Ordnance Department. Spencers were also bought with private funds and shipped to state units.

69. W. L. Curry, *Four Years in the Saddle: History of the First Regiment Ohio Volunteer Cavalry* (Columbus, Ohio, 1898), p. 213.

70. F. W. Morse, *Personal Experiences of the War of the Great Rebellion* (Albany, N.Y., 1866), p. 124.

71. William Sipes, *The Seventh Pennsylvania's Veteran Volunteer Cavalry: Its Record, Reminiscences, and Roster* (Pottsville, Pa., n.d.), p. 150.

72. Scott, *Fourth Iowa*, p. 369.

73. Scott, *Fourth Iowa*, p. 370; Harold Peterson, *The American Sword, 1775–1945* (New Hope, Pa., 1954), pp. 35, 93; Lieutenant Hinricks's report on January 24 indicated receiving twenty-two cavalry sabers and seven saber belts for Company L, Tenth Missouri, Hinricks Mss.

74. *OR*, ser. 1, vol. XLIX, pt. 1, pp. 409–410.

75. *Clarke County Journal* (Grove Hill, Ala.), March 2, 16, 1865; *Selma Morning Reporter*, February 7, 1865.

76. Larson, *4th Cavalry*, p. 289.

77. Pepper Diary, February 23–25, 1865, Pepper Mss.

78. Stephen V. Shipman Diary, March 1, 1865, Shipman Mss., Wisconsin State Historical Library, Madison.

79. Shipman Diary, March 3, 5, 1865, Shipman Mss.

80. Pepper Diary, March 1–4, 1865, Pepper Mss.

81. *OR*, ser. 1, vol. XLIX, pt. 1, p. 356.

82. *Macon Daily Telegraph and Confederate*, April 4, 1865; Hosea, "Campaign of Selma," p. 80, reported that the *Columbus* (Mississippi) *Republic* carried an identical story.

83. Pepper Diary, March 5, 1865, Pepper Mss.; Henry Newhall to Sister, February 25, 1865, Newhall Mss.

84. *OR*, ser. 1, vol. XLIX, pt. 1, p. 825, 840.

85. Wilson, *Old Flag*, II: 183.

86. *OR*, ser. 1, vol. XLIX, pt. 1, pp. 689–690.

87. Ibid., p. 711.

88. Wilson, *Old Flag*, II:184.

89. Lewis M. Hosea, "Some Side Lights on the War for the Union," *Papers Read Before the Ohio Commandery of the Military Order of the Loyal Legion of the United States* (Cleveland, 1912), p. 9.

90. Ibid., p. 11.

91. Ibid., p. 12.

92. Ibid.

93. Wilson, *Old Flag*, II:185; Robert S. Henry, *"First with the Most" Forrest* (Indianapolis, 1944), pp. 423–425.

94. Wilson, *Old Flag*, II:184.

95. *OR*, ser. 1, vol. XLIX, pt. 1, p. 908.

96. Pepper Dairy, March 8–11, 1865, Pepper Mss.

97. Shipman Diary, March 1–8, 1865, Shipman Mss.

98. *OR*, ser. 1, vol. XLIX, pt. 1, p. 355.

99. JHW to Adam Badeau, March 7, 1865, Wilson Mss., Library of Congress.

100. Pepper Diary, March 11–12, 1865, Pepper Mss.

101. Ibid., March 13–15, 1865.

102. Wilson, *Old Flag*, II:175.

103. Atkins, "Wilson's Famous Raid," p. 7.

104. McGee, *72nd Indiana*, p. 521.

105. Wilson Diary, March 19–20, 1865, Wilson Mss., D.S.H.S.

106. JHW to Adam Badeau, March 20, 1865, Wilson Mss., Library of Congress.

107. Pepper Diary, March 12, 1865, Pepper Mss.; Hosea, "Campaign of Selma," p. 80.

108. Michie, *Upton*, pp. 137–138.

CHAPTER II

1. Wilson, *Old Flag*, II:170.

2. Ibid., p. 172.

3. Ibid., p. 168.

4. Ibid., p. 190.

5. Wilson, *Old Flag*, II:191; *OR*, ser. 1, vol. XLIX, pt. 1, pp. 355–356.

6. Morse, *Personal Experiences*, p. 126.

7. Brown, *Grierson's Raid*, p. 9; Herr and Wallace, *U.S. Cavalry*, p. 118.

8. Brown, *Grierson's Raid*, p. 10.

9. Bell I. Wiley, *The Life of Billy Yank: Common Soldier of the Union* (Indianapolis, 1951), pp. 209, 222. See also Pepper, Hinricks, and Shipman Diaries.

10. Scott, *Fourth Iowa*, pp. 26–27.

11. Fred A. Shannon, *The Organization and Administration of the Union Army, 1861–1865* (Cleveland, 1928), vol. II, pp. 270–271; Brown, *Grierson's Raid*, pp. 9–11.

12. Wiley, *Billy Yank*, pp. 326–327.

13. Shannon, *Organization and Administration*, II:270–271.

14. Taylor, *Destruction and Reconstruction*, p. 241; Andrew N. Lytle, *Bedford Forrest and His Critter Company* (New York, 1931), p. 371.

15. John W. Morton, *The Artillery of Nathan Bedford Forrest's Cavalry* (Nashville, Tenn., 1909), p. 305.

16. Robert S. Henry, ed., *As They Saw Forrest: Some Recollections and Comments of Contemporaries* (Jackson, Tenn., 1956), pp. 751–752.

17. Morton, *Artillery*, p. 303; Henry, *"First with the Most,"* p. 425.

18. Henry, *"First with the Most,"* p. 13.

19. Frank A. Montgomery, *Reminiscences of a Mississippian in Peace and War* (Cincinnati, 1901), p. 225.

20. See: Albert Castel, "The Ft. Pillow Massacre: A Fresh Examination of the Evidence," *Civil War History*, vol. IV, no. 1 (March, 1958), pp. 37–50.

21. *OR*, ser. 1, vol. XXXIX, pt. 1, p. 121.

22. Morton, *Artillery*, p. 303.

23. *Columbus Daily Enquirer*, March 4, 1865; *Southwestern Baptist* (Tuskegee, Ala.), March 16, 1865.

24. *Jacksonville* (Alabama) *Republican*, March 16, 1865.

25. Montgomery, *Reminiscences*, p. 234.

26. Robert F. Durden, *The Gray and the Black: The Confederate Debate on Emancipation* (Baton Rouge, 1972), deals with both emancipation and the discussion of arming the slaves.

27. *New York Times*, February 12, 1865. The *Times* reported such a story in the Richmond *Whig*.

28. *Memphis Appeal*, February 28, 1865; *Eutaw* (Alabama) *Whig and Observer*, March 9, 1865.

29. Montgomery, *Reminiscences*, p. 228.

30. *OR*, ser. 1, vol. XLIX, pt. 1, p. 972; Charles E. Hooker, *Missis-*

sippi, vol. VII of *Confederate Military History,* Clement A. Evans, ed. (Atlanta, 1899), pp. 224–225; John A. Wyeth, *Life of Lieutenant-General Nathan Bedford Forrest* (New York, 1899), p. 587.

31. *OR,* ser. 1, vol. XLIX, pt. 1, p. 972; James D. Porter, *Tennessee,* vol. VIII of *Confederate Military History.* Clement A. Evans, ed. (Atlanta, 1899), pp. 251–252.

32. *OR,* ser. 1, vol. XLIX, pt. 1, p. 992; *Montgomery Daily Mail,* March 29, 1865; V. Y. Cook, "Forrest's Efforts to Save Selma," *Confederate Veteran,* XXVI (April, 1918), p. 151; Edward M. Coffman, ed., "Memoirs of Hylan B. Lyon, Brigadier General, C.S.A.," *Tennessee Historical Quarterly,* vol. XVIII, no. 1 (March, 1959), p. 43.

33. *Clarke County Journal* (Grove Hill, Ala.), March 2, 1865.

34. *Montgomery Daily Mail,* March 15, 1865.

35. *OR,* ser. 1, vol. XLIX, pt. 1, pp. 342, 1048; Montgomery, *Reminiscences,* p. 233; James R. Chalmers, "Forrest and His Campaigns," *Southern Historical Society Papers,* VII (October, 1879), p. 485.

36. *Alabama Beacon* (Greensboro), February 10, 1865.

37. Henry, ed., *As They Saw Forrest,* p. 284.

38. John M. Hubbard, *Notes of a Private* (St. Louis, 1913), p. 181.

39. John P. Young, *The Seventh Tennessee Cavalry, Confederate* (Nashville, 1890), p. 131.

40. *Wilcox Banner* (Camden, Ala.), August 12, 1903; *Columbus Weekly Sun,* March 28, 1865; Hubbard, *Notes,* p. 180.

41. Henry, ed., *As They Saw Forrest,* p. 284.

42. Wyeth, *Forrest,* p. 578.

43. Young, *Seventh Tennessee,* p. 132.

44. Montgomery, *Reminiscences,* pp. 233–234.

45. *OR,* ser. 1, vol. XLIX, pt. 1, p. 953; Thomas Jordan and J. P. Pryor, *The Campaigns of Lieutenant General N. B. Forrest, and of Forrest's Cavalry* (New Orleans, 1868), p. 656.

46. *Montgomery Daily Mail,* February 18, March 8, 1865.

47. *Clarke County Journal* (Grove Hill, Ala.), March 2, 1865.

48. *Alabama Beacon* (Greensboro), February 21, 1865.

49. *OR,* ser. 1, vol. XLIX, pt. 1, p. 1014; *Jacksonville* (Alabama) *Republican,* March 16, 1865.

50. *Autauga Citizen* (Prattville, Ala.), March 16, 1865; *Clarke County Journal* (Grove Hill, Ala.), March 23, 1865; *Jacksonville* (Ala.) *Republican,* March 16, 1865.

51. *OR,* ser. 1, vol. XLIX, pt. 1, p. 953.

52. Ibid., pp. 953, 969–970.

53. Ibid., pp. 1005, 1012.

54. Ibid., pp. 1031–1032.

55. Wyeth, *Forrest*, p. 585; Chalmers, "Forrest and His Campaigns," p. 485.

56. *Clarke County Journal* (Grove Hill, Ala.), March 30, 1865; Michie, *Upton*, p. 142; Wyeth, *Forrest*, p. 588.

57. Wyeth, *Forrest*, p. 588; Wilson, *Old Flag*, II:195.

58. Hubbard, *Notes of a Private*, pp. 183–184.

59. Montgomery, *Reminiscences*, pp. 233–234; *Wilcox Banner* (Camden, Ala.), August 12, 1903; Wilson, *Old Flag*, II:199; Hubbard, *Notes of a Private*, p. 186.

60. *OR*, ser. 1, vol. XLIX, pt. 1, p. 1160.

61. Ibid., p. 357.

62. Wilson, *Old Flag*, II:192.

63. Pepper Diary, March 23, 1865, Pepper Mss.; Shipman Diary, March 23, 1865, Shipman Mss.

64. *OR*, ser. 1, vol. XLIX, pt. 1, p. 357.

65. Wilson Diary, March 24, 1865, Wilson Mss., D.S.H.S.

66. Larson, *4th Cavalry*, p. 290; Wilson, *Old Flag*, II:194; Hosea, "Campaign of Selma," p. 87.

67. Shipman Diary, March 23, 24, 1865, Shipman Mss.

68. Hinricks Diary, March 24, 25, 1865, Hinricks Mss.

69. *OR*, ser. 1, vol. XLIX, pt. 1, p. 411; Shipman Diary, March 23, 25, 1865, Shipman Mss.

70. Hinricks Diary, March 26, 1865, Hinricks Mss.

71. Scott, *Fourth Iowa*, p. 431.

72. Pepper Diary, March 23, 1865, Pepper Mss.; Shipman Diary, March 24, 1865, Shipman Mss.

73. Shipman Diary, March 23, 1865, Shipman Mss.

74. *OR*, ser. 1, vol. XLIX, pt. 1, p. 419; Charles D. Mitchell, "Field Notes on the Selma Campaign," *Sketches of War History, 1861–1865, Papers Read Before the Ohio Commandery of the Military Order of the Loyal Legion of the United States, 1903–1908*, Theodore F. Allen, et al., eds. (Cincinnati, 1908), VI:179.

75. Hinricks Diary, March 25, 1865, Hinricks Mss.

76. *OR*, ser. 1, vol. XLIX, pt. 1, pp. 357, 404–405; Wilson, *Old Flag*, II:204.

77. Morse, *Personal Experiences*, p. 127.

CHAPTER III

1. Wilson Diary, March 27, 1865, Wilson Mss., D.S.H.S. The general wrote: "banks were not merely precipituous, but mountainous."

2. Hinricks Diary, March 27, 1865, Hinricks Mss.

3. Atkins, "Wilson's Famous Raid," p. 7; Wilson, *Old Flag*, ii:203; Vale, *Minty and the Cavalry*, p. 428.

4. Hinricks Diary, March 27, 1865, Hinricks Mss.

5. Hinricks Diary, March 28, 1865, Hinricks Mss.; *OR*, ser. 1, vol. XLIX, pt. 1, p. 405.

6. *Historical Sketch of the Chicago Board of Trade Battery, Horse Artillery, Illinois Volunteers* (Chicago, 1902), p. 47; *OR*, ser. 1, vol. XLIX, pt. 1, p. 411.

7. *OR*, ser. 1, vol. XLIX, pt. 1, pp. 404–405; McGee, *72nd Indiana*, p. 534.

8. Shipman Diary, March 25, 27, 1865, Shipman Mss.

9. *Chicago Board of Trade Battery*, p. 47.

10. Shipman Diary, March 27, 1865, Shipman Mss.

11. Taylor, *Destruction and Reconstruction*, p. 311.

12. *OR*, ser. 1, vol. XLIX, pt. 1, p. 405; Hinricks Diary, March 28, 1865, Hinricks Mss.

13. Hinricks Diary, March 8, 1865, Hinricks Mss.

14. Elyton is the site of the modern city of Birmingham.

15. Wilson, *Old Flag*, ii:204.

16. Shipman Diary, March 29, 1865, Shipman Mss.; Wilson Diary, March 30, 1865, Wilson Mss., D.S.H.S. reported of the area: "forage plenty."

17. *OR*, ser. 1, vol. XLIX, pt. 2, p. 1160.

18. Ibid., pp. 1160–1161.

19. Ibid., p. 1169.

20. Taylor, *Destruction and Reconstruction*, p. 268.

21. *Southwestern Baptist* (Tuskegee, Ala.), March 30, 1865.

22. Andrews, *Campaign of Mobile*, p. 246; Wilson, *Old Flag*, ii:199. Wilson charged that part of Forrest's loss of time was due to his review of troops and that this loss was "both irreparable and fatal."

23. *OR*, ser. 1, vol. XLIX, pt. 2, p. 1165; Montgomery, *Reminiscences*, p. 236.

24. Henry, *"First with the Most,"* p. 429; Hubbard, *Notes of a Private*, p. 183.

25. *OR*, ser. 1, vol. XLIX, pt. 1, pp. 13–14, 357; Hosea, "Campaign of Selma," p. 87.

26. *OR*, ser. 1, vol. XLIX, pt. 1, p. 419.

27. Shipman Diary, March 30, 1865, Shipman Mss.

28. *OR*, ser. 1, vol. XLIX, pt. 1, pp. 419–420; James A. Anderson, "The Federal Raid Into Central Alabama April, 1865, Including Wilson's Raid on Selma and Montgomery, and Croxton's Raid on Tuscaloosa," Unpublished Mss. of speech delivered in 1935. Anderson Mss., University of Alabama Library, Tuscaloosa.

29. *OR*, ser. 1, vol. XLIX, pt. 1, p. 420.

30. Thomas P. Clinton, "The Military Operations of General John T. Croxton in West Alabama, 1865," *Transactions of the Alabama Historical Society*, Thomas M. Owen, ed., IV (1904), p. 499.

31. *OR*, ser. 1, vol. XLIX, pt. 1, p. 420.

32. Hubbard, *Notes of a Private*, p. 186; Andrews, *Campaign of Mobile*, p. 248.

33. *OR*, ser. 1, vol. XLIX, pt. 2, p. 174.

34. *OR*, ser. 1, vol. XLIX, pt. 1, p. 421; Clinton, "Military Operations of Croxton," p. 450.

35. Clinton, "Military Operations of Croxton," p. 450; Andrews, *Campaign of Mobile*, p. 261; *OR*, ser. 1, vol. XLIX, pt. 1, p. 421.

36. *OR*, ser. 1, vol. XLIX, pt. 1, p. 420; Marshall P. Thatcher, *A Hundred Battles in the West, St. Louis to Atlanta, 1861–1865* (Detroit, 1884), p. 243; Clinton, "Military Operations of Croxton," p. 450. Croxton did not rejoin Wilson at Selma. For the rest of the "Lost Brigade's" march across Alabama and Georgia see chapter VII.

37. Scott, *Fourth Iowa*, p. 432; Hinricks Diary, March 30, 1865, Hinricks Mss.

38. *Chicago Board of Trade Battery*, p. 47.

39. Wilson, *Old Flag*, II:205; *OR*, ser. 1, vol. XLIX, pt. 1, p. 405; McGee, *72nd Indiana*, p. 537.

40. Morse, *Personal Experiences*, p. 126.

41. Scott, *Fourth Iowa*, p. 435; Gilpin, "The Last Campaign," pp. 633–634.

42. Shipman Diary, March 31, 1865, Shipman Mss.

43. Ibid., March 30, 1865.

44. Scott, *Fourth Iowa*, p. 435.

45. Wilson, *Old Flag*, II:207; McGee, *72nd Indiana*, pp. 534–536; Clinton, "Military Operations of Croxton," p. 449; Ethel Armes, *The*

Story of Coal and Iron in Alabama (Birmingham, 1910), pp. 161, 186;
Joseph H. Woodward, "Alabama Iron Manufacturing," *Alabama Review*, vol. VII, no. 3 (July, 1954), pp. 204–206; Frank E. Vandiver,
"The Shelby Iron Company in the Civil War: A Study of Confederate
Industry," *Alabama Review*, vol. I, nos. 1, 2, 3 (January, April, July,
1948), pp. 204, 214.

46. *Memphis Appeal*, March 30, 1865.

47. Willis Brewer, *Alabama: Her History, Resources, War Record,
and Public Men* (Montgomery, 1872), pp. 681–688; D. B. Castleberry,
"Last Review of Forrest's Cavalry," *Confederate Veteran*, vol. XXIV
(July, 1916), p. 301.

48. JHW to Joseph T. Dickman, June 16, 1913, Wilson Mss., Library of Cong.

49. Michie, *Upton*, pp. 150–151.

50. *OR*, ser. 1, vol. XLIX, pt. 1, p. 500; Wilson, *Old Flag*, II:208; Wilson Diary, March 31, 1865, Wilson Mss., D.S.H.S.

51. *OR*, ser. 1, vol. XLIX, pt. 1, p. 357; Jordan and Pryor, *The Campaigns of Forrest*, pp. 662–663; Cook, "Forrest's Efforts," pp. 151–152;
J. M. Browne, "Forrest's Last Exploit," *Confederate Veteran*, vol. XXV
(November, 1917), p. 491.

52. Jordan and Pryor, *The Campaigns of Forrest*, pp. 663–664;
Henry, *"First with the Most,"* p. 430; *OR*, ser. 1, vol. XLIX, pt. 1,
p. 479.

53. Wilson, *Old Flag*, II:208.

54. *OR*, ser. 1, vol. XLIX, pt. 1, p. 358.

55. Hinricks Diary, March 31, 1865, Hinricks Mss.

56. *OR*, ser. 1, vol. XLIX, pt. 1, p. 350.

57. Michie, *Upton*, p. 149; Wilson, *Old Flag*, II:213.

58. *OR*, ser. 1, vol. XLIX, pt. 2, p. 1182.

59. *OR*, ser. 1, vol. XLIX, pt. 1, pp. 350–351; Wilson, *Old Flag*,
II:211.

60. *OR*, ser. 1, vol. XLIX, pt. 1, p. 358.

61. Shipman Diary, April 1, 1865, Shipman Mss.

62. *OR*, ser. 1, vol. XLIX, pt. 1, pp. 427, 435–436.

63. Hubbard, *Notes of a Private*, p. 187.

64. *OR*, ser. 1, vol. XLIX, pt. 1, pp. 416–417, 431.

65. Shipman Diary, April 2, 1865, Shipman Mss.

66. *OR*, ser. 1, vol. XLIX, pt. 1, pp. 416–417, 428; Young, *Seventh
Tennessee*, pp. 135–136.

67. Henry, *"First with the Most,"* p. 430.

68. Chalmers, "Forrest and His Campaigns," p. 485.

69. *OR*, ser. 1, vol. XLIX, pt. 1, p. 359; E. C. Faulkner, "The Last Time I Saw General Forrest," *Confederate Veteran*, vol. v (February, 1897) , p. 83.

70. Hubbard, *Notes of a Private*, p. 189.

71. Confederate estimates are from the *Columbus Sun*, April 6, 1865 and from Henry, *"First with the Most,"* p. 431. The Union estimate is from *OR*, ser. 1, vol. XLIX, pt. 1, p. 359 and from Scott, *Fourth Iowa*, p. 443. Scott estimated four thousand men and chastised the rebels for the "habit of . . . minimizing their numbers."

72. Wilson, *Old Flag*, II:211.

73. Ibid., p. 213.

74. *OR*, ser. 1, vol. XLIX, pt. 1, pp. 351, 358; Wilson, *Old Flag*, II:215.

75. *OR*, ser. 1, vol. XLIX, pt. 1, p. 437; Hosea, "Campaign of Selma," p. 92.

76. *OR*, ser. 1, vol. XLIX, pt. 1, p. 359.

77. Wilson, *Old Flag*, II:216–217; Sipes, *Seventh Pennsylvania*, p. 150.

78. Wilson, *Old Flag*, II:217. Wilson believed that White could have bested Forrest in hand-to-hand combat, but the "younger and slighter" Taylor could not.

79. Browne, "Forrest's Last Exploit," p. 492; McGee, *72nd Indiana*, p. 542; *OR*, ser. 1, vol. XLIX, pt. 1, p. 359; Henry, *"First with the Most,"* p. 431; Hosea, "Campaign of Selma," p. 93; Lytle, *Bedford Forrest*, p. 374.

80. *OR*, ser. 1, vol. XLIX, pt. 1, p. 447; Atkins, "Wilson's Famous Raid," p. 7.

81. Hosea, "Campaign of Selma," p. 94.

82. *OR*, ser. 1, vol. XLIX, pt. 1, p. 500.

83. Ibid., p. 1012.

84. Scott, *Fourth Iowa*, p. 443; *OR*, ser. 1, vol. XLIX, pt. 1, p. 479.

85. Pepper Diary, April 1, 1865, Pepper Mss.

86. *Montgomery Daily Mail*, April 2, 1865; *Alabama Beacon* (Greensboro) , April 5, 1865.

87. *OR*, ser. 1, vol. XLIX, pt. 1, p. 351; McGee, *72nd Indiana*, p. 543.

88. *OR*, ser. 1, vol. XLIX, pt. 1, p. 406.

89. Wilson, *Old Flag*, II:220.

90. Pepper Diary, April 1, 1865, Pepper Mss.

91. Wilson, *Old Flag*, II:211.

CHAPTER IV

1. Hinricks Diary, April 2, 1865, Hinricks Mss.

2. Wirt A. Cate, *Two Soldiers* (Chapel Hill, N.C., 1938), p. 36; Shipman Diary, April 7, 1865, Shipman Mss.

3. Marie Bankhead Owen, *The Story of Alabama: A History of the State* (New York, 1949), 11:140–148; Henry, *"First with the Most,"* p. 442.

4. U.S. Bureau of the Census, *Eighth Census of the United States: 1860* (Washington, 1864), p. 3; John Hardy, *Selma: Her Institutions and Her Men* (Selma, 1879), p. 47.

5. James A. Carpenter, "James D. Lynch in War and Peace," *Alabama Historical Quarterly*, vol. xx, No. 1 (Spring, 1958), p. 75.

6. Shipman Diary, April 7, 1865, Shipman Mss.; Hinricks Diary, April 8, 1865, Hinricks Mss.

7. *OR*, ser. 1, vol. xlix, pt. 1, p. 484.

8. Walter M. Jackson, *The Story of Selma* (Birmingham, 1954), p. 199; Hardy, *Selma*, p. 46.

9. *OR*, ser. 1, vol. xlix, pt. 1, p. 484; William A. Albraugh and Edward N. Simmons, *Confederate Arms* (Harrisburg, Pa., 1957), p. 261.

10. C. E. Landis, "The Siege and Fall of Selma, Alabama," *Confederate Veteran*, vol. xxi (March, 1923), p. 96.

11. *OR*, ser. 1, vol. xlix, pt. 1, p. 484; Armes, *Coal and Iron in Alabama*, p. 186; Hardy, *Selma*, pp. 44–46; Scrapbook no. ii, Wilson's Raid, Carnegie Library, Selma. The ten factories not named above were: Pierce's Foundries; the Tennessee Iron Works; the Washington Iron Works; the Phelan and McBride Works; the Horseshoe Manufactory; the Selma Shovel Factory; Campbell's Foundry; the Brooks and Gainor Iron Works; the Central City Iron Works and Foundry; and the Dallas Iron Works.

12. Albert B. Moore, *History of Alabama* (Tuscaloosa, 1934), p. 446; Hardy, *Selma*, p. 47; Scrapbook no. 1, Wilson's Raid, Carnegie Library, Selma.

13. Owen, *The Story of Alabama*, 1:418; Moore, *History of Alabama*, p. 446.

14. *OR*, ser. 1, vol. xlix, pt. 1, p. 484.

15. Hardy, *Selma*, p. 46.

16. *OR*, ser. 1, vol. xlix, pt. 1, pp. 360–361, 438.

17. *OR*, ser. 1, vol. xlix, pt. 1, pp. 360–361; *Official Atlas*, vol. lxx.

18. Scrapbook no. i, Wilson's Raid, Carnegie Library, Selma; Alice

V. D. Pierrepont, *Reuben Vaughan Kidd: Soldier of the Confederacy* (Petersburg, Va., 1947), p. 369; Larson, *4th Cavalry*, p. 293.

19. *Selma Evening Reporter*, March 28, 1865.

20. Jordan and Pryor, *Campaigns of Forrest*, pp. 671–672.

21. Chalmers, Forrest and His Campaigns," p. 485.

22. W. F. Ross, "Lack of Co-operation at Selma, 1865," *Confederate Veteran*, vol. xxvi (July, 1918), p. 322.

23. Taylor, *Destruction and Reconstruction*, p. 268.

24. Ibid.

25. Andrews, *Campaign of Mobile*, p. 253.

26. Hardy, *Selma*, p. 51; Wilson, *Old Flag*, ii:232; Thomas F. Dornblaser, *Saber Strokes of the Pennsylvania Dragoons in the War of 1861–1865, Interspersed with Personal Reminiscences* (Philadelphia, 1884), p. 213.

27. *Montgomery Daily Mail*, April 2, 1865.

28. Hardy, *Selma*, p. 51; Henry, "*First with the Most*," pp. 431–432; Scott, *Fourth Iowa*, p. 449; *OR*, ser. 1, vol. xlix, pt. 1, p. 361; Vale, *Minty*, p. 431. Longacre, *Union Stars*, settles on a figure of six thousand, p. 206.

29. Landis, "Siege and Fall," p. 96; Jackson, *Selma*, pp. 214–215.

30. Taylor, *Destruction and Reconstruction*, p. 268.

31. Pierrepont, *Kidd*, p. 370.

32. Montgomery, *Reminiscences*, p. 240. The lieutenant colonel states that some men were so late moving into the line that if Long had struck one-half hour sooner he would have attacked an empty parapet.

33. Hosea, "Campaign of Selma," p. 96.

34. Hinricks Diary, April 2, 1865, Hinricks Mss.

35. Pepper Diary, April 2, 1865, Pepper Mss.

36. *OR*, ser. 1, vol. xlix, pt. 1, pp. 359–360.

37. Longacre, *Union Stars*, p. 206.

38. *OR*, ser. 1, vol. xlix, pt. 1, p. 351; Wilson, *Old Flag*, ii:221–222; E. N. Gilpin, "The Last Campaign," p. 634.

39. Wilson, *Old Flag*, ii:224.

40. *OR*, ser. 1, vol. xlix, pt. 1, pp. 461–462, 470.

41. Charles O. Brown, "Narrative of Personal Experiences in the Battle of Selma," unpublished typescript, Brown Mss., Illinois State Historical Library, Springfield.

42. Montgomery, *Reminiscences*, p. 241.

43. *OR*, ser. 1, vol. xlix, pt. 1, p. 480.

44. Scott, *Fourth Iowa*, p. 445; Hinricks Diary, April 2, 1865, Hinricks Mss.

45. *OR*, ser. 1, vol. XLIX, pt. 1, p. 360.

46. Dornblaser, *Saber Strokes*, p. 210; *OR*, ser. 1, vol. XLIX, pt. 1, pp. 360, 438, 439.

47. JHW to Charles O. Brown, February 28, 1910, Wilson Mss., Library of Congress. In *OR*, ser. 1, vol. XLIX, pt. 1, p. 360, Wilson praised Long for "admirable judgement."

48. Wilson, *Old Flag*, II:221; Montgomery, *Reminiscences*, pp. 241, 242.

49. Hosea, "Campaign of Selma," p. 98.

50. *OR*, ser. 1, vol. XLIX, pt. 1, p. 395.

51. Atkins, "Wilson's Famous Raid," p. 7.

52. *Columbus Daily Sun*, April 8, 1865.

53. Montgomery, *Reminiscences*, pp. 243, 250.

54. Larson, *4th Cavalry*, p. 295.

55. Eli Long to JHW, January 30, 1878, Wilson Mss., Library of Congress; Curry, *1st Ohio*, p. 387.

56. *OR*, ser. 1, vol. XLIX, pt. 1, pp. 343, 351.

57. Hinricks Diary, April 2, 1865, Hinricks Mss.

58. *OR*, ser. 1, vol. XLIX, pt. 1, p. 473; Hosea, "Side Lights," p. 16; Hinricks Diary, April 2, 1865, Hinricks Mss.

59. Wilson, *Old Flag*, II:229.

60. JHW to James E. Kelly, February 9, 1910, Wilson Mss., Library of Congress.

61. Atkins, "Wilson's Famous Raid," p. 7; Larson, *4th Cavalry*, pp. 296, 297.

62. *OR*, ser. 1, vol. XLIX, pt. 1, p. 360; Wilson, *Old Flag*, II:229, 230; *Chicago Board of Trade Battery*, p. 48. "Sheridan" went through the campaign and died in May at Macon as a result of the Selma wounds. Wilson called him the "prince of horses and acknowledged to be the best in the corps." Wilson to Adam Badeau, May 13, 1865, Wilson Mss., Library of Congress.

63. Brown, "Narrative," p. 3.

64. *OR*, ser. 1, vol. XLIX, pt. 1, pp. 351, 473; W. H. H. Benefiel, *Sou-Ven-ir: History of the 17th Regiment Indiana Volunteer Infantry During the Civil War from 1861 to 1865* (n.p., 1913), p. 3.

65. Ona S. Morrison, *The Battle of Selma* (Selma, n.d.), p. 3; Hosea, "Side Lights," p. 16; *OR*, ser. 1, vol. XLIX, pt. 1, pp. 351, 473.

66. Wilson Diary, April 2, 1865, Wilson Mss., D.S.H.S.

67. *OR*, ser. 1, vol. XLIX, pt. 1, p. 351.

68. Hinricks Diary, April 2, 1865, Hinricks Mss.

69. *OR*, ser. 1, vol. XLIX, pt. 1, p. 361; *Alabama Beacon* (Greensboro), 5 April 1865.

70. Hardy, *Selma*, p. 51; *OR*, ser. 1, vol. XLIX, pt. 1, p. 351.

71. Morrison, *Battle of Selma*, p. 4.

72. Montgomery, *Reminiscences*, p. 250.

73. Ibid., p. 245, 251.

74. *OR*, ser. 1, vol. XLIX, pt. 1, pp. 351, 360; Robert U. Johnson and Clarence C. Buel, eds., *Battles and Leaders of the Civil War* (New York, 1887–1888), IV:760.

75. *OR*, ser. 1, vol. XLIX, pt. 1, p. 393.

76. Vale, *Minty*, p. 434.

77. Larson, *4th Cavalry*, p. 299.

78. Larson, *4th Cavalry*, pp. 298–299; Montgomery, *Reminiscences*, p. 248; Wilson, *Old Flag*, II:232–233.

79. *Alabama Beacon* (Greensboro), April 21, 1865; Walter L. Fleming, *Civil War and Reconstruction in Alabama* (New York, 1905), p. 72.

80. Speech of Governor Lewis Parsons in New York City, n.d., in Folder, "Raids-Wilson," Alabama Department of Archives and History, Montgomery. The governor's speech was entitled, "The Sacking of Selma."

81. Hardy, *Selma*, p. 52.

82. Annie G. Coombs's Scrap Book, 1866 in Folder, "Raids-Wilson," in Alabama Department of Archives and History, Montgomery.

83. Sarah Ellen Phillips Memoir, Phillips Mss., Southern Historical Collection, University of North Carolina, Chapel Hill.

84. For several views of the problem see: Wilson, *Old Flag*, II:232–233; Landis, "Siege and Fall," p. 97; Mitchell, "Field Notes," p. 184; Fleming, *Civil War and Reconstruction in Alabama*, pp. 72–73; Andrews, *The Campaign of Mobile*, p. 256.

85. Hosea, "Campaign of Selma," p. 101–102; Wilson, *Old Flag*, II:233.

86. Hardy, *Selma*, p. 53.

87. Wilson, *Old Flag*, II:234, 237; Owen, *The Story of Alabama*, I:419; Hinricks Diary, April 3, 1865, Hinricks Mss.

88. Wilson, *Old Flag*, II:232. Longacre, *Union Stars*, p. 208, observes that Wilson led the fight to halt the fires and that he "decreed capital punishment for all housebreakers."

89. *Selma Evening Reporter*, March 28, 1865.

90. *Columbus Daily Sun*, April 9, 1865; *Alabama Beacon* (Greensboro), April 21, 1865.

91. *Southern Advertiser* (Troy, Ala.), April 7, 1865; Hardy, *Selma*, p. 52.

92. James S. Clark, *Life in the Middle West: Reminiscences of James S. Clark* (Chicago, n.d.), p. 128; Joseph O. Jackson, ed., *"Some of the Boys:" The Civil War Letters of Isaac Jackson* (Carbondale, Ill., 1960), p. 248.

93. Gilpin, "The Last Campaign," p. 640.

94. Jackson, *Selma*, p. 217.

95. Jackson, *Selma*, p. 214; Rankin, *7th Ohio*, p. 27. In 1942, during World War II, Selma residents dove in the river to salvage some of this metal for use in the production of war material. *Atlanta Constitution*, October 9, 1942.

96. *OR*, ser. 1, vol. XLIX, pt. 1, p. 484; Wilson, *Old Flag*, II:168; McGee, *72nd Indiana*, pp. 562, 565.

97. Larson, *4th Cavalry*, pp. 300–301.

98. Wilson, *Old Flag*, II:232–233; Hinricks Diary, April 6, 1865, Hinricks Mss.

99. *OR*, ser. 1, vol. XLIX, pt. 1, p. 484.

100. Shipman Diary, April 9, 1865, Shipman Mss.; Hinricks Diary, April 7, 1865, Hinricks Mss.

101. *Clarke County Journal* (Grove Hill, Ala.), April 6, 13, 1865.

102. *Southern Advertiser* (Troy, Ala.), April 7, 1865.

103. *OR*, ser. 1, vol. XLIX, pt. 1, p. 406; Henry, *"First with the Most,"* pp. 432–433; Jordan and Pryor, *The Campaigns of Forrest*, p. 677; Scott, *Fourth Iowa*, p. 459.

104. Larson, *4th Cavalry*, p. 299.

105. *OR*, ser. 1, vol. XLIX, pt. 1, p. 406.

106. Hubbard, *Notes of a Private*, p. 191.

107. Wilson Diary, April 4, 1865, Wilson Mss., D.S.H.S.

108. *OR*, ser. 1, vol. XLIX, pt. 1, pp. 351, 361.

109. Shipman Diary, April 6, 1865, Shipman Mss.

110. Wilson Diary, April 8, 1865, Wilson Mss., D.S.H.S.

111. *OR*, ser. 1, vol. XLIX, pt. 1, p. 362; Wilson, *Old Flag*, II:241–242; Hosea, "Side Lights," p. 18; Wilson Diary, April 8, 1865, Wilson Mss., D.S.H.S.

112. Wilson, *Old Flag*, II:238; Wilson Diary, April 4, 1865, Wilson Mss., D.S.H.S.

113. *OR*, ser. 1, vol. XLIX, pt. 1, p. 361.

114. Ibid., p. 362.

115. Hinricks Diary, April 8, 1865, Hinricks Mss.

116. *OR*, ser. 1, vol. XLIX, pt. 1, p. 410.

117. *OR*, ser. 1, vol. XLIX, pt. 1, p. 412; Pepper Diary, April 9, 1865, Pepper Mss.; Scott, *Fourth Iowa*, p. 468; Wilson, *Old Flag*, II:245.

118. Eli Long to JHW, January 30, 1878, Wilson Mss., Library of Congress.

119. Jackson, *"Some of the Boys,"* p. 248.

120. Wilson, *Old Flag*, II:246–247; Scott, *Fourth Iowa*, p. 468; Montgomery, *Reminiscences*, p. 251.

121. Wilson, Old Flag, II:248.

122. Jackson, *"Some of the Boys,"* p. 248.

CHAPTER V

1. *OR*, ser. 1, vol. XLIX, pt. 1, p. 393.

2. Hinricks Diary, April 10, 1865, Hinricks Mss.

3. *OR*, ser. 1, vol. XLIX, pt. 1, pp. 407, 431; Brewer, *Alabama*, p. 684; Shipman Diary, April 10, 1865, Shipman Mss.

4. *OR*, ser. 1, vol. XLIX, pt. 1, p. 431.

5. *OR*, ser. 1, vol. XLIX, pt. 1, p. 442; Wilson, *Old Flag*, II:249; Scott, *Fourth Iowa*, pp. 471–472; Hinricks Diary, April 11, 1865, Hinricks Mss.

6. *OR*, ser. 1, vol. XLIX, pt. 1, p. 407.

7. Scott, *Fourth Iowa*, pp. 472–473.

8. Gilpin, "The Last Campaign," p. 648; *OR*, ser. 1, vol. XLIX, pt. 1, pp. 370–371, 407; Montgomery *Daily Mail*, April 17, 1865: Wilson Diary, April 11, 1865, Wilson Mss., D.S.H.S.

9. Montgomery, *Reminiscences*, p. 251.

10. Shipman Diary, April 11, 1865, Shipman Mss.

11. Hinricks Diary, April 11, 1865, Hinricks Mss.

12. Shipman Diary, April 11, 1865, Shipman Mss.

13. Pepper Diary, April 11, 1865, Pepper Mss.

14. *Gilpin*, "The Last Campaign," p. 647; *OR*, ser. 1, vol. XLIX, pt. 1, p. 433.

15. Albraugh and Simmons, *Confederate Arms*, pp. 195–196; Fleming, *The Civil War and Reconstruction in Alabama*, p. 151.

16. *Memphis Daily Appeal*, March 30, 1865.

17. *Montgomery Daily Mail*, April 2, 1865.

18. Diary of Ellen Blue, April 2, 3, 1865, Diary in possession of Mrs. Charles M. Smith, Jr., Montgomery.

19. Virginia K. Jones, ed., "The Journal of Sarah G. Follansbee," *Alabama Historical Quarterly*, vol. xxviii, nos. 3 and 4 (Fall and Winter, 1965) , p. 229.

20. *Southern Advertiser* (Troy, Ala.) , April 7, 1865.

21. Blue Diary, April 4, 1865, Diary in possession of Mrs. Smith, Montgomery.

22. *Montgomery Daily Mail*, April 11, 1865.

23. Ibid.

24. *Alabama Beacon* (Greensboro) , April 21, 1865.

25. *Columbus Sun*, April 6, 9, 1865; *Southern Advertiser* (Troy, Ala.) , April 14, 1865.

26. *Columbus Sun*, April 6, 8, 1865; *Columbus Daily Enquirer*, April 12, 1865; *OR*, ser. 1, vol. xlix, pt. 1, p. 505; Blue Diary, April 3, 1865, Diary in possession of Mrs. Smith, Montgomery.

27. Samuel Walker Catts, "Wilson's Raid and Other Recital," *Alabama Historical Quarterly*, vol. v, no. 4 (Winter, 1943) , p. 430.

28. Wilson, *Old Flag*, ii:252; *Columbus Sun*, April 8, 1865.

29. *Southern Advertiser* (Troy, Ala.) , April 14, 1865.

30. Blue Diary, April 5, 1865, Diary in possession of Mrs. Smith, Montgomery; *Southern Advertiser* (Troy, Ala.) , April 14, 1865.

31. *Columbus Sun*, April 6, 9, 1865.

32. *Columbus Sun*, April 11, 1865; *Montgomery Daily Mail*, April 11, 1865.

33. *OR*, ser. 1, vol. xlix, pt. 1, p. 1239.

34. *Montgomery Advertiser*, April 18, 1865.

35. *OR*, ser. 1, vol. xlix, pt. 1, pp. 504–505; *Montgomery Advertiser*, April 18, 1865; *Montgomery Daily Mail*, April 17, 1865; Jones, "Journal of Sarah Follansbee," p. 231.

36. Jones, "Journal of Sarah Follansbee," p. 230.

37. *Columbus Sun*, April 14, 1865.

38. *Columbus Sun*, April 14, 1865; *Montgomery Daily Mail*, April 17, 1865.

39. Wilson, *Old Flag*, ii:249. The city's surrender also surprised the men. See Scott, *Fourth Iowa*, p. 473.

40. *OR*, ser. 1, vol. xlix, pt. 1, p. 352; *Montgomery Daily Mail*, April 17, 1865.

41. *Montgomery Daily Mail*, April 17, 1865.

42. Shipman Diary, April 12, 1865, Shipman Mss.; Wilson, *Old Flag*, II:250.

43. Wilson, *Old Flag*, II:250; Hinricks Diary, April 12, 1865, Hinricks Mss.

44. Andrews, *Campaign of Mobile*, p. 259.

45. Hinricks Diary, April 12, 1865, Hinricks Mss.

46. Ibid.

47. Jones, "Journal of Sarah Follansbee," p. 232.

48. Scott, *Fourth Iowa*, p. 474; Shipman Diary, April 12, 1865, Shipman Mss.; Atkins, "Wilson's Famous Raid," p. 7; *Montgomery Daily Mail*, April 17, 1865; *OR*, ser. 1, vol. XLIX, pt. 1, p. 407; Wilson, *Old Flag*, II:251.

49. Blue Diary, April 13, 1865, Diary in possession of Mrs. Smith, Montgomery.

50. *OR*, ser. 1, vol. XLIX, pt. 1, pp. 430, 434, 504–505.

51. Wilson, *Old Flag*, II:252.

52. *OR*, ser. 1, vol. XLIX, pt. 1, pp. 363, 433; Shipman Diary, April 12, 1865, Shipman Mss.

53. *Montgomery Daily Mail*, April 17, 1865.

54. *Montgomery Advertiser*, April 18, 1865; *Montgomery Daily Mail*, April 17, 1865.

55. Pepper Diary, April 12, 13, 1865, Pepper Mss.

56. Hinricks Diary, April 13, 1865, Hinricks Mss.

57. *Montgomery Advertiser*, April 18, 1865; Shipman Diary, April 13, 1865, Shipman Mss.; *New York Tribune*, April 29, 1865; *OR*, ser. 1, vol. XLIX, pt. 1, p. 407; Jones, "Journal of Sarah Follansbee," p. 233.

58. Wilson Diary, April 12, 13, 1865, Wilson Mss., D.S.H.S.

59. Cloyd Bryner, *Bugle Echoes: The Story of Illinois' 47th* (Springfield, Ill., 1905), p. 157.

60. Shipman Diary, April 13, 1865, Shipman Mss.

61. Mitchell, "Field Notes," p. 187.

62. *OR*, ser. 1, vol. XLIX, pt. 1, pp. 363, 434; McGee, *72nd Indiana*, p. 577.

63. Wilson, *Old Flag*, II:253.

64. Shipman Diary, April 14, 1865, Shipman Mss.

65. *OR*, ser. 1, vol. XLIX, pt. 2, p. 344.

66. Wilson, *Old Flag*, II:254.

67. *OR*, ser. 1, vol. XLIX, pt. 1, p. 345; Michie, *Upton*, p. 165.

68. *OR*, ser. 1, vol. XLIX, pt. 1, p. 408.

69. Ibid., pp. 428, 436.

70. *OR*, ser. 1, vol. XLIX, pt. 1, p. 432; Wilson, *Old Flag*, II:255.

71. McGee, *72nd Indiana*, p. 580; Wilson, *Old Flag*, II:255.

72. Shipman Diary, April 15, 1865, Shipman Mss.

73. Rhoda Coleman Ellison, "Huntingdon College, 1860–1865," *Alabama Review*, vol. VII, no. 1 (January 1954), pp. 15–17.

74. Wilson, *Old Flag*, II:255–257. Wilson says that she posted a $5,000 bond and the paper was drawn up by Col. John Noble, "a rising young lawyer," and later Secretary of the Interior under Benjamin Harrison.

75. *OR*, ser. 1, vol. XLIX, pt. 1, pp. 370–371; Wilson Diary, April 15, 1865, Wilson Mss., D.S.H.S.

76. Montgomery, *Reminiscences*, pp. 252–253.

77. *OR*, ser. 1, vol. XLIX, pt. 1, pp. 370–371.

78. McGee, *72nd Indiana*, p. 579.

79. McGee, *72nd Indiana*, p. 578; Dornblaser, *Saber Strokes*, pp. 218–223.

80. Hinricks Diary, April 15, 1865, Hinricks Mss.

81. *OR*, ser. 1, vol. XLIX, pt. 1, pp. 363, 428.

82. Scott, *Fourth Iowa*, p. 480; L. B. M'Farland, "Battle of West Point," *Confederate Veteran*, vol. XXIII (August, 1915), p. 353; Earl Edwards, "The Battle of West Point," *Chattahoochee Valley Historical Society*, Bulletin, no. 3 (1957), pp. 3, 12.

83. *OR*, ser. 1, vol. XLIX, pt. 1, pp. 364, 429; M'Farland, "Battle of West Point," p. 353; Edwards, "Battle of West Point," p. 4.

84. *OR*, ser. 1, vol. XLIX, pt. 1, p. 429; *Battles and Leaders of the Civil War*, IV:761. M'Farland, in "Battle of West Point," says only 121 men served in the fort. The others included in LaGrange's figure were, according to M'Farland, sick and wounded soldiers in the West Point area.

85. *OR*, ser. 1, vol. XLIX, pt. 1, p. 428.

86. Ibid., p. 429.

87. Scott, *Fourth Iowa*, p. 480; *OR*, ser. 1, vol. XLIX, pt. 1, p. 429.

88. M'Farland, "Battle of West Point," p. 354; Scott, *Fourth Iowa*, p. 481.

89. *OR*, ser. 1, vol. XLIX, pt. 1, pp. 429, 436; Edwards, "Battle of West Point," pp. 3, 5; W. J. Slatter, "Last Battle of the War," *Confederate Veteran*, vol. IV (November, 1896), p. 382.

90. *OR*, ser. 1, vol. XLIX, pt. 1, p. 429; Wilson, *Old Flag*, II:268.

91. *OR*, ser. 1, vol. XLIX, pt. 1, p. 429. Robert C. Black in *The Rail-*

roads of the Confederacy (Chapel Hill, N.C., 1952), pp. 287–290, wrote that the destruction at West Point was one of the most shattering blows to the Southern rail system delivered during the war.

CHAPTER VI

1. Hinricks Diary, April 15, 1865, Hinricks Mss.

2. Ibid., April 16.

3. Scott, *Fourth Iowa*, p. 488.

4. *OR*, ser. 1, vol. XLIX, pt. 1, p. 364; Wilson, *Old Flag*, II:265.

5. John H. Martin (comp.), *Prominent Incidents in the History of Columbus, Georgia, from its First Settlement in 1827, to Wilson's Raid, in 1865* (Columbus, 1874), II:120, 159, 174.

6. Albraugh and Simmons, *Confederate Arms*, p. 217; Diffee W. Standard, *Columbus, Georgia in the Confederacy* (New York, 1953), pp. 27–28; 33–34; Nancy Telfair, *A History of Columbus, Georgia, 1828–1928* (Columbus, 1929), p. 118.

7. Standard, *Columbus*, pp. 29–30; Telfair, *Columbus*, pp. 118–119.

8. Albraugh and Simmons, *Confederate Arms*, p. 226; Standard, *Columbus*, p. 39; Telfair, *Columbus*, p. 116; T. Conn Bryan, *Confederate Georgia* (Athens, 1953), pp. 102–104.

9. Standard, *Columbus*, pp. 37–39.

10. Standard, *Columbus*, p. 43; Albraugh and Simmons, *Confederate Arms*, pp. 211–212; *OR*, ser. 1, vol. XLIX, pt. 1, p. 487. Also see William Still, *Iron Afloat* (Nashville, 1971).

11. I. W. Avery, *The History of Georgia from 1850–1851* (New York, 1881), p. 297.

12. Telfair, *Columbus*. p. 128; *Columbus Sun*, April 13, 1865.

13. *Columbus Sun*, March 31, 1865.

14. Ibid., April 4, 1865.

15. Ibid., April 8, 1865.

16. Ibid., April 15, 1865.

17. Ibid., April 16, 1865.

18. Standard, *Columbus*, p. 26.

19. *OR*, ser. 1, vol. XXVIII, pt. 2, p. 553.

20. *Columbus Sun*, April 13, 1865.

21. Ibid., April 8, 1865.

22. Ibid., April 15, 1865.

23. Allen D. Candler (comp.), *The Confederate Records of the State of Georgia* (Atlanta, 1910), III:712.

24. *OR*, ser. 1, vol. XLIX, pt. 1, p. 364; Martin, *Incidents*, II:178.

25. Martin, *Incidents*, II:178; Columbus *Times*, March 28, 1865; W. W. Grant, "Recollections of the Last Battle," *Confederate Veteran*, vol. XXIII (April, 1915), p. 164.

26. *OR*, ser. 1, vol. XLIX, pt. 1, p. 474; Scott, *Fourth Iowa*, p. 485.

27. Telfair, *Columbus*, p. 294.

28 Standard, *Columbus*, p. 60.

29. Curry, *1st Ohio*, p. 223.

30. Ibid.

31. *OR*, ser. 1, vol. XLIX, pt. 1, p. 363; Wilson, *Old Flag*, II:260. Curry in *1st Ohio*, p. 221 says that the bridge caught fire from Union shots since the span was saturated with turpentine.

32. Scott, *Fourth Iowa*, p. 483.

33. *OR*, ser. 1, vol. XLIX, pt. 1, p. 363; Scott, *Fourth Iowa*, pp. 490, 492; Charles J. Swift, *The Last Battle of the Civil War* (Columbus, 1915), pp. 24–25. Also see Chapter III for "Upton's tactics," and Wilson, *Old Flag*, II:260–261.

34. *OR*, ser. 1, vol. XLIX, pt. 1, p. 474; Michie, *Upton*, p. 166.

35. *OR*, ser. 1, vol. XLIX, pt. 1, p. 363; Scott, *Fourth Iowa*, p. 492.

36. Wilson, *Old Flag*, II:260.

37. Martin, *Incidents*, II:179.

38. *OR*, ser. 1, vol. XLIX, pt. 1, p. 480; Wilson, *Old Flag*, II:260.

39. Hinricks Diary, April 16, 1865, Hinricks Mss.

40. Macon *Daily Telegraph and Confederate*, April 18, 1865; *OR*, ser. 1, vol. XLIX, pt. 1, p. 363; Wilson, *Old Flag*, II:261–262.

41. Wilson, *Old Flag*, II:264; Scott, *Fourth Iowa*, p. 496.

42. Hinricks Diary, April 16, 1865, Hinricks Mss.

43. Martin, *Incidents*, II:180.

44. Scott, *Fourth Iowa*, p. 499.

45. Scott, *Fourth Iowa*, p. 499; *OR*, ser. 1, vol. XLIX, pt. 1, p. 482.

46. JHW to Charles J. Swift, January 13, 1865, Wilson Mss., Library of Congress.

47. Wilson Diary, April 16, 1865, Wilson Mss., D.S.H.S.

48. Shipman Diary, April 16, 1865, Shipman Mss.; Montgomery, *Reminiscences*, p. 255.

49. Kate Cumming, *A Journal of Hospital Life in the Confederate Army of Tennessee from the Battle of Shiloh to the End of the War* (Louisville, 1866), p. 272.

50. Hinricks Diary, April 16, 1865, Hinricks Mss.

51. *OR*, ser. 1, vol. XLIX, pt. 2, p. 383; Scott, *Fourth Iowa*, p. 500.

52. This is what Wilson labeled his battle in JHW to Adam Badeau, April 22, 1865, Wilson Mss., Library of Congress. There is some conflict in the prisoner figure. They range from one thousand to fifteen hundred. *OR*, ser. 1, vol. XLIX, pt. 1, pp. 344, 364, 478; *Battles and Leaders*, IV:761.

53. *OR*, ser. 1, vol. XLIX, pt. 1, p. 398; Scott, *Fourth Iowa*, p. 491.

54. Montgomery, *Reminiscences*, p. 253.

55. Hinricks Diary, April 17, 1865, Hinricks Mss.

56. *OR*, ser. 1, vol. XLIX, pt. 1, pp. 364, 476; ser. 1, vol. XLII, pt. 2, p. 383; *Battles and Leaders*, IV:761; Martin, *Incidents*, II:180.

57. Hinricks Diary, April 17, 1865, Hinricks Mss.

58. Wilson, *Old Flag*, II:266. In JHW to Theodore F. Allen, 20 January 1908, Wilson Mss., Library of Congress. Wilson wrote that he had revisited Columbus with the First Army Corps before going to Cuba in the Spanish-American War. The town "looked quite natural, though somewhat diminished in size. The hills on the opposite side of the river also seemed somewhat lower than I should have said, speaking from recollection."

59. Wilson, *Old Flag*, II:266.

60. Ibid.

61. *OR*, ser. 1, vol. XLIX, pt. 1, pp. 365, 478; Scott, *Fourth Iowa*, pp. 502–503; Wilson, *Old Flag*, II:268; Still, *Iron Afloat*, p. 223; Etta B. Worsley, *Columbus on the Chattahoochee* (Columbus, 1951), appendix D.

62. Wilson, *Old Flag*, II:266.

63. JHW to John Dozier Pou, October 1, 1909, Wilson Mss., Library of Congress.

64. *OR*, ser. 1, vol. XLIX, pt. 1, p. 416; Martin, *Incidents*, II:182. Some places say 125,000 but in JHW to Adam Badeau, April 22, 1865, Wilson Mss., Library of Congress, the general says about 100,000 bales.

65. McGee, *72nd Indiana*, pp. 581–582.

66. Morse, *Personal Experiences*, p. 142.

67. Shipman Diary, April 16, 17, 1865, Shipman Mss.

68. *OR*, ser. 1, vol. XLIX, pt. 1, pp. 365, 487.

69. Ibid., ser. 1, vol. XLIX, pt. 2, p. 38.

70. Telfair, *Columbus*, p. 141.

71. Hinricks Diary, April 17, 1865, Hinricks Mss.

72. Montgomery, *Reminiscences*, p. 254; *OR*, ser. 1, vol. XLIX, pt. 1, p. 487.

73. Mitchell, "Field Notes," p. 192.

74. *OR*, ser. 1, vol. XLIX, pt. 1, p. 487.

75. *OR*, ser. 1, vol. XLIX, pt. 2, p. 383; Hinricks Diary, April 17, 1865, Hinricks Mss.

76. Longacre, *Union Stars*, p. 34.

77. Swift, *Last Battle* and Theodore F. Allen, "The Last Battle of the Civil War," *Journal of the United States Cavalry Association*, vol. XIII (April, 1908), p. 785 support the last battle theory. Accepting the Texas action at Palo Alto on May 13, 1865, as the war's last battle are: E. Merton Coulter, *The Confederate States of America, 1861–1865* (Baton Rouge, La., 1950), p. 563; Davis, *Rise and Fall*, II:698–699; R. A. Brock, ed., "The Last Battle of the War," *Southern Historical Society Papers*, vol. XXI (January, December, 1893), pp. 226–227; and Luther Conyer, "Last Battle of the War," *Southern Historical Society Papers*, vol. XXIV (January, December, 1896), pp. 309–315.

78. JHW to L. H. Chappell, April 7, 1865, Wilson Mss., Library of Congress.

CHAPTER VII

1. *OR*, ser. 1, vol. XLIX, pt. 1, p. 419.

2. See Chapter III for the action on April 1.

3. Andrews, *Campaign of Mobile*, pp. 260–261. Anderson, "Federal Raid," Anderson Mss., says this message never reached Tuscaloosa, p. 9.

4. *OR*, ser. 1, vol. XLIX, pt. 1, p. 421; Thomas P. Clinton, "Military Operations of Croxton," p. 451.

5. Ibid.

6. See Chapter III for McCook's movement to Scottsville.

7. Thatcher, *Hundred Battles*, p. 243.

8. *OR*, ser. 1, vol. XLIX, pt. 1, p. 421; Thomas P. Clinton, "Military Operations of Croxton," p. 451.

9. *OR*, ser. 1, vol. XLIX, pt. 1, p. 421; Thomas P. Clinton, "Military Operations of Croxton," p. 452–454; Anderson, "Federal Raid," Anderson Mss., p. 9.

10. Joseph Wheeler, *Alabama*, vol. VII in *Confederate Military History*, edited by Clement A. Evans (Atlanta, 1899), p. 252; *OR*, ser. 1, vol. XLIX, pt. 1, p. 505.

11. *OR*, ser. 1, vol. XLIX, pt. 1, p. 421; Matthew W. Clinton, *Tusca-*

loosa, Alabama: Its Early Days, 1816–1865 (Tuscaloosa, 1958), p. 161.

12. Mead, *Eighth Iowa*, p. 18.

13. Thomas P. Clinton, "Military Operations of Croxton," p. 453; *OR*, ser. 1, vol. XLIX, pt. 1, pp. 421, 505.

14. *OR*, ser. 1, vol. XLIX, pt. 1, pp. 421, 426, 505; Thomas P. Clinton, "Military Operations of Croxton," p. 453.

15. *OR*, ser. 1, vol. XLIX, pt. 1, p. 421.

16. Thomas P. Clinton, "Military Operations of Croxton," p. 452.

17. Thomas P. Clinton, "Military Operations of Croxton," p. 454; *OR*, ser. 1, vol. XLIX, pt. 1, p. 421.

18. *OR*, ser. 1, vol. XLIX, pt. 1, p. 419.

19. *Wilcox Banner* (Camden, Alabama), August 12, 1903; Henry, *"First with the Most,"* p. 453.

20. Thomas P. Clinton, "Military Operations of Croxton," p. 454.

21. Thomas P. Clinton, "Military Operations of Croxton," p. 454; Matthew Clinton, *Tuscaloosa*, p. 162.

22. *OR*, ser. 1, vol. XLIX, pt. 1, p. 421; Thomas P. Clinton, "Military Operations of Croxton," pp. 455–456; Anderson, "Federal Raid," Anderson Mss., p. 11. Anderson reported that the students marched to Marion where they heard of the Confederate surrender. They then disbanded and returned to the university.

23. *OR*, ser. 1, vol. XLIX, pt. 1, pp. 421, 426, 505.

24. Thatcher, *Hundred Battles*, pp. 367–368; Wilson, *Old Flag*, II: 206; Anderson, "Federal Raid," Anderson Mss., pp. 16–19.

25. Matthew Clinton, *Tuscaloosa*, p. 163; Owen, *The Story of Alabama*, II:429; Thomas P. Clinton, "Military Operations of Croxton," p. 457; Anderson, "Federal Raid," Anderson Mss., p. 11; *Alabama Beacon* (Greensboro), April 5, 1865.

26. *OR*, ser. 1, vol. XLIX, pt. 1, pp. 426, 505; Thomas P. Clinton, "Military Operations of Croxton," p. 457; Matthew Clinton, *Tuscaloosa*, p. 163.

27. Armes, *Story of Coal and Iron*, pp. 159, 186; Woodward, "Alabama Iron Manufacturing," p. 205.

28. Thomas Maxwell to Thomas McWhan, December 2, 1865, Anderson Mss.

29. John L. Hunnicutt, *Reconstruction in West Alabama: The Memoirs of John L. Hunnicutt*, ed. by William Stanley Hoole (Tuscaloosa, 1959), p. 40.

30. Ibid.

31. *OR*, ser. 1, vol. XLIX, pt. 1, pp. 421, 505; Thomas P. Clinton,

"Military Operations of Croxton," p. 460; Matthew Clinton, *Tusca-loosa*, p. 163.

32. *OR*, ser. 1, vol. XLIX, pt. 1, p. 426; Thomas P. Clinton, "Military Operations of Croxton," p. 454; Matthew Clinton, *Tuscaloosa*, p. 162; Anderson, "Federal Raid," Anderson Mss., pp. 1, 2, 4, 15.

33. Anderson, "Federal Raid," Anderson Mss., p. 14.

34. Muster Roll, Eighth Iowa Cavalry, Company K, Richard H. Mead Mss., Illinois State Historical Library, Springfield.

35. *OR*, ser. 1, vol. XLIX, pt. 1, p. 422; Jordan and Pryor, *Campaigns of Forrest*, p. 679; Thomas P. Clinton, "Military Operations of Croxton," p. 461.

36. Anderson, "Federal Raid," Anderson Mss., p. 20.

37. *OR*, ser. 1, vol. XLIX, pt. 1, p. 422; Thomas P. Clinton, "Military Operations of Croxton," p. 461.

38. Ibid.

39. *OR*, ser. 1, vol. XLIX, pt. 1, p. 422; ser. 1, vol. XLIX, pt. 2, p. 1207.

40. *OR*, ser. 1, vol. XLIX, pt. 1, p. 422; Thomas P. Clinton, "Military Operations of Croxton," p. 461; Andrews, *Campaign of Mobile*, p. 262; Thatcher, *Hundred Battles*, p. 358.

41. Thatcher, *Hundred Battles*, pp. 358–359; *OR*, ser. 1, vol. XLIX, pt. 1, p. 422.

42. Thomas P. Clinton, "Military Operations of Croxton," p. 462.

43. *OR*, ser. 1, vol. XLIX, pt. 2, p. 271; Andrews, *Campaign of Mobile*, p. 262.

44. *OR*, ser. 1, vol. XLIX, pt. 1, pp. 1217, 1220; Andrews, *Campaign of Mobile*, p. 264.

45. *OR*, ser. 1, vol. XLIX, pt. 1, pp. 422, 426–427; Thomas P. Clinton, "Military Operations of Croxton," p. 462.

46. *OR*, ser. 1, vol. XLIX, pt. 1, p. 422; Thomas P. Clinton, "Military Operations of Croxton," p. 462.

47. Hunnicutt, *Reconstruction*, p. 39.

48. *OR*, ser. 1, vol. XLIX, pt. 1, p. 422; Thomas P. Clinton, "Military Operations of Croxton," p. 462.

49. Andrews, *Campaign of Mobile*, p. 267.

50. Armes, *Coal and Iron in Alabama*, pp. 180–186; *OR*, ser. 1, vol. XLIX, pt. 1, p. 423.

51. Thatcher, *Hundred Battles*, p. 361.

52. Mead, *8th Iowa*, pp. 17–18.

53. *OR*, ser. 1, vol. XLIX, pt. 1, p. 423; Thatcher, *Hundred Battles*, pp. 243, 361.

CHAPTER VIII

1. Wilson, *Old Flag*, II:254.
2. *OR*, ser. 1, vol. XLIX, pt. 1, p. 442.
3. Ibid., pp. 352, 465.
4. Hinricks Diary, April 19, 1865, Hinricks Mss.
5. Sipes, *Seventh Pennsylvania*, pp. 163–164.
6. *OR*, ser. 1, vol. XLIX, pt. 1, p. 409; McGee, *72nd Indiana*, p. 583; Scott, *Fourth Iowa*, p. 508.
7. McGee, *72nd Indiana*, p. 484; *OR*, ser. 1, vol. XLIX, pt. 1, p. 442; Hinricks Diary, April 20, 1865, Hinricks Mss.
8. Cumming, *A Journal of Hospital Life*, p. 176; Scott, *Fourth Iowa*, p. 509.
9. Cumming, *A Journal of Hospital Life*, p. 274.
10. Hinricks Diary, April 20, 1865, Hinricks Mss.
11. *OR*, ser. 1, vol. XLIX, pt. 1, pp. 365, 442; Scott, *Fourth Iowa*, p. 509.
12. *OR*, ser. 1, vol. XLIX, pt. 1, pp. 443, 457; Wilson, *Old Flag*, II:272; Benefiel, *Sou-Ven-ir*, p. 41.
13. *Macon Daily Telegraph and Confederate*, March 22, 28, 1865.
14. Ibid., April 18, 1865.
15. Ibid.
16. Eliza Frances Andrews, *The Wartime Journal of a Georgia Girl*, ed. by Spencer King (Macon, 1960), pp. 148–149; George Mercer Diary, April 16, 1865, George Mercer Mss., Southern Historical Collection, University of North Carolina, Chapel Hill.
17. *Macon Daily Telegraph and Confederate*, April 13, 14, 17, 18, 19, 1865.
18. *Macon Daily Telegraph and Confederate*, April 18, 19, 1865; *Macon Telegraph and Messenger*, April 18, 20, 1875.
19. Andrews, *Journal*, pp. 152–155.
20. Swift, *Last Battle*, pp. 12.
21. *Macon Telegraph and Messenger*, April 20, 1875; *OR*, ser. 1, vol. XLIX, pt. 1, pp. 366, 459; John A. Cobb, "Civil War Incidents in Macon," *Georgia Historical Quarterly*, vol. VII, no. 3 (September, 1923), p. 283.
22. *OR*, ser. 1, vol. XLIX, pt. 1, pp. 366, 458–459; Wilson, *Old Flag*, II:277.
23. *OR*, ser. 1, vol. XLIX, pt. 1, pp. 458–459; Scott, *Fourth Iowa*,

p. 511; McGee, *72nd Indiana*, p. 586; *Macon Telegraph and Messenger*, April 20, 1875.

24. *OR*, ser. 1, vol. XLIX, pt. 1, p. 459; *Macon Telegraph and Messenger*, April 20, 1875; Wilson, *Old Flag*, II:279.

25. Wilson, *Old Flag*, II:279.

26. *OR*, ser. 1, vol. XLIX, pt. 1, pp. 352, 366; Wilson, *Old Flag*, II: 279–281; JHW to Adam Badeau, April 22, 1865, Wilson Mss., Library of Congress; Wilson Diary, April 20, 1865, Wilson Mss., D.S.H.S.

27. *OR*, ser. 1, vol. XLIX, pt. 1, p. 460; JHW to Adam Badeau, April 22, 1865, Wilson Mss., Library of Congress.

28. *Macon Daily Telegraph and Confederate*, April 20, 1865; *Macon Daily Telegraph*, May 4, 11, 1865.

29. *OR*, ser. 1, vol. XLIX, pt. 1, p. 352; Wilson Diary, April 21, 1865, Wilson Mss., D.S.H.S.

30. Atkins, "Wilson's Famous Raid," p. 7

31. Scott, *Fourth Iowa*, p. 521.

32. JHW to Adam Badeau, April 22, 1865, Wilson Mss., Library of Congress. Edward G. Longacre's biography of Wilson questions Wilson's friendship with Badeau. Longacre, without specific examples and without complete footnotes, alleges that Wilson became "childishly jealous" of Badeau. Yet after that evaluation of their relationship Longacre writes, "To his friend Badeau he wrote . . ." Longacre, *Union Stars*, pp. 108, 154, 214. The January–May, 1865 correspondence between the two men indicates warmth and confidence in the relationship. See: James P. Jones, ed., " 'Your Left Arm': James H. Wilson's Letters to Adam Badeau," *Civil War History*, vol. XX, no. 3 (September, 1966) , pp. 230–245.

33. Ibid., April 29, 1865.

34. Hinricks Diary, April 21, 1865, Hinricks Mss.

35. Wilson, *Old Flag*, II:284–285.

36. *Macon Telegraph and Messenger*, April 20, 1875.

37. Wilson Diary, April 22, 1865, Wilson Mss., D.S.H.S.

38. Thatcher, *Hundred Battles*, p. 361.

39. *OR*, ser. 1. vol. XLIX, pt. 1, p. 417.

40. Scott, *Fourth Iowa*, pp. 510–513.

41. Wilson, *Old Flag*, II:306.

42. Ibid., p. 407.

43. Curry, *1st Ohio*, pp. 248–249.

44. *OR*, ser. 1, vol. XLIX, pt. 2, pp. 601–602; Wilson, *Old Flag*, II: 312–313.

45. Wilson, *Old Flag*, II:319; *OR*, ser. 1, vol. XLIX, pt. 1, pp. 517–519.

46. Wilson, *Old Flag*, II:325.

47. Wilson, *Old Flag*, II:325; JHW to Julian Dickinson, August 16, 1910; JHW to Adam Badeau, May 13, 1865, Wilson Mss., Library of Congress.

48. Davis, *Rise and Fall*, pp. 700–701.

49. Hudson Strode, *Jefferson Davis* (New York, 1964), III:221; Davis, *Rise and Fall*, p. 702.

50. Wilson, *Old Flag*, II:330.

51. Wilson Diary, May 12, 1865, Wilson Mss., D.S.H.S.

52. *OR*, ser. 1, vol. XLIX, pt. 2, p. 732; JHW to Adam Badeau, May 12, 1865, Wilson Mss., Library of Congress.

53. *OR*, ser. 1, vol. XLIX, pt. 2, p. 743; JHW to Adam Badeau, May 13, 1865, Wilson Mss., Library of Congress.

54. Wilson, *Old Flag*, II:331.

55. Wilson, *Old Flag*, II:332; *OR*, ser. 1, vol. XLIX, pt. 2, pp. 721, 743.

56. *Harpers Weekly* (New York), June 17, 1865.

57. Strode, *Jefferson Davis*, III:224; Davis, *Rise and Fall*, p. 703.

58. *Macon Daily Telegraph*, May 14, 1865.

59. Mead, *8th Iowa*, p. 19.

60. Wilson, *Old Flag*, II:335.

61. Wilson, *Old Flag*, II:355; Davis, *Rise and Fall*, p. 703.

62. Wilson, *Old Flag*, II:357–359.

63. Ibid., pp. 339, 343.

64. Scott, *Fourth Iowa*, p. 530; *OR*, ser. 1, vol. XLIX, pt. 1, p. 379; ser. 1, vol. XLIX, pt. 2, p. 750.

65. JHW to Adam Badeau, May 12, 1865, Wilson Mss., Library of Congress.

66. *OR*, ser. 1, vol. XLIX, pt. 1, pp. 369, 379; Scott, *Fourth Iowa*, p. 530.

67. JHW to Adam Badeau, May 13, 1865, Wilson Mss., Library of Congress.

68. *OR*, ser. 1, vol. XLIX, pt. 2, p. 800; Ovid L. Futch, *History of Andersonville Prison* (Gainesville, Fla., 1968), p. 117.

69. *OR*, ser. 1, vol. XLIX, pt. 1, p. 379; Wilson Diary, May 7, 1865, Wilson Mss., D.S.H.S.

70. Michie, *Upton*, p. 173.

71. *OR*, ser. 1, vol. XLIX, pt. 2, pp. 601–602.

72. Ellen Call Long, *Florida Breezes; or Florida, New and Old* (Gainesville, Fla., 1962), pp. 380–381.

73. *OR*, ser. 1, vol. XLIX, pt. 2, p. 944; *Florida Union* (Jacksonville), May 27, 1865.

74. Wilson Diary, May 5, 1865, Wilson Mss., D.S.H.S.

75. Wilson Diary, May 5, 6, 1865, Wilson Mss., D.S.H.S.; Longacre, *Union Stars*, pp. 226, 227.

76. JHW to Joseph E. Brown, May 3, 9, 1865, Joseph E. Brown Mss., Duke University Library, Durham, North Carolina; Wilson Diary, May 9, 1865, Wilson Mss., D.S.H.S.

77. *OR*, ser. 1, vol. XLIX, pt. 1, p. 365; Wilson, *Old Flag*, II:298.

78. James C. Bonner, ed., *Journal of a Milledgeville Girl, 1861–1867* (Athens, Ga., 1964), p. 79.

79. *Macon Daily Telegraph*, May 4, 1865.

80. Longacre, *Union Stars*, pp. 219–220.

81. Wilson, *Old Flag*, II:300.

82. Hinricks Diary, April 21, 1865, Hinricks Mss.

83. Cumming, *A Journal of Hospital Life*, p. 279.

84. Shipman Diary, April 24, 25, 27, 1865, Shipman Mss.; Hinricks Diary, April 22, 1865, Hinricks Mss.

85. Longacre, *Union Stars*, p. 218.

86. *Macon Daily Telegraph*, May 21, 24, 1865.

87. Ibid., May 24, 1865.

88. *Chicago Board of Trade Battery*, p. 48; *OR*, ser. 1, vol. XLIX, pt. 1, p. 379.

89. Michie, *Upton*, p. 174.

90. *OR*, ser. 1, vol. XLIX, pt. 2, p. 1059.

91. Ibid., ser. 1, vol. XLIX, pt. 1, p. 369.

92. Ibid.

93. Robert C. Black, *Railroads of the Confederacy* (Chapel Hill, N. C., 1952), pp. 287–290.

94. There were seventeen iron manufacturies in the state in 1865. See: Woodward, "Alabama Iron Manufacturing," pp. 54, 207. Also see: Robert H. McKenzie, "Reconstruction of the Alabama Iron Industry, 1865–1880," *Alabama Review*, vol. XXV, no. 3 (July, 1972), pp. 178–191. McKenzie emphasized, in his recent study, that Wilson's destruction, while complete, was not the major factor in the slowness of the industry's recovery. The raiders did not have "time nor energy" to

completely dismantle the works. The financial chaos following the war's end, McKenzie felt, was more dislocating, in the long run, than Wilson's wreckers.

95. *OR*, ser. 1, vol. XLIX, pt. 1, p. 369.

96. Davis, *Rise and Fall*, p. 697.

97. Clifford Dowdey, *The Land They Fought For* (New York, 1955), p. 408.

98. JHW to James M. Swales, February 2, 1910, Wilson Mss., Library of Congress.

99. JHW to Charles Francis Adams, November 30, 1901; September 15, 1902; February 22, 1908, Wilson Mss., Library of Congress.

100. A. R. Chaffee, "James Harrison Wilson, Cavalryman," *The Cavalry Journal*, vol. XXXIV, no. 140 (July, 1925), pp. 271, 289.

101. Taylor, *Destruction and Reconstruction*, p. 269.

102. Wilson, *Old Flag*, II:296; Ulysses S. Grant, *Personal Memoirs of U. S. Grant* (New York, 1895), II:368; William T. Sherman, *Memoirs of General W. T. Sherman* (New York, 1875), II:345, 368.

103. G. F. R. Henderson, *The Civil War: A Soldier's View*, ed. by Jay Luvaas (Chicago, 1958), p. 220.

104. Johnson and Bill, *Horsemen*, pp. 3, 202; Allan Nevins, *War for the Union* (New York, 1971), IV:277.

105. Herr and Wallace, *U.S. Cavalry*, pp. 138, 139; Bruce Catton, *This Hallowed Ground* (New York, 1956), pp. 458, 467.

106. Longacre, *Union Stars*, p. 15.

Critical Essay on Sources

I. PRIMARY SOURCES

Manuscripts

Much of this study is based on unpublished manuscripts. The James Harrison Wilson Papers of the Library of Congress were indispensable. General Wilson lived until 1925, and his correspondence covers a sixty-year period. He exchanged letters with a widely varied group and often commented on cavalry theory in general and his own application of mounted strategy and tactics in particular. Great insight into Wilson's mind was found in a series of letters written in the spring of 1865 to a friend, Adam Badeau, Grant's military secretary. Some of these letters have been published (James P. Jones, ed., " 'Your Left Arm': James H. Wilson's Letters to Adam Badeau," *Civil War History*, xx, no. 3, September, 1966, 230–245), and those and others, still unpublished, were major sources for this work. The James H. Wilson Diary in the Delaware State Historical Society, Wilmington, was also a useful source. The general's daily entries are brief, and much of the diary was directly incorporated into his autobiography published after the war; nevertheless, a few comments made in the diary are available nowhere else.

Two long diaries provided an excellent day-to-day picture of the entire course of the raid. Capt. Charles F. Hinricks, an inquisitive German-American, rode with the Tenth Missouri and commented daily on everything from the grimness of battle to the beauty of a waterfall. His diary is in the Western Historical Manuscripts Collection, University of Missouri, Columbia. Maj. Stephen V. Shipman, a Wisconsin architect, served with the First Wisconsin Cavalry. Shipman criticized the enemy and his own commander alike. His comments on the cities and towns through which the campaign rolled are as good as those in any Civil War diary. Major Shipman's diary is in the Wisconsin State Historical Society, Madison. Not as complete as the Hinricks and Shipman accounts is that of the 123rd Illinois' Will Pepper. Pepper's diary in the Illinois State Historical Library, Springfield, is excellent for the period of preparation, with scattered later entries from Selma and Montgomery. But Sgt. Pepper's diary is particularly important in supplying a view from the ranks. The brief lapse of discipline in Wilson's corps in March is all the more graphic when seen through Pepper's eyes.

Confederate resistance to Wilson is to be seen in the Diary of Ellen Blue of Montgomery. Miss Blue's diary, in the possession of Mrs. Charles M. Smith, Jr., of Montgomery, was made available to the author by Milo Howard, director of the Alabama Department of Archives and History. It reflects the sadness and hatred involved in the fall of the Confederacy's first capital and the entry of Union troops. The Sarah Ellen Phillips Papers in the Southern Historical Collection, University of North Carolina, Chapel Hill, also afford a picture of the hatred of the Union raiders. Miss Phillips's memoir of the fall of Selma, although distorted and inaccurate, clearly delineates the depths of the scars caused by the war.

Also valuable was the folder marked "Raids-Wilson," in the Alabama Department of Archives and History, Montgomery, and Scrapbooks I and II in the Carnegie Library, Selma.

Documents

Any study of a Civil War campaign is greatly indebted to the U.S. Department of War, *The War of the Rebellion: A Compilation of the Official Records of the Union and Confederate Armies* (Washington, 1880–1901). Volume XLIX, parts 1 and 2 of series 1 contains the dispatches, reports, and orders of the months of preparation, the raid itself, and the dispersal of the corps. Also found there are the reports and dispatches pertaining to the capture of Jefferson Davis and other Confederate leaders. The *Atlas to Accompany the Official Records of Union and Confederate Armies of the War of the Rebellion* (Washington, 1891–1895), contains eight maps and diagrams of various phases of the campaign.

Newspapers

Newspapers have been used chiefly as a source to clarify the picture of Confederate resistance. It was a desperate time for the shrinking Confederacy, and newspapers urged Alabamans and Georgians to fight to the last. Useful Alabama journals were the *Alabama Beacon* (Greensboro); *Autauga Citizen* (Prattville); *Clarke County Journal* (Grove Hill); *Eutaw Whig and Observer*; *Southern Advertiser* (Troy); and *Southwestern Baptist* (Tuskegee). Also useful were the Montgomery and Selma presses. The *Montgomery Advertiser* and the *Montgomery Daily Mail* and the *Selma Evening* and *Morning Reporter* reflected the South's desperation of 1865.

Several Georgia newspapers were also consulted. The *Columbus Times, Columbus Daily Enquirer*, and *Columbus Daily* and *Weekly Sun* called for resistance. In Macon the transition from division to reunion can be seen in the *Macon Daily Telegraph and Confederate* and its successor the *Macon Daily Telegraph*.

A curious Civil War journalistic phenomenon was the *Memphis Appeal*. Called the "Moving *Appeal*," because of its flight from the Yankee tide, the journal was published in both Alabama and Georgia. The despair of the dying nation, mingled with its futile hopes, can be seen in its columns.

Books

The best account of Wilson's Raid is to be found in the general's own extremely readable autobiography, *Under the Old Flag*, 2 vols. (New York, 1912). Wilson wrote clearly and with vigor of his long military career which included the Spanish-American War and the Boxer Rebellion as well as the Civil War. The two volumes are among the finest Civil War reminiscences and are vital to any reconstruction of his 1865 ride across Alabama and Georgia.

Union regimental histories poured off the presses in the half-century after Appomattox. They ranged from well-written, highly accurate accounts to biased and misleading cases of special pleading. The former can add a dimension of breadth to any military study since the story of the enlisted man can be told so well from biographies of the Union Army's basic unit—the regiment. Four of Wilson's regiments have excellent histories. They are W. L. Curry, *Four Years in the Saddle: History of the First Regiment Ohio Volunteer Cavalry* (Columbus, Ohio, 1898); Benjamin F. McGee, *History of the 72nd Indiana Volunteer Infantry of the Mounted Lightning Brigade* (Lafayette, Indiana, 1882); William F. Scott, *The Story of a Cavalry Regiment: The Career of the Fourth Iowa Veteran Volunteers, from Kansas to Georgia, 1861–1865* (New York, 1893); and William Sipes, *The Seventh Pennsylvania's Veteran Volunteer Cavalry: Its Record, Reminiscences and Roster* (Pittsville, Pennsylvania, n.d.). Other regimental memoirs of assistance were: Cloyd Bryner, *Bugle Echoes: The Story of Illinois' 47th* (Springfield, Illinois, 1905); *Historical Sketch of the Chicago Board of Trade Battery, Horse Artillery, Illinois Volunteers* (Chicago, 1902); Homer Mead, *The Eighth Iowa Cavalry in the Civil War* (Carthage, Illinois, n.d.); and Marshall P. Thatcher, *A Hundred Battles in the West: St. Louis to Atlanta, 1861–1865* (Detroit, 1884).

Several men who rode with Wilson published reminiscences after the war. Two, James Larson, *Sergeant Larson, 4th Cavalry* (San Antonio, Texas, 1935), and F. W. Morse, *Personal Experiences of the War of the Great Rebellion* (Albany, New York, 1866), are excellent. Sgt. Larson was an acute observer who wrote with engaging humor.

Two fine sources of material on Wilson's best-known brigadier, Emory Upton, are Peter Michie, ed., *The Life and Letters of Emory Upton* (New York, 1885), and Stephen Ambrose, *Upton and the Army* (Baton Rouge, 1964).

The horsemen who rode with Forrest in his vain effort to stop Wilson have had their memoirists. John M. Hubbard's *Notes of a Private* (St. Louis, 1913); John M. Morton's *The Artillery of Nathan Bedford Forrest's Cavalry* (Nashville, Tennessee, 1909); John P. Young's *The Seventh Tennessee Cavalry, Confederate* (Nashville, Tennessee, 1890); and Robert S. Henry's edition of *As They Saw Forrest: Some Recollections and Comments of Contemporaries* (Jackson, Tennessee, 1956) are valuable in outlining the troubles the Confederate cavalry genius had in putting a force in the field. Of particular value is Frank A. Montgomery, *Reminiscences of a Mississippian in Peace and War* (Cincinnati, 1901). Colonel Montgomery fought Wilson and then traveled with the Union column as a prisoner after his capture at Selma. The despair of those who had fought so well only to see the "lost cause" die is a theme of this memoir.

Richard Taylor's *Destruction and Reconstruction: Personal Experiences of the Late War* (New York, 1955), edited by Richard B. Harwell, is of great value for an account of Confederate resistance in Alabama, and Jefferson Davis's *The Rise and Fall of the Confederate Government* (New York, 1958) supplies the best picture of the Confederate leader's intentions to fight on in the deep South. The latter is, of course, invaluable in recreating the pursuit and capture of the Davis party.

The journals of two Southern women portray the chaos and fear in Georgia at war's end. They are Eliza Frances Andrews, *The Wartime Journal of a Georgia Girl* (Macon, 1960), edited by Spencer King; and Kate Cumming, *A Journal of Hospital Life in the Confederate Army of Tennessee: from the Battle of Shiloh to the End of the War* (Louisville, 1866).

Articles

Six primary articles are more valuable than many books as sources for the raid. Edward Smith Atkins, "Wilson's Famous Raid," *The National Tribune*, Washington, D.C., June 2, 1910; E. N. Gilpin, "The Last Campaign—A Cavalryman's Journal," *Journal of the United States Cavalry Association*, XIII (April, 1908), 617–675; and Charles D. Mitchell, "Field Notes on the Selma Campaign," *Sketches of War History, 1861–1865, Papers Read Before the Ohio Commandery of the Loyal Legion of the United States, 1903–1908*, VI, ed. Theodore F. Allen et al. (Cincinnati, 1908), are excellent. The two papers of Capt. Lewis Hosea, "The Campaign of Selma," *Sketches of War History, Papers Read before the Ohio Commandery of the Loyal Legion of the United States*, I (Cincinnati, 1888), and "Some Side Lights on the War for the Union," *Papers Read before the Ohio Commandery of the Loyal Legion of the United States* (Cleveland, 1912), are by Wilson's reliable staff officer. They are among the best-known sources on the raid and on General Forrest. Hosea saw "That Devil Forrest" twice, and one of the most revealing portraits of the legendary Forrest came from the Yankee captain. It was Hosea who reported Forrest's "first with the most" statement.

"The Journal of Sarah G. Follansbee," edited by Virginia K. Jones, in the *Alabama Historical Quarterly*, XXVIII, nos. 3 and 4 (Fall and Winter, 1965), 213–239, was of special aid. Miss Follansbee, a Northerner who lived in Montgomery, watched the blue-coats ride into the city with some pride in the victory of the Union and a great deal of sorrow for the trials of her Alabama friends.

II. SECONDARY SOURCES

Books

First among the secondary sources is Edward G. Longacre's new biography of Wilson, *From Union Stars to Top Hat: A Biography of the Extraordinary General James Harrison Wilson* (Harrisburg, Pennsylvania, 1972). The biographer traces the general's entire career and places great emphasis on Wilson's character. Longacre devotes twenty pages to the 1865 raid. Longacre's book is not footnoted fully, and some of his evaluations of Wilson's character are subject to challenge. Overall, however, the work affords a valuable picture of the "boy general" who led the Civil War's most successful mounted campaign.

Secondary sources added greatly to an understanding of the history of cavalry in the United States. John K. Herr and Edward S. Wallace, *The Story of the U.S. Cavalry* (Boston, 1953), and James R. Johnson and Alfred H. Bill, *Horsemen, Blue and Gray* (New York, 1960), were very general, but useful. Dee Alexander Brown, *Grierson's Raid* (Urbana, Illinois, 1954), though about a very different kind of cavalry mission, is a brilliant study and was a great aid. Fairfax Downey, *Clash of Cavalry: The Battle of Brandy Station, June 9, 1863* (New York, 1959), closely studies conflicting theories of cavalry operations and adds much on the myth and lore of Civil War horsemen. Fred A. Shannon, *The Organization and Administration of the Union Army, 1861–1865*, 2 vols. (Cleveland, 1928), provided information on the ideal composition of a cavalry unit.

Weaponry is a highly specialized subject, and three such studies were consulted. William Albraugh and Edward N. Simmons, *Confederate Arms* (Harrisburg, Pennsylvania, 1957), was informative on the weapons of Wilson's opponents, as well as on the kinds of weapons the raiders destroyed. Harold Peterson, *The American Sword, 1775–1945* (New Hope, Pennsylvania, 1954), and Arcadi Gluckman, *United States Muskets, Rifles and Carbines* (Buffalo, New York, 1948), helped in understanding the raiders' armament. Gluckman's section on the Spencer Carbine was especially helpful.

The thoroughness of Wilson's destruction was outlined in Ethel Armes, *The Story of Coal and Iron in Alabama* (Birmingham, 1910), and in Robert C. Black, *The Railroads of the Confederacy* (Chapel Hill, 1952). Wilson's Raid was conducted simultaneously with Gen. E. R. S. Canby's assault on Mobile. C. C. Andrews, *History of the Campaign of Mobile, Including the Cooperative Operations of General Wilson's Cavalry in Alabama* (New York, 1867) covered both these Union strikes.

Biographies of Forrest and studies of various aspects of his career are numerous. From five works a picture emerged of the tough fighter Wilson faced. These works are Robert S. Henry, *"First with the Most" Forrest* (Indianapolis, 1944) ; Thomas Jordan and J. P. Pryor, *The Campaigns of Lieutenant-General N. B. Forrest and of Forrest's Cavalry* (New Orleans, 1868) ; Andrew N. Lytle, *Bedford Forrest and His Critter Company* (New York, 1931) ; and John A. Wyeth, *Life of Lieutenant General Nathan Bedford Forrest* (New York, 1899) . An excellent coverage of Forrest's career in the wider context of the western war is to be found in Thomas L. Connelly, *Autumn of Glory: The Army of Tennessee, 1862–1865* (Baton Rouge, 1971) .

The two states Wilson invaded have been amply studied. For Alabama, Marie Bankhead Owen, *The Story of Alabama: A History of the State* (New York, 1949) ; Willis Brewer, *Alabama: Her History, Resources, War Record, and Public Men* (Montgomery, 1872) ; Walter L. Fleming, *Civil War and Reconstruction in Alabama* (New York, 1905) ; John Hardy, *Selma: Her Institutions and Her Men* (Selma, 1879) ; Walter M. Jackson, *The Story of Selma* (Birmingham, 1954) ; Albert B. Moore, *History of Alabama* (Tuscaloosa, 1934) , were used.

Consulted for Georgia were T. Conn Bryan, *Confederate Georgia* (Athens, 1953) ; I. W. Avery, *The History of Georgia from 1850–1881* (New York, 1881) ; Diffee W. Standard, *Columbus, Georgia in the Confederacy* (New York, 1953) ; and Nancy Telfair, *A History of Columbus, Georgia, 1828–1928* (Columbus, 1929) .

Finally, several general studies of the war were used for views of the place of Wilson's Raid in the Civil War. Four were used in the final chapter. Clifford Dowdey, *The Land They Fought For*

(New York, 1955), saw Wilson's force as a "Tartar Horde" heedlessly ravaging the land. Allan Nevins, *The War for the Union*, IV (New York, 1971), praised the young major general; and Bruce Catton, *This Hallowed Ground* (New York, 1956), likened the raiders to a twentieth-century blitzkrieg moved by horses instead of tanks. G. F. R. Henderson in *The Civil War: A Soldier's View*, edited by Jay Luvaas (Chicago, 1958), favorably compared the Civil War's mounted rifleman to his European contemporary and described Wilson's movement as the classic operation by mounted riflemen.

Articles

Only five secondary articles were of much value in the study. Wilson's trail of destruction is examined and its lasting effect on the economy of Alabama discussed in three excellent articles in the *Alabama Review*. They are Robert H. McKenzie, "Reconstruction of the Alabama Iron Industry, 1865–1880," *Alabama Review*, XXV, no. 3 (July, 1972), 178–191; Frank E. Vandiver, "The Shelby Iron Company in the Civil War: A Study of Confederate Industry," *Alabama Review*, I, nos. 1, 2, and 3 (January, April, and July, 1948), 12–27; 111–128; 203–218; and Joseph H. Woodward, "Alabama Iron Manufacturing," *Alabama Review*, VII, no. 3 (July, 1954), 199–208.

Particularly helpful in following the meanderings of Gen. John T. Croxton's "Lost Brigade" was Thomas P. Clinton, "The Military Operations of General John T. Croxton in West Alabama, 1865," *Transactions of the Alabama Historical Society*, Thomas M. Owen, ed., IV (1904), 449–463.

A. R. Chaffee, a U.S. cavalry major in 1925, offered a eulogy of Wilson in "James Harrison Wilson, Cavalryman," *The Cavalry Journal*, XXXIV, no. 140 (July, 1925), 271–289, published just after the general's death. The article indicated that Wilson's strategy and tactics were still being studied sixty years after his horsemen rode from the Tennessee River to Macon.

Bibliography

I. PRIMARY MATERIALS

Manuscripts

Anderson Mss. Papers of James Anderson, University of Alabama Library, Tuscaloosa.

Blue Mss. Diary of Ellen Blue, in possession of Mrs. Charles M. Smith, Jr., Montgomery, Alabama.

Brown Mss. "Narrative of Personal Experiences in the Battle of Selma," unpublished typescript by Charles O. Brown in Illinois State Historical Library, Springfield.

Brown Mss. Papers of Joseph E. Brown, Duke University Library, Durham, North Carolina.

Hinricks Mss. Diary of Charles F. Hinricks, Western Historical Manuscripts Collection, University of Missouri, Columbia.

Mead Mss. Papers of Richard H. Mead, Illinois State Historical Library, Springfield.

Mercer Mss. Diary of George Mercer, Southern Historical Collection, University of North Carolina, Chapel Hill.

Newhall Mss. Papers of Henry M. Newhall, Illinois State Historical Library, Springfield.

Pepper Mss. Diary of William Pepper, Illinois State Historical Library, Springfield.

Phillips Mss. Papers of Sarah Ellen Phillips, Southern Historical Collection, University of North Carolina, Chapel Hill.

"Raids–Wilson" Folder, Alabama Department of Archives and History, Montgomery. Annie Coombs's Scrapbook, 1866.

"Raids–Wilson" Folder, Alabama Department of Archives and History, Montgomery. "The Sacking of Selma," Speech of Governor Lewis Parsons, New York, n.d.

Scrapbook no. i, Wilson's Raid, Carnegie Library, Selma, Alabama.

Scrapbook no. ii, Wilson's Raid, Carnegie Library, Selma, Alabama.

Shipman Mss. Diary of Stephen V. Shipman, Wisconsin State Historical Society, Madison.

Wilson Mss. Diary of James Harrison Wilson, Delaware State Historical Society, Wilmington.

Wilson Mss. Papers of James Harrison Wilson, Library of Congress.

Government Documents

Georgia. *The Confederate Records of the State of Georgia.* Allen D. Candler (comp.). 3 vols. Atlanta: Charles P. Byrd, 1910.

U.S., Bureau of the Census. *Eighth Census of the United States: 1860.* Washington: Government Printing Office, 1864.

U.S., War Department. *Atlas to Accompany the Official Records of the Union and Confederate Armies.* 2 vols. Washington: Government Printing Office, 1891–1895.

U.S., War Department. *The War of the Rebellion: A Compilation of the Official Records of the Union and Confederate Armies.* 129 vols. Washington: Government Printing Office, 1880–1901.

Newspapers and Periodicals

Alabama Beacon, Greensboro, Alabama.
Atlanta Constitution, Atlanta, Georgia.
Autauga Citizen, Prattville, Alabama.
Clarke County Journal, Grove Hill, Alabama.
Columbus Daily Enquirer, Columbus, Georgia.
Columbus Daily Sun, Columbus, Georgia.
Columbus Times, Columbus, Georgia.

Eutaw Whig and Observer, Eutaw, Alabama.
Florida Union, Jacksonville, Florida.
Harpers Weekly, New York, New York.
Jacksonville Republican, Jacksonville, Alabama.
Macon Daily Telegraph, Macon, Georgia.
Macon Daily Telegraph and Confederate, Macon, Georgia.
Macon Telegraph and Messenger, Macon, Georgia.
Memphis Appeal, Memphis, Tennessee. Publishing in 1865 in
   Montgomery and Columbus.
Montgomery Advertiser, Montgomery, Alabama.
Montgomery Daily Mail, Montgomery, Alabama.
New York Times, New York, New York.
New York Tribune, New York, New York.
Selma Evening Reporter, Selma, Alabama.
Selma Morning Reporter, Selma, Alabama.
Southern Advertiser, Troy, Alabama.
Southwestern Baptist, Tuskegee, Alabama.
Wilcox Banner, Camden, Alabama.

Books

Andrews, Eliza Frances. *The Wartime Journal of a Georgia Girl.*
   Edited by Spencer King. Macon: Ardivan Press, 1960.
Benefiel, W. H. H. *Sou-Ven-ir: History of the 17th Regiment Indi-
   ana Volunteer Infantry During the Civil War from 1861 to 1865.*
   n.p.: n.d., 1913.
Bonner, James C., ed., *Journal of a Milledgeville Girl, 1861–1867.*
   Athens: University of Georgia Press, 1964.
Bryner, Cloyd. *Bugle Echoes: The Story of Illinois' 47th.* Spring-
   field: Phillips Brothers, 1905.
Cate, Wirt A. *Two Soldiers.* Chapel Hill: University of North Car-
   olina Press, 1938.
Clark, James S. *Life in the Middle West: Reminiscences of James
   S. Clark.* Chicago: Advance Publishing, n.d.
Cumming, Kate. *A Journal of Hospital Life in the Confederate*

Army of Tennessee from the Battle of Shiloh to the End of the War. Louisville: John P. Norton, 1866.

Curry, W. L. *Four Years in the Saddle: History of the First Regiment Ohio Volunteer Cavalry.* Columbus, Ohio: Champlin Printing, 1898.

Davis, Jefferson. *The Rise and Fall of the Confederate Government.* New York: Thomas Yoseloff, 1958.

Dornblaser, Thomas F. *Saber Strokes of the Pennsylvania Dragoons in the War of 1861–1865, Interspersed with Personal Reminiscences.* Philadelphia: Lutheran Publication Society, 1884.

Grant, Ulysses S. *Personal Memoirs of U. S. Grant.* 2 vols., 2nd ed. New York: Century, 1895.

Historical Sketch of the Chicago Board of Trade Battery, Horse Artillery, Illinois Volunteers. Chicago: n.p., 1902.

Henry, Robert S., ed., *As They Saw Forrest: Some Recollections and Comments of Contemporaries.* Jackson, Tenn.: McCowat, Mercer Press, 1956.

Hubbard, John M. *Notes of a Private.* St. Louis: Nixon–Jones Printing, 1913.

Hunnicutt, John L. *Reconstruction in West Alabama: The Memoirs of John L. Hunnicutt.* Edited by William Stanley Hoole. Tuscaloosa: Confederate Publishing, 1959.

Jackson, Joseph O., ed., *"Some of the Boys": The Civil War Letters of Isaac Jackson, 1862–1865.* Carbondale: Southern Illinois University Press, 1960.

Johnson, Robert U., and Buel, Clarence C., eds., *Battles and Leaders of the Civil War.* 4 vols. New York: Century, 1887–1888.

Larson, James. *Sergeant Larson, 4th Cavalry.* San Antonio: Southern Literary Institute, 1935.

Long, Ellen Call. *Florida Breezes; or Florida, New and Old.* Gainesville: University of Florida Press, 1962.

Martin, John H., comp., *Prominent Incidents in the History of Columbus, Georgia from Its Earliest Settlements in 1827, to*

Wilson's Raid, in 1865. 2 vols. Columbus: Thomas Gilbert, 1874.

McGee, Benjamin F. *History of the 72nd Indiana Volunteer Infantry of the Mounted Lightning Brigade.* Lafayette, Ind.: S. Vater, 1882.

Mead, Homer. *The Eighth Iowa Cavalry in the Civil War.* Carthage, Ill.: S. C. Davidson, n.d.

Michie, Peter, ed. *The Life and Letters of Emory Upton.* New York: D. Appleton, 1885.

Montgomery, Frank A. *Reminiscences of a Mississippian in Peace and War.* Cincinnati: Robert Clarke, 1901.

Morse, F. W. *Personal Experiences of the War of the Great Rebellion.* Albany, N.Y.: Munsell Printer, 1866.

Morton, John W. *The Artillery of Nathan Bedford Forrest's Cavalry.* Nashville, Tenn.: Methodist Episcopal Church, 1909.

Rankin, R. C. *History of the 7th Ohio Volunteer Cavalry.* Ripley, Ohio: J. C. Newcomb, 1881.

Scott, William F. *The Story of a Cavalry Regiment: The Career of the Fourth Iowa Veteran Volunteers, from Kansas to Georgia, 1861–1865.* New York: G. P. Putnam's, 1893.

Sherman, William T. *Memoirs of General W. T. Sherman.* 2 vols. 1st ed. New York: D. Appleton, 1875.

Sipes, William. *The Seventh Pennsylvania's Veteran Volunteer Cavalry: Its Records, Reminiscences, and Roster.* Pottsville, Pa.: Miners' Journal Printer, n.d.

Taylor, Richard. *Destruction and Reconstruction: Personal Experiences of the Late War.* Edited by Richard B. Harwell. New York: Longmans, Green, 1955.

Thatcher, Marshall P. *A Hundred Battles in the West, St. Louis to Atlanta, 1861–1865.* Detroit: L. F. Kilroy, 1884.

Vale, Joseph G. *Minty and the Cavalry: A History of Cavalry Campaigns in the Western Armies.* Harrisburg, Pa.: Edwin K. Meyers, 1886.

Wilson, James Harrison. *Under the Old Flag.* 2 vols. New York: D. Appleton, 1912.

Young, John P. *The Seventh Tennessee Cavalry, Confederate.* Nashville, Tenn.: Publishing House of the Methodist Episcopal Church, 1890.

Articles

Atkins, Edward Smith. "Wilson's Famous Raid." *National Tribune,* June 2, 1910.

Castleberry, D. B. "Last Review of Forrest's Cavalry." *Confederate Veteran* xxiv (July, 1916) : 301–308.

Chalmers, James R. "Forrest and His Campaigns." *Southern Historical Society Papers* vii (October, 1879) : 451–487.

Coffman, Edward M., ed. "Memoirs of Hylan B. Lyon, Brigadier General, C.S.A." *Tennessee Historical Quarterly* xviii, no. 1 (March, 1959) : 35–54.

Cook, V. Y. "Forrest's Efforts to Save Selma." *Confederate Veteran* xxvi (April, 1918) : 151–152.

Faulkner, E. C. "The Last Time I Saw General Forrest." *Confederate Veteran* v (February, 1897) :83.

Gilpin, E. N. "The Last Campaign—A Cavalryman's Journal." *Journal of the United States Cavalry Association* xiii (April, 1908) : 617–675.

Grant, W. W. "Recollections of the Last Battle." *Confederate Veteran* xxiii (April, 1915) : 163–165.

Hosea, Lewis M. "The Campaign of Selma." *Sketches of War History, 1861–1865, Papers Read Before the Ohio Commandery of the Military Order of the Loyal Legion of the United States* i. Cincinnati, 1888: 77–95.

———. "Some Side Lights on the War for the Union." *Papers Read Before the Ohio Commandery of the Military Order of the Loyal Legion of the United States.* Cleveland, Ohio, 1912: 1–20.

Jones, Virginia K., ed. "The Journal of Sarah G. Follansbee." *Ala-*

bama Historical Quarterly XXVIII, nos. 3 and 4 (Fall and Winter, 1965): 213–239.

Landis, C. E. "The Siege and Fall of Selma, Alabama." *Confederate Veteran* XXI (March, 1923) : 96–98.

M'Farland, L. B. "The Battle of West Point." *Confederate Veteran* XXIII (August, 1915) : 353–355.

Mitchell, Charles D. "Field Notes on the Selma Campaign." *Sketches of War History, 1861–1865, Papers Read Before the Ohio Commandery of the Loyal Legion of the United States.* Cincinnati, Ohio, 1908.

Ross, W. F. "Lack of Co–operation at Selma, 1865." *Confederate Veteran* XXVI (July, 1918) : 3–22.

Slatter, W. J. "Last Battle of the War." *Confederate Veteran* IV (November, 1896) : 308–312.

II. SECONDARY MATERIALS

Books

Albraugh, William and Simmons, Edward N. *Confederate Arms.* Harrisburg, Penn.: Stackpole, 1957.

Ambrose, Stephen. *Upton and the Army.* Baton Rouge: Louisiana State University Press, 1964.

Andrews, C. C. *History of the Campaign of Mobile, Including the Cooperative Operations of General Wilson's Cavalry in Alabama.* New York: D. Van Nostrand, 1867.

Armes, Ethel. *The Story of Coal and Iron in Alabama.* Birmingham: Chamber of Commerce, 1910.

Avery, I. W. *The History of Georgia from 1850–1881.* New York: Brown and Derby, 1881.

Black, Robert C. *Railroads of the Confederacy.* Chapel Hill: University of North Carolina Press, 1952.

Brewer, Willis. *Alabama: Her History, Resources, War Record, and Public Men.* Montgomery: Barrett and Brown, 1872.

Brown, Dee Alexander. *Grierson's Raid*. Urbana: University of Illinois Press, 1954.

Bryan, T. Conn. *Confederate Georgia*. Athens: University of Georgia Press, 1953.

Catton, Bruce. *This Hallowed Ground*. New York: Pocket Books, 1956.

Clinton, Matthew W. *Tuscaloosa, Alabama: Its Early Days, 1816–1865*. Tuscaloosa: The Zonta Club, 1958.

Connelly, Thomas L. *Autumn of Glory: The Army of Tennessee, 1862–1865*. Baton Rouge: Louisiana State University Press, 1972.

Coulter, E. Merton. *The Confederate States of America, 1861–1865*. Baton Rouge: Louisiana State University Press, 1950.

Dowdey, Clifford. *The Land They Fought For*. New York: Doubleday, 1955.

Downey, Fairfax. *Clash of Cavalry: The Battle of Brandy Station, June 9, 1863*. New York: David McKay, 1959.

Durden, Robert F. *The Gray and the Black: The Confederate Debate on Emancipation*. Baton Rouge: Louisiana State University Press, 1972.

Fleming, Walter L. *Civil War and Reconstruction in Alabama*. New York: Columbia University Press, 1905.

Futch, Ovid L. *History of Andersonville Prison*. Gainesville: University of Florida Press, 1968.

Gluckman, Arcadi. *United States Muskets, Rifles and Carbines*. Buffalo, N.Y.: Otto Ullrich, 1948.

Hardy, John. *Selma: Her Institutions and Her Men*. Selma: Times Book and Job Office, 1879.

Henderson, G. F. R. *The Civil War: A Soldier's View*. Edited by Jay Luvaas. Chicago: University of Chicago Press, 1958.

Henry, Robert S. *"First With the Most" Forrest*. Indianapolis: Bobbs-Merrill, 1944.

Herr, John K. and Wallace, Edward S. *The Story of the U.S. Cavalry, 1775–1942*. Boston: Little, Brown, 1953.

Hooker, Charles E. *Mississippi*. Vol. vii of Confederate Military History. Edited by Clement A. Evans. Atlanta: 1899.

Horn, Stanley F. *The Decisive Battle of Nashville*. Baton Rouge: Louisiana State University Press, 1956.

Jackson, Walter M. *The Story of Selma*. Birmingham: Birmingham Printing, 1954.

Johnson, James R. and Bill, Alfred H. *Horsemen, Blue and Gray*. New York: Oxford University Press, 1960.

Jordan, Thomas and Pryor, J. P. *The Campaigns of Lieutenant-General N. B. Forrest, and of Forrest's Cavalry*. New Orleans: Blalock, 1868.

Longacre, Edward G. *From Union Stars to Top Hat: A Biography of the Extraordinary General James Harrison Wilson*. Harrisburg, Pa.: Stackpole, 1972.

Lytle, Andrew N. *Bedford Forrest and His Critter Company*. New York: Minton, Balch, 1931.

Moore, Albert B. *History of Alabama*. Tuscaloosa: Alabama Book Store, 1934.

Morrison, Ona S. *The Battle of Selma*. Selma, n.p., n.d.

Nevins, Allan. *The War for the Union*. 4 vols. New York: Scribner's, 1959–1971.

Owen, Marie Bankhead. *The Story of Alabama: A History of the State*. 5 vols. New York: Lewis Historical Publishing, 1949.

Peterson, Harold. *The American Sword, 1775–1945*. New Hope, Pa.: Robert Halter, The River House, 1954.

Pierrepont, Alice V. D. *Reuben Vaughan Kidd: Soldier of the Confederacy*. Petersburg, Va.: n.p., 1947.

Porter, James D. *Tennessee*. Vol. viii of Confederate Military History. Edited by Clement A. Evans. Atlanta: Confederate Publishing, 1899.

Shannon, Fred A. *The Organization and Administration of the Union Army, 1861–1865*. 2 vols. Cleveland: Clark, 1928.

Standard, Diffee W. *Columbus, Georgia in the Confederacy*. New York: William Frederick Press, 1953.

Still, William. *Iron Afloat*. Nashville: Vanderbilt University Press, 1971.

Strode, Hudson. *Jefferson Davis*. 3 vols. New York: Harcourt, Brace and World, 1964.

Swift, Charles J. *The Last Battle of the Civil War*. Columbus, Ga.: Gilbert Printing, 1915.

Telfair, Nancy. *A History of Columbus, Georgia, 1828–1928*. Columbus, Ga.: Historical Publishing, 1929.

Wheeler, Joseph. *Alabama*. Vol. VII of Confederate Military History. Edited by Clement A. Evans. Atlanta: Confederate Publishing, 1899.

Wiley, Bell I. *The Life of Billy Yank: Common Soldier of the Union*. Indianapolis: Bobbs–Merrill, 1951.

Worsley, Etta B. *Columbus on the Chattahoochee*. Columbus, Ga.: Columbus Office Supply, 1951.

Wyeth, John A. *Life of Lieutenant General Nathan Bedford Forrest*. New York: Harper, 1899.

Articles

Allen, Theodore F. "The Last Battle of the Civil War." *Journal of the United States Cavalry Association* XIII (April, 1908) : 785–786.

Brock, R. A. "The Last Battle of the War." *Southern Historical Society Papers* XXI (January-December, 1893) : 226–227.

Browne, J. M. "Forrest's Last Exploit." *Confederate Veteran* XXV (November, 1917) : 491–492.

Carpenter, James A. "James D. Lynch in War and Peace." *Alabama Historical Quarterly* XX, no. 1 (Spring, 1958) : 73–90.

Castel, Albert. "The Ft. Pillow Massacre: A Fresh Examination of the Evidence." *Civil War History* IV, no. 1 (March, 1958) : 37–50.

Catts, Samuel Walker. "Wilson's Raid and Other Recital." *Alabama Historical Quarterly* V (Winter, 1943) :430–437.

Chaffee, A. R. "James Harrison Wilson, Cavalryman." *The Cavalry Journal* xxxiv, no. 140 (July, 1925) :271–289.

Clinton, Thomas P. "The Military Operations of General John T. Croxton in West Alabama, 1865." *Transactions of the Alabama Historical Society*, iv. Edited by Thomas M. Owen. (1904): 449–463.

Cobb, John A. "Civil War Incidents in Macon." *Georgia Historical Quarterly* vii, no. 3 (September, 1923) : 282–284.

Conyer, Luther, "Last Battle of the War." *Southern Historical Society Papers* xxiv (January-December, 1896) : 309–315.

Edwards, Earl. "The Battle of West Point." *Chattahoochee Valley Historical Society* Bulletin no. 3 (1957) : 1–16.

Ellison, Rhoda Coleman. "Huntingdon College, 1860–1865." *Alabama Review* vii, no. 1 (January, 1954) : 3–22.

McKenzie, Robert H. "Reconstruction of the Alabama Iron Industry, 1865–1880." *Alabama Review* xxv, no. 3 (July, 1972) : 178–191.

Vandiver, Frank E. "The Shelby Iron Company in the Civil War: A Study of Confederate Industry." *Alabama Review* i, nos. 1, 2, and 3 (January, April, and July, 1948) : 12–27; 111–128; 203–218.

Woodward, Joseph H. "Alabama Iron Manufacturing." *Alabama Review* vii, no. 3 (July, 1954) : 199–208.

Index

Abbeville, Ga., 174, 175
Abbeville, S.C., 172
Adams, Charles Francis, 187
Adams, Gen. Daniel W.: 58, 81, 82; prewar career, 46; Civil War career, 46; calls troops inadequate, 49–50; correspondence with Taylor, 49; at Montevallo, 65; in battle of Ebenezer Church, 69–72; and cotton burning, 94; promises to defend Montgomery, 108; organizes defense of Montgomery, 109–111; abandons Montgomery, 111
Adams, Gen. Wirt, 44, 51, 154–156
Alabama, Fourth Cavalry Regiment, 104, 114
Alabama, Seventh Cavalry Regiment, 104, 114, 132, 133
Alabama and Florida Railroad, 107, 117
Alabama and Mississippi Railroad, 60, 91, 153
Alabama and Tennessee River Railroad, 63, 64, 69, 70, 76, 80, 82, 84, 158
Alabama Arms Manufacturing Company, 107
Alabama River, 19, 75, 76, 79, 80, 100, 106, 108, 110, 113, 160
Albany, Ga., 172
Alexander, Gen. Andrew J.: Civil War career, 32, 34; personality, 34; commands at Montevallo, 65; and

battle of Ebenezer Church, 72; at Selma, 86; injured in leaving Selma, 100; at Columbus, 134; pursues Jefferson Davis, 170, 172
Andersonville Prison, 180
Andrews, Eliza Frances, 165
Antietam, battle of, 4, 10
Apalachicola, Fla., 127
Armistead, Col. Charles G., 45
Armstrong, Gen. Frank C.: 50, 81; prewar career, 44; Civil War career, 44; described in press, 46; reacts to invasion from Florida, 51; and battle of Ebenezer Church, 69–72; at Selma, 83, 86
Atlanta, Ga., 44, 45, 172, 184, 187
Atlanta and West Point Railroad, 122
Atlanta Campaign, 11, 30, 34, 44, 45, 85, 131–132
Atlantic Monthly, 2
Auburn, Ala., 118, 122
Augusta, Ga., 170, 172, 179

Badeau, Adam, 1, 5, 6, 17, 26, 168, 176, 177, 191n, 214n, 219n
Barnesville, Ga., 169, 170
Beauregard, Gen. P. G. T., 165, 179
Beck, Capt. Moses M., 31, 123–124
Bell, Gen. Tyree H., 45, 68
Benjamin, Judah P., 170, 180
Benteen, Lt. Col. Fred W.: commands Tenth Missouri, 32; destroys Montevallo factories, 64, 65; at